we are the people

we are
the people

voices from the other side
of american history

edited by **nathaniel may** & **clint willis**
introduction by **james w. loewen**

thunder's mouth press
new york

WE ARE THE PEOPLE:
VOICES FROM THE OTHER SIDE OF AMERICAN HISTORY

Compilation copyright © 2003 by Nathaniel May and Clint Willis
Book Introduction copyright © 2003 by James W. Loewen
Introductions copyright © 2003 by Nathaniel May and Clint Willis

Published by
Thunder's Mouth Press
An Imprint of Avalon Publishing Group Incorporated
245 West 17th St.
11th floor
New York, NY 10011

Library of Congress Cataloging-in-Publication Data is available.

ISBN 1-56025-505-6

Interior design by Simon M. Sullivan

Printed in the United States of America

Distributed by Publishers Group West

We dedicate this book to Edna Coleman,
and to other people whose stories remain untold

contents

native americans

slavery

peace

women

labor

civil rights

poverty

civil liberties

introduction

I studied twelve high school American history textbooks for my 1995 book, *Lies My Teacher Told Me: Everything Your American History Textbook Got Wrong*. Indeed, I am the only American ever to have read twelve high school American history textbooks! It was literally heavy going: they average almost five pounds and 888 pages. They would have averaged over a thousand pages, had it not been that a couple were shorter books intended for "slow" classes.

Yet for all their heft, rarely do these books allow the past to speak. They devote seven paragraphs and two photographs to the Lincoln-Douglas debates, on average, but all twelve books combined provide just three sentence fragments from Stephen A. Douglas. Instead, the authors supply summaries, expurgated of any content that might make Lincoln, Douglas, or the United States look bad.

The textbooks are reluctant to quote leaders like Lincoln and Douglas. Even less likely are they to allow "regular folks" to speak. For instance, virtually the only people whom textbooks quote on the Vietnam War are Presidents Johnson and Nixon. In a typical passage (in *The American Pageant)* Nixon says, "America cannot—and will not—conceive all the plans, design all the programs, execute all the decisions, and undertake all the defense of the free nations of the world." That passage hardly helps to clarify either the war or the opposition to it.

We Are the People supplies what the textbooks leave out. From a Native American speaking in 1822 to a civil libertarian writing in

2003, alternative voices can now be heard. Teachers can supplement the dead prose of the usual textbook author with the very lively speeches, memoirs, interviews, and articles collected herein. The rest of us, now well beyond high school, can learn here what we missed there, and have a good time in the process.

A caution: as with history textbooks themselves, you must read these selections thoughtfully and critically. The very first, Pawnee leader Sharitarish's 1822 address to President James Monroe, presents an American Indian view but not *the* American Indian view. Some 80 percent of Native Americans were agricultural peoples—not Plains nomads such as Sharitarish—when Europeans (and Africans) came on the scene. The next selection, the fascinating 1850 California law for the "Government and Protection of the Indians," contains clauses that directly contradict each other. I leave it for you to sort out these clauses, bearing in mind that the enslavement of American Indians in California persisted at least until 1863.

Some of the pieces are almost beyond criticism, because they so clearly present their authors' actual experience. Luther Standing Bear's account of his education, for example, encapsulates the story of his people. Sallie Tisdale's "We Do Abortions Here" will please neither those who favor a woman's right to terminate any pregnancy at any point nor opponents who deem all abortions murder—but the people and situations she describes have the ring of truth.

Isn't it interesting that the editors have included sections on "Peace" and "Civil Liberties?" While doing the research for my book, *Lies Across America: What Our Historic Sites Get Wrong,* I found that the history written on our landscape is largely the history of our wars. Maybe I should not be too surprised, since the United States has been at war somewhere on the globe almost every year since I was born (1942). We must recognize that some Americans have opposed each of this country's wars, however, and we need to hear those Americans' arguments in their own words.

From first ("Native Americans") to last ("Civil Liberties"), the editors also take care to bring the issues down to now. American history is far from over. American Indians still struggle against oppressions. Poverty still grasps at the heels of maids and food service workers. Our civil liberties are hardly secure. Americans of our era continue to fight for justice on all fronts. *We Are the People* gives us some much needed provisions for this struggle.

—JAMES W. LOEWEN
July 22, 2003

native americans

1822
from Address to President Monroe

by Chief Sharitarish

A large delegation of Pawnees and other Indian tribes in
November of 1821 traveled to Washington to meet with
President James Monroe. Sharitarish led the delegation. He
returned home to become chief of the Grand Pawnee
nation, but died several months later, probably of cholera.

My Great Father:—I have travelled a great distance to see you—I
have seen you and my heart rejoices. I have heard your words—they
have entered one ear and shall not escape the other, and I will carry
them to my people as pure as they came from your mouth.

My Great Father— . . . If I am here now and have seen your
people, your houses, your vessels on the big lake, and a great many
wonderful things far beyond my comprehension, which appear to
have been made by the Great Spirit and placed in your hands, I am
indebted to my Father [Major Benjamin O'Fallon] here, who invited
me from home, under whose wings I have been protected . . . but
there is still another Great Father to whom I am much indebted—it
is the Father of us all. . . . The Great Spirit made us all—he made my
skin red, and yours white; he placed us on this earth, and intended
that we should live differently from each other.

He made the whites to cultivate the earth, and feed on domestic
animals; but he made us, red skins, to rove through the uncultivated
woods and plains; to feed on wild animals; and to dress with their

skins. He also intended that we should go to war—to take scalps—steal horses from and triumph over our enemies—cultivate peace at home, and promote the happiness of each other.

My Great Father:—Some of your good chiefs, as they are called [missionaries], have proposed to send some of their good people among us to change our habits, to make us work and live like the white people. . . . You love your country—you love your people—you love the manner in which they live, and you think your people brave. I am like you, my Great Father, I love my country—I love my people—I love the manner in which we live, and think myself and warriors brave. Spare me then, my Father; let me enjoy my country, and I will trade skins with your people. I have grown up, and lived thus long without work—I am in hopes you will suffer me to die without it. We have plenty of buffalo, beaver, deer, and other wild animals—we have an abundance of horses—we have everything we want—we have plenty of land, if you will keep your people off of it. . . .

There was a time when we did not know the whites—our wants were then fewer than they are now. They were always within our control—we had then seen nothing which we could not get. Before our intercourse with the whites, who have caused such a destruction in our game, we could lie down to sleep, and when we awoke we would find the buffalo feeding around our camp—but now we are killing them for their skins, and feeding the wolves with their flesh, to make our children cry over their bones.

Here, my Great Father, is a pipe which I present you, as I am accustomed to present pipes to all the red skins in peace with us. It is filled with such tobacco as we were accustomed to smoke before we knew the white people. It is pleasant, and the spontaneous growth of the most remote parts of our country. I know that the robes, leggings, moccasins, bear claws, etc., are of little value to you, but we wish you to have them deposited and preserved in some conspicuous part of your lodge, so that when we are gone and the sod turned over our bones, if our children should visit this place, as we do now, they may see and recognize with pleasure the deposits of their fathers; and reflect on the times that are past.

1850
A California Law for the Government and Protection of the Indians

THE PEOPLE OF the State of California, represented in Senate and Assembly, do enact as follows:

1. Justices of the Peace shall have jurisdiction in all cases of complaints by, for, or against Indians, in their respective Townships in this State.

2. Persons and proprietors of land on which Indians are residing, shall permit such Indians peaceably to reside on such lands, unmolested in the pursuit of their usual avocations for the maintenance of themselves and families: *Provided,* the white person or proprietor in possession of lands may apply to a Justice of the Peace in the Township where the Indians reside, to set off to such Indians a certain amount of land, and, on such application, the Justice shall set off a sufficient amount of land for the necessary wants of such Indians, including the site of their village or residence, if they so prefer it; and in no case shall such selection be made to the prejudice of such Indians, nor shall they be forced to abandon their homes or villages where they have resided for a number of years; and either party feeling themselves aggrieved, can appeal to the County

Court from the decision of the Justice: and then divided, a record shall be made of the lands so set off in the Court so dividing them, and the Indians shall be permitted to remain thereon until otherwise provided for.

3. Any person having or hereafter obtaining a minor Indian, male or female, from the parents or relations of such Indian minor, and wishing to keep it, such person shall go before a Justice of the Peace in his Township, with the parents or friends of the child, and if the Justice of the Peace becomes satisfied that no compulsory means have been used to obtain the child from its parents or friends, shall enter on record, in a book kept for that purpose, the sex and probable age of the child, and shall give to such person a certificate, authorizing him or her to have the care, custody, control, and earnings of such minor, until he or she obtains the age of majority. Every male Indian shall be deemed to have attained his majority at eighteen, and the female at fifteen years.

4. Any person having a minor Indian in his care, as described in the foregoing Section of this Act, who shall neglect to clothe and suitably feed such minor Indian, or shall inhumanly treat him or her, on conviction thereof shall be subject to a fine not less than ten dollars, at the discretion of a Court or Jury; and the Justice of the Peace, in his discretion, may place the minor Indian in the care of some other person, giving him the same rights and liabilities that the former master of said minor was entitled and subject to.

5. Any person wishing to hire an Indian, shall go before a Justice of the Peace with the Indian, and make such contract as the Justice may approve, and the Justice shall file such contract in writing in his office, and all contracts so made shall be binding between the parties; but no contract between a white man and an Indian, for labor, shall otherwise be obligatory on the part of an Indian.

6. Complaints may be made before a Justice of the Peace, by white persons or Indians; but in no case shall a white man be convicted of any offence upon the testimony of an Indian.

7. If any person forcibly conveys any Indian from his home, or compels him to work, or perform any service against his will, in this State, except as provided in this Act, he or they shall, on conviction, be fined in any sum not less than fifty dollars, at the discretion of the Court or jury.

8. It shall be the duty of the Justices of the Peace, once in six months in every year, to make a full and correct statement to the Court of Sessions of their county, of all moneys received for fines imposed on Indians, and all fees allowed for services rendered under the provisions of this Act; and said Justices shall pay over to the County Treasurer of their respective counties, all money they may have received for fines and not appropriated, or fees for services rendered under this Act; and the Treasurer shall keep a correct statement of all money so received, which shall be termed the "Indian Fund" of the county. The Treasurer shall pay out any money of said funds in his hands, on a certificate of a Justice of the Peace of his county, for fees and expenditures incurred in carrying out the provisions of this law.

9. It shall be the duty of Justices of the Peace, in their respective townships, as well as all other peace officers in this State, to instruct the Indians in their neighborhood in the laws which relate to them, giving them such advice as they may deem necessary and proper; and if any tribe or village of Indians refuse or neglect to obey the laws, the Justice of the Peace may punish the guilty chiefs or principal men by reprimand or fine, or otherwise reasonably chastise them.

10. If any person or persons shall set the prairie on fire, or refuse to use proper exertions to extinguish the fire when the prairies are burning, such person or persons shall be subject to fine or punishment, as a Court may adjudge proper.

11. If any Indian shall commit an unlawful offence against a white person, such person shall not inflict punishment for such offence,

but may, without process, take the Indian before a Justice of the Peace, and on conviction, the Indian shall be punished according to the provisions of this Act.

12. In all cases of trial between a white man and an Indian, either party may require a jury.

13. Justices may require the chiefs and influential men of any village to apprehend and bring before them or him any Indian charged or suspected of an offence.

14. When an Indian is convicted of an offence before a Justice of the Peace punishable by fine, any white person may, by consent of the Justice, give bond for said Indian, conditioned for the payment of said fine and costs, and in such case the Indian shall be compelled to work for the person so bailing, until he has discharged or cancelled the fine assessed against him: *Provided,* the person bailing shall treat the Indian humanely, and clothe and feed him properly; the allowance given for such labor shall be fixed by the Court, when the bond is taken.

15. If any person in this State shall sell, give, or furnish to any Indian, male or female, any intoxicating liquors (except when administered in sickness), for good cause shown, he, she, or they so offending shall, on conviction thereof, be fined not less than twenty dollars for each offence, or be imprisoned not less than five days, or fined and imprisoned, as the Court may determine.

16. An Indian convicted of stealing horses, mules, cattle, or any valuable thing, shall be subject to receive any number of lashes not exceeding twenty-five, or shall be subject to a fine not exceeding two hundred dollars, at the discretion of the Court or Jury.

17. When an Indian is sentenced to be whipped, the Justice may appoint a white man, or an Indian at his discretion, to execute the sentence in his presence, and shall not permit unnecessary cruelty in the execution of the sentence.

18. All fines, forfeitures, penalties recovered under or by this Act,

shall be paid into the treasury of the county, to the credit of the Indian Fund as provided in Section Eight.

19. All white persons making application to a Justice of the Peace, for confirmation of a contract with or in relation to an Indian, shall pay the fee, which shall not exceed two dollars for each contract determined and filed as provided in this Act, and for all other services, such fees as are allowed for similar services under other law of this State. *Provided,* the application fee for hiring Indians, or keeping minors, and fees and expenses for setting off lands to Indians, shall be paid by the white person applying.

20. Any Indian able to work and support himself in some honest calling, not having wherewithal to maintain himself, who shall be found loitering and strolling about, or frequenting public places where liquors are sold, begging, or leading an immoral or profligate course of life, shall be liable to be arrested on the complaint of any resident citizen of the county, and brought before any Justice of the Peace of the proper county, Mayor or Recorder of any incorporated town or city, who shall examine said accused Indian, and hear the testimony in relation thereto, and if said Justice, Mayor or Recorder shall be satisfied that he is a vagrant, as above set forth, he shall make out a warrant under his hand and seal, authorizing and requiring the officer having him in charge or custody, to hire out such vagrant within twenty-four hours to the best bidder, by public notice given as he shall direct, for the highest price that can be had, for any term not exceeding four months; and such vagrant shall be subject to and governed by the provisions of this Act, regulating guardians and minors, during the time which he has been so hired. The money received for his hire, shall, after deducting the costs, and the necessary expense for clothing for said Indian, which may have been purchased by his employer, be, if he be without a family, paid into the County Treasury, to the credit of the Indian fund. But if he have a family, the same shall be appropriated for their use and benefit:

Provided, that any such vagrant, when arrested, and before judgment, may relieve himself by giving to such Justice, Mayor, or Recorder, a bond, with good security, conditioned that he will, for the next twelve months, conduct himself with good behavior, and betake to some honest employment for support.

1864
Sand Creek Massacre
BY JOHN S. SMITH

The Cheyenne camped at Sand Creek, Colorado, had surrendered their arms for a promise of federal protection. That made them easy prey for the Colorado militia who attacked the camp on November 29, 1864, slaughtering 450 Cheyenne—mostly women and children. John S. Smith, an Indian agent, offered the following testimony to an 1865 Congressional committee.

I LEFT TO go to this village of Indians on the 26th of November last. I arrived there on the 27th and remained there the 28th. On the morning of the 29th, between daylight and sunrise—nearer sunrise than daybreak—a large number of troops were discovered from three-quarters of a mile to a mile below the village. The Indians, who discovered them, ran to my camp, called me out, and wanted me to go and see what troops they were, and what they wanted. The head chief of the nation, Black Kettle, and head chief of the Cheyennes, was encamped there with us. Some years previous he had been presented with a fine American flag by Colonel Greenwood, a commissioner, who had been sent out there. Black Kettle ran this American flag up to the top of his lodge, with a small white flag tied right under it, as he had been advised to do in case he should meet with any troops out on the prairies. I then left my own camp and started for that portion of the troops that was nearest the village, supposing I could go up to them. I did not know but they might be strange troops, and thought my presence and explantations could reconcile matters. Lieutenant Wilson was in command of the detachment to which I tried to make my approach; but they fired several volleys at me, and I returned back to my camp and entered my lodge.

After I had left my lodge to go out and see what was going on, Colonel Chivington rode up to within fifty or sixty yards of where I was camped; he recognized me at once. They all call me Uncle John in that country. He said, "Run here, Uncle John; you are all right." I went to him as fast as I could. He told me to get in between him and his troops, who were then coming up very fast; I did so; directly another officer who knew me—Lieutenant Baldwin, in command of a battery—tried to assist me to get a horse; but there was no loose horse there at the time. He said, "Catch hold of the caisson, and keep up with us."

By this time the Indians had fled; had scattered in every direction. The troops were some on one side of the river and some on the other, following up the Indians. We had been encamped on the north side of the river; I followed along, holding on the caisson, sometimes running, sometimes walking. Finally, about a mile above the village, the troops had got a parcel of the Indians hemmed in under the bank of the river; as soon as the troops overtook them, they commenced firing on them; some troops had got above them, so that they were completely surrounded. There were probably a hundred Indians hemmed in there, men, women, and children; the most of the men in the village escaped.

By the time I got up with the battery to the place where these Indians were surrounded there had been some considerable firing. Four or five soldiers had been killed, some with arrows and some with bullets. The soldiers continued firing on these Indians, who numbered about a hundred, until they had almost completely destroyed them. I think I saw altogether some seventy dead bodies lying there; the greater portion women and children. There may have been thirty warriors, old and young; the rest were women and small children of different ages and sizes.

The troops at that time were very much scattered. There were not over two hundred troops in the main fight, engaged in killing this body of Indians under the bank. The balance of the troops were scattered in different directions, running after small parties of Indians who were trying to make their escape. I did not go to see how many they might have killed outside of this party under the bank of the river. Being still quite weak from my last sickness, I returned with the first body of troops that went back to the camp.

QUESTION. *Were the women and children slaughtered indiscriminately, or only so far as they were with the warriors?*

ANSWER. Indiscriminately.

QUESTION. *Were there any acts of barbarity perpetrated there that came under your own observation?*

ANSWER. Yes, sir; I saw the bodies of those lying there cut all to pieces, worse mutilated than any I ever saw before; the women cut all to pieces.

By Mr. Buckalew:

QUESTION. *How cut?*

ANSWER. With knives; scalped; their brains knocked out; children two or three months old; all ages lying there, from sucking infants up to warriors. . . . They were terribly mutilated, lying there in the water and sand; most of them in the bed of the creek, dead and dying, making many struggles. They were so badly mutilated and covered with sand and water that it was very hard for me to tell one from another. . . .

By Mr. Gooch:

QUESTION. *Did you see it done?*

ANSWER. Yes, sir; I saw them fall.

QUESTION. *Fall when they were killed?*

ANSWER. Yes, sir.

QUESTION. *Did you see them when they were mutilated?*

ANSWER. Yes, sir.

QUESTION. *By whom were they mutilated?*

ANSWER. By the United States troops.

QUESTION. *Do you know whether or not it was done by the direction or consent of any of the officers?*

ANSWER. I do not; I hardly think it was. . . .

QUESTION. *Were there any other barbarities or atrocities committed there other than those you have mentioned, that you saw?*

ANSWER. Yes, sir; I had a half-breed son there, who gave himself up. He started at the time the Indians fled; being a half-breed he had but little hope of being spared, and seeing them fire at me, he ran away with the Indians for the distance of about a mile. During the fight up there he walked back to my camp and went into the lodge. It was surrounded by soldiers at the time. He came in quietly and sat down; he remained there that day, that night, and the next day in the afternoon; about four o'clock in the evening, as I was sitting inside the camp, a soldier came up outside of the lodge and called me by name. I got up and went out; he took me by the arm and walked towards Colonel Chivington's camp, which was about sixty yards from my camp. Said he, "I am sorry to tell you, but they are going to kill your son Jack." I knew the feeling towards the whole camp of Indians, and that there was no use to make any resistance. I said, "I can't help it." I then walked on towards where Colonel Chivington was standing by his camp-fire; when I had got within a few feet of him I heard a gun fired, and saw a crowd run to my lodge, and they told me that Jack was dead.

QUESTION. *What action did Colonel Chivington take in regard to that matter?*

ANSWER. Major Anthony, who was present, told Colonel Chivington that he had heard some remarks made, indicating that they were desirous of killing Jack; and that he (Colonel Chivington) had it in his power to save him, and that by saving him he might make him a very useful man, as he was well acquainted with all the Cheyenne and Arapahoe country, and he could be used as a guide or interpreter. Colonel Chivington replied to Major Anthony, as the Major himself told me, that he had no orders to receive and no advice to give.

1877
from An Indian's Views of Indian Affairs

BY CHIEF JOSEPH

In 1877, General Oliver O. Howard gave Young Joseph's band of Nez Percé thirty days to join the rest of their tribe on a reservation. This passage is from an article in the April 1879 *North American Review.*

MY FRIENDS AMONG white men have blamed me for the war. I am not to blame. When my young men began the killing, my heart was hurt. Although I did not justify them, I remembered all the insults I had endured, and my blood was on fire. Still I would have taken my people to the buffalo country without fighting, if possible.

I could see no other way to avoid a war. We moved over to White Bird Creek, sixteen miles away, and there encamped, intending to collect our stock before leaving; but the soldiers attacked us, and the first battle was fought. We numbered in that battle sixty men, and the soldiers a hundred. The fight lasted but a few minutes, when the soldiers retreated before us for twelve miles. They lost thirty-three killed, and had seven wounded. When an Indian fights, he only shoots to kill; but soldiers shoot at random. None of the soldiers were scalped. We do not believe in scalping, nor in killing wounded men. Soldiers do not kill many Indians unless they are wounded and left upon the battle-field. Then they kill Indians.

Seven days after the first battle, General Howard arrived in the Nez Percés' country, bringing seven hundred more soldiers. It was now war in earnest. We crossed over Salmon River, hoping General Howard would follow. We were not disappointed. He did follow us, and we got back between him and his supplies, and cut him off for three days. He sent out two companies to open the way. We attacked them, killing one officer, two guides, and ten men.

We withdrew, hoping the soldiers would follow, but they had got fighting enough for that day. They intrenched themselves, and next day we attacked them again. The battle lasted all day, and was renewed next morning. We killed four and wounded seven or eight.

About this time General Howard found out that we were in his rear. Five days later he attacked us with three hundred and fifty soldiers and settlers. We had two hundred and fifty warriors. The fight lasted twenty-seven hours. We lost four killed and several wounded. General Howard's loss was twenty-nine men killed and sixty wounded.

The following day the soldiers charged upon us, and we retreated with our families and stock a few miles, leaving eighty lodges to fall into General Howard's hands.

Finding that we were outnumbered, we retreated to Bitter Root Valley. Here another body of soldiers came upon us and demanded our surrender. We refused. They said, "You can not get by us." We answered, "We are going by you without fighting if you will let us, but we are going by you anyhow." We then made a treaty with these soldiers. We agreed not to molest any one, and they agreed that we might pass through the Bitter Root country in peace. We bought provisions and traded stock with white men there.

We understood that there was to be no more war. We intended to go peaceably to the buffalo country, and leave the question of returning to our country to be settled afterward.

With this understanding we traveled on for four days, and, thinking that the trouble was all over, we stopped and prepared tent-poles to take with us. We started again, and at the end of two days we saw three white men passing our camp. Thinking that peace had been made, we did not molest them. We could have killed or taken them prisoners, but we did not suspect them of being spies, which they were.

That night the soldiers surrounded our camp. About daybreak one of my men went out to look after his horses. The soldiers saw him and shot him down like a coyote. I have since learned that these soldiers were not those we had left behind. They had come upon us from another direction. The new white war-chief's name was Gibbon. He charged upon us while some of my people were still asleep. We had a hard fight. Some of my men crept around and attacked the soldiers from the rear. In this battle we lost nearly all our lodges, but we finally drove General Gibbon back.

Finding that he was not able to capture us, he sent to his camp a few miles away for his big guns (cannons), but my men had captured them and all the ammunition. We damaged the big guns all we could, and carried away the powder and lead. In the fight with General Gibbon we lost fifty women and children and thirty fighting men. We remained long enough to bury our dead. The Nez Percés never make war on women and children; we could have killed a great many women and children while the war lasted, but we would feel ashamed to do so cowardly an act.

We never scalp our enemies, but when General Howard came up and joined General Gibbon, their Indian scouts dug up our dead and scalped them. I have been told that General Howard did not order this great shame to be done.

We retreated as rapidly as we could toward the buffalo country. After six days General Howard came close to us, and we went out and attacked him, and captured nearly all his horses and mules (about two hundred and fifty head). We then marched on to the Yellowstone Basin.

On the way we captured one white man and two white women. We released them at the end of three days. They were treated kindly. The women were not insulted. Can the white soldiers tell me of one time when Indian women were taken prisoners, and held three days and then released without being insulted? Were the Nez Percés women who fell into the hands of General Howard's soldiers treated with as much respect? I deny that a Nez Percé was ever guilty of such a crime.

A few days later we captured two more white men. One of them stole a horse and escaped. We gave the other a poor horse and told him he was free.

Nine days' march brought us to the mouth of Clarke's Fork of the Yellowstone. We did not know what had become of General Howard, but we supposed that he had sent for more horses and mules. He did not come up, but another new war-chief (General Sturgis) attacked us. We held him in check while we moved all our women and children and stock out of danger, leaving a few men to cover our retreat.

Several days passed, and we heard nothing of General Howard, or Gibbon, or Sturgis. We had repulsed each in turn, and began to feel secure, when another army, under General Miles, struck us. This was the fourth army, each of which outnumbered our fighting force, that we had encountered within sixty days.

We had no knowledge of General Miles's army until a short time before he made a charge upon us, cutting our camp in two, and capturing nearly all of our horses. About seventy men, myself among them, were cut off. My little daughter, twelve years of age, was with me. I gave her a rope, and told her to catch a horse and join the others who were cut off from the camp. I have not seen her since, but I have learned that she is alive and well.

I thought of my wife and children, who were now surrounded by soldiers, and I resolved to go to them or die. With a prayer in my mouth to the Great Spirit Chief who rules above, I dashed unarmed through the line of soldiers. It seemed to me that there were guns on every side, before and behind me. My clothes were cut to pieces and my horse was wounded, but I was not hurt. As I reached the door of my lodge, my wife handed me my rifle, saying: "Here's your gun. Fight!"

The soldiers kept up a continuous fire. Six of my men were killed in one spot near me. Ten or twelve soldiers charged into our camp and got possession of two lodges, killing three Nez Percés and losing three of their men, who fell inside our lines. I called my men to drive them back. We fought at close range, not more than twenty steps apart, and drove the soldiers back upon their main line, leaving their dead in our hands. We secured their arms and ammunition. We lost, the first day and night, eighteen men and three women. General Miles lost twenty-six killed and forty wounded. The following day General Miles sent a messenger into my camp under protection of a white flag. I sent my friend Yellow Bull to meet him.

Yellow Bull understood the messenger to say that General Miles wished me to consider the situation; that he did not want to kill my people unnecessarily. Yellow Bull understood this to be a demand for me to surrender and save blood. Upon reporting this message to me, Yellow Bull said he wondered whether General Miles was in earnest. I sent him back with my answer, that I had not made up my mind, but would think about it and send word soon. A little later he sent some Cheyenne scouts with another message. I went out to meet them. They said they believed that General Miles was sincere and really wanted peace. I walked on to General Miles's tent. He met me and we shook hands. He said, "Come, let us sit down by the fire and talk this matter over." I remained with him all night; next morning Yellow Bull came over to see if I was alive, and why I did not return.

General Miles would not let me leave the tent to see my friend alone.

Yellow Bull said to me: "They have got you in their power, and I am afraid they will never let you go again. I have an officer in our camp, and I will hold him until they let you go free."

I said: "I do not know what they mean to do with me, but if they kill me you must not kill the officer. It will do no good to avenge my death by killing him."

Yellow Bull returned to my camp. I did not make any agreement that day with General Miles. The battle was renewed while I was with him. I was very anxious about my people. I knew that we were near Sitting Bull's camp in King George's land, and I thought maybe the Nez Percés who had escaped would return with assistance. No great damage was done to either party during the night.

On the following morning I returned to my camp by agreement, meeting the officer who had been held a prisoner in my camp at the flag of truce. My people were divided about surrendering. We could have escaped from Bear Paw Mountain if we had left our wounded, old women, and children behind. We were unwilling to do this. We had never heard of a wounded Indian recovering while in the hands of white men.

On the evening of the fourth day General Howard came in with a small escort, together with my friend Chapman. We could now talk understandingly. General Miles said to me in plain words, "If you will come out and give up your arms, I will spare your lives and send you to your reservation." I do not know what passed between General Miles and General Howard.

I could not bear to see my wounded men and women suffer any longer; we had lost enough already. General Miles had promised that we might return to our own country with what stock we had left. I thought we could start again. I believed General Miles, or *I never would have surrendered.* I have heard that he has been censured for making the promise to return us to Lapwai. He could not have made any other terms with me at that time. I would have held him in check until my friends came to my assistance, and then neither of the generals nor their soldiers would have ever left Bear Paw Mountain alive.

On the fifth day I went to General Miles and gave up my gun, and said, "From where the sun now stands I will fight no more." My people needed rest—we wanted peace.

I was told we could go with General Miles to Tongue River and stay there until spring, when we would be sent back to our country. Finally it was decided that we were to be taken to Tongue River. We had nothing to say about it. After our arrival at Tongue River, General Miles received orders to take us to Bismarck. The reason given was, that subsistence would be cheaper there.

General Miles was opposed to this order. He said: "You must not blame me. I have endeavored to keep my word, but the chief who is over me has given the order, and I must obey it or resign. That would do you no good. Some other officer would carry out the order."

I believe General Miles would have kept his word if he could have done so. I do not blame him for what we have suffered since the surrender. I do not know who is to blame. We gave up all our horses—over eleven hundred—and all our saddles—over one hundred—and we have not heard from them since. Somebody has got our horses.

General Miles turned my people over to another soldier, and we were taken to Bismarck. Captain Johnson, who now had charge of us, received an order to take us to Fort Leavenworth. At Leavenworth we were placed on a low river bottom, with no water except river-water to drink and cook with. We had always lived in a healthy country, where the mountains were high and the water was cold and clear. Many of my people sickened and died, and we buried them in this strange land. I can not tell how much my heart suffered for my people while at Leavenworth. The Great Spirit Chief who rules above seemed to be looking some other way, and did not see what was being done to my people.

During the hot days (July, 1878) we received notice that we were to be moved farther away from our own country. We were not asked if we were willing to go. We were ordered to get into the railroad-cars. Three of my people died on the way to Baxter Springs. It was worse to die there than to die fighting in the mountains.

We were moved from Baxter Springs (Kansas) to the Indian Territory, and set down without our lodges. We had but little medicine, and we were nearly all sick. Seventy of my people have died since we moved there.

We have had a great many visitors who have talked many ways. Some of the chiefs (General Fish and Colonel Stickney) from Washington came to see us, and selected land for us to live upon. We have not moved to that land, for it is not a good place to live.

The Commissioner Chief (E.A. Hayt) came to see us. I told him, as I told every one, that I expected General Miles's word would be carried out. He said it "could not be done; that white men now lived in my country and all the land was taken up; that, if I returned to Wallowa, I could not live in peace; that law-papers were out against my young men who began the war, and that the Government could not protect my people." This talk fell like a heavy stone upon my heart. I saw that I could not gain anything by talking to him. Other law chiefs (Congressional Committee) came to see me and said they would help me to get a healthy country. I did not know who to believe. The white people have too many chiefs. They do not understand each other. They do not all talk alike.

The Commissioner Chief (Mr. Hayt) invited me to go with him and hunt for a better home than we have now. I like the land we found (west of the Osage reservation) better than any place I have seen in that country; but it is not a healthy land. There are no mountains and rivers. The water is warm. It is not a good country for stock. I do not believe my people can live there. I am afraid they will all die. The Indians who occupy that country are dying off. I promised Chief Hayt to go there, and do the best I could until the Government got ready to make good General Miles's word. I was not satisfied, but I could not help myself.

Then the Inspector Chief (General McNiel) came to my camp and we had a long talk. He said I ought to have a home in the mountain country north, and that he would write a letter to the Great Chief at Washington. Again the hope of seeing the mountains of Idaho and Oregon grew up in my heart.

At last I was granted permission to come to Washington and bring my friend Yellow Bull and our interpreter with me. I am glad we came. I have shaken hands with a great many friends, but there are some things I want to know which no one seems able to explain. I can not understand how the Government sends a man out to fight us, as it did General Miles, and then breaks his word. Such a Government has something wrong about it. I can not understand why so many chiefs are allowed to talk so many different ways and promise so many different things. I have seen the Great Father Chief (the President), the next Great Chief (Secretary of the Interior), the Commissioner Chief (Hayt), the Law Chief (General Butler), and many other law chiefs (Congressmen), and they all say they are my friends, and that I shall have justice, but while their mouths all talk right I do not understand why nothing is done for my people. I have heard talk and talk, but nothing is done. Good words do not last long unless they amount to something. Words do not pay for my dead people. They do not pay for my country, now overrun by white men. They do not protect my father's grave. They do not pay for all my horses and cattle. Good words will not give me back my children. Good words will not make good the promise of your War Chief General Miles. Good words will not give my people good health and stop them from dying. Good words will not get my people a home where they can live in peace and take care of themselves. I am tired of talk that comes to nothing. It makes my heart sick when I remember all the good words and all the broken promises. There has been too much talking by men who had no right to talk. Too many misrepresentations have been made, too many misunderstandings have come up between the white men about the Indians. If the white man wants to live in peace with the Indian he can live in peace. There need be no trouble. Treat all men alike. Give them all the same law. Give them all an even chance to live and grow. All men were made by the same Great Spirit Chief. They are all brothers. The earth is the mother of all people, and all people should have equal rights upon it. You might as well expect the rivers to run backward as that any man who was born a free man should be contented when penned up and denied liberty to go where he pleases. If you tie a horse to a stake, do you expect he will grow fat? If you pen an Indian up on a squall spot of earth, and compel him to stay there, he will not be contented, nor will he grow and prosper. I have asked some of the great white chiefs where they got their authority to say to the Indian that he shall stay in one place, while he sees white men going where they please. They can not tell me.

I only ask of the Government to be treated as all other men are treated. If I can not go to my own home, let me have a home in some country where my people will not die so fast. I would like to go to Bitter Root Valley. There my people would be healthy; where they are now they are dying. Three have died since I left my camp to come to Washington.

When I think of our condition my heart is heavy. I see men of my race treated as outlaws and driven from country to country, or shot down like animals.

I know that my race must change. We can not hold our own with the white men as we are. We only ask an even chance to live as other men live. We ask to be recognized as men. We ask that the same law shall work alike on all men. If the Indian breaks the law, punish him by the law. If the white man breaks the law, punish him also.

Let me be a free man—free to travel, free to stop, free to work, free to trade where I choose, free to choose my own teachers, free to follow the religion of my fathers, free to think and talk and act for myself—and I will obey every law, or submit to the penalty.

Whenever the white man treats the Indian as they treat each other, then we will have no more wars. We shall all be alike—brothers of one father and one mother, with one sky above us and one country around us, and one government for all. Then the Great Spirit Chief who rules above will smile upon this land, and send rain to wash out the bloody spots made by brothers' hands from the face of the earth. For this time the Indian race are waiting and praying. I hope that no more groans of wounded men and women will ever go to the ear of the Great Spirit Chief above, and that all people may be one people.

In-mut-too-yah-lat-lat has spoken for his people.

Young Joseph.
Washington City, D.C.

1885
from *Indeh: An Apache Odyssey*

BY EVE BALL, WITH NORA HENN AND LYNDA SANCHEZ

Geronimo, a Bedonkohe Apache leader of the Chiricahua Apache, led his people during the last days of their struggle for freedom.

DAKLUGIE
NOT UNTIL AFTER the death of my father, Juh, did Geronimo become very prominent. After that he just took over. He was a Bedonkohe and never was elected to the chieftainship. Naiche was chief, but he was very young—too young for the leadership. It took a man to lead the Chiricahua. Geronimo was of middle age, a well-known fighter and superb leader, and he was also a Medicine Man. No White Eyes seem

to understand the importance of that in controlling Apaches. Naiche was not a Medicine Man; so he needed Geronimo as Geronimo needed *him*. It was a good combination. Geronimo saw that Naiche was accorded the respect and recognition due a chief and that he always occupied the seat of honor; but Geronimo planned the strategy, with Naiche's help, and made the decisions. Of course, had Juh or Geronimo been chief, nobody could have usurped their prerogatives. But don't forget that not being a Medicine Man was a great handicap to Naiche.

Several years after our capture, and after I returned from school, I lived in Geronimo's village and was his confidant and interpreter. I accompanied him everywhere he went. When he took pneumonia at Fort Sill and was sent to the hospital, Eugene Chihuahua sat beside him during the day and I at night. And he died with his hand in mine. Even in his delirium, he talked of those seventeen men who had eluded five thousand men of the army of the United States for many years; and eluded not only them, but also twenty-five hundred Mexican soldiers—seventy-five hundred men, well armed, well trained, and well equipped against seventeen whom they regarded as naked savages. The odds were only five hundred to one against Geronimo, but still they could not whip him nor could they capture him.

But I am Geronimo's nephew and there are people who might think that I am biased. Go see Charlie Smith. As a child he and his mother were captured by Geronimo's band. Charlie was with Geronimo and Naiche about a year, I think, before going to Florida.

CHARLIE SMITH

My father, Ne-do-bilt-yo, or Conceals His Tracks, was a Chiricahua scout who was stationed at Fort Stanton for a long time. The officer who enlisted him was unable to either spell or pronounce his name, so he just recorded him as Charlie Smith. In some books he is mentioned as Corporal or Sergeant Charlie; in others he is Alabama Charlie.

While at the fort, he met and married my mother, Cumpah, a

Mescalero; and according to Indian way that made him a Mescalero too. She had a home at White Tail, and my father went there as often as he was permitted. It was there that I was born.

There had been no piñon crop in our mountains for four or five years; you know that the trees don't bear often. My father learned from a scout, who came in from western New Mexico, that there was a big piñon crop out there. About forty Mescaleros got passes from the agency for a trip to last thirty days, and my father's captain let him go with us. To make sure that he did not over-stay his time, he tied thirty knots in a buckskin thong and each day untied one.

We went on horseback, of course; there were many more wild horses on the reservation then than now, and my parents had several. They had given me the best-broken of the lot, and I was old enough to ride alone.[*] Each of them had a mount, and they took pack horses. I do not know what year it was, but I think it was 1885.

We met the others at the Rinconada and rode over the saddle of the Sacred Mountain [Sierra Blanca] and down past the Shanta place, and then we struck out between the White Sands and the Malpais [lava flow].

We went on to the Rio Grande, crossed it, and started up the long slope of the Black Range. We crossed the divide on the old primitive trail and camped on the west side. From where we stopped we could see the lights at the copper mine and dim lights as though from small fires further to the southwest. Somebody jokingly said that they might be from Geronimo's camp, but nobody took it seriously. Still, the next night we stopped in a deep canyon where we could build a fire for cooking without danger of its being seen. We were still eating dried food that we had brought with us.

---

[*] Charlie guessed his age as four or five. Apache children of necessity learned to ride when very young.

The next morning, usually by twos, the men left to hunt. My father and a few others preferred going alone. The women also divided into small groups. With Mother and me were Ih-tedda, or Young Girl, and a young mother with her baby. We began our harvest of piñons by finding trails of pack rats and tracking them to their dens. The nests were sometimes two and a half feet high, and about that in diameter. Sometimes we got as many as two gallons or more of the tiny nuts from one cache. The rats never carry a faulty piñon to their hoard. When we could find no more nests, we placed skins under the trees and beat the lower limbs with clubs; and we even picked up some one by one.

When the men returned in the evening, the women dressed the game and hung it on bushes and low branches to dry. They scraped the fat from the hides and pegged them out. The tanning would be done after our return. Both meat and piñons were obtained in abundance, and people were thinking of returning to Mescalero when two families asked to stay just one more day to complete their harvest.

On our last evening, as my mother's party started for camp, strange warriors swooped down the mountain and we scattered. I was running toward some chaparral when a bullet nicked the calf of my leg. I still have the scar. The next thing I knew a man leaned from his mount and lifted me in front of him. Riders were forcing the women to mount behind them; and they carried us to the camp of Geronimo.

As was the custom, the chief got first choice of the women; but Naiche was well supplied and yielded to Geronimo. He took Ih-tedda and a warrior named Juan-si-got-si chose my mother and me. What became of the other woman and the baby I don't know.

My mother warned me that I was not to let my unhappiness be known. I was to be very obedient to my stepfather; I was to anticipate his every need. Already I had learned that when he rode in I was to meet him, take his horse, and care for it. I was to build fires, gather wood, and, above all, obey instantly. I was to ask no questions. I was to eat any portion of food given me without complaint. All Apache boys were expected to do these things. My stepfather was a strict disciplinarian but neither mother nor I resented that; had we felt it, we would not have shown it. And I am sure that he liked me. He told my mother that I would make a good warrior and that I must become a good shot. He made a bow and arrows for me—arrows with blunt points—and he required me to practice shooting several hours a day. I was too young, he said, to have real points, but if I continued to gain skill he would provide me with some. Imagine my delight when one evening he rode in with a pony for me!

I'll never forget that winter. Geronimo would line up the boys on the bank, have us build a fire and undress by it, and then make us plunge into the stream, breaking the ice as we went. The first time he did this, I thought that the ordeal would be over when he let us get out of the water. But no—time after time we warmed ourselves by the fire and returned to the icy water. There were times when I just hated him. Geronimo would stand there on the bank, with a stick in his hand. What for, I don't know; I never saw him strike anybody. But we knew he might and that was enough. Nobody defied Geronimo.[*]

Was I present during the fighting? Geronimo had the women and children along, and of course they saw what happened. If pursued, he, as did all Apaches, tried to protect them by sending them ahead; but ordinarily, when fighting occurred, it was because he laid an ambush, and every one of the band was there. Some of the women were very good shots—good fighters, too. Lozen, sister of Victorio, was called

---

[*] Apaches very seldom whipped a child.

The Woman Warrior; and though she may not have had as much strength as one of the men she was as good as a shot as any of them.[*]

When actually on the warpath the Apaches were under very strict rules. Even words for common things were different. Women could go with their husbands, but they could not live together. No unmarried woman was permitted to go with them. Lozen? No, she was not married; she never married. But to us she was as a Holy Woman and she was regarded and treated as one. White Painted Woman herself was not more respected. And she was brave! Geronimo sent her on missions to the military officers to arrange for meetings with him, or to carry messages.[**]

When Geronimo crossed the border into New Mexico or Arizona, it was usually to get ammunition. I do not think that he wanted to kill, but there were cases when he had no choice. If he were seen by a civilian, it meant that he would be reported to the military and they'd be after us. So there was nothing to do but kill the civilian and his entire family. It was terrible to see little children killed. I do not like to talk of it. I do not like to think of it. But the soldiers killed our women and children, too. Don't forget that. There were times that I hated Geronimo for that, too; but when I got older, I knew that he had no choice.

Stealing horses was fun. I was not quite old enough to get in on that, and how I envied those who were! It was usually the boys, too, who shot the fire-arrows to set houses ablaze. I never saw that done but twice, though. I did see many, many people killed. I wish I could forget it. Even babies were killed; and I love babies.

---

[*]   Lozen never married. She died at Mr. Vernon Barracks. (I am in error having corrected Kaywaykla in *In the Days of Victorio* and stating that Lozen married Calvin Zhunni and died on the Mescalero Reservation. However, Zhunni's wife was also named Lozen and she did die at Mescalero. Ball, *Victorio,* p. 207.)

[**]   I have frequently been asked why nobody but Kaywaykla mentioned Lozen (see Ball, *Victorio*). His explanation was that the Apaches respected her and were protecting her from criticism. Only wives of warriors went on the warpath with their husbands.

But Geronimo was fighting not only to avenge his murdered mother, wife, and children, but for his people and his tribe. Later there were Apaches who were bitter against Geronimo, saying that it was his fault that they were sent to Florida and were prisoners of war for twenty-seven years. Well, if they'd had the fighting spirit of Geronimo, they need not have been sent. The big difference was that he had the courage to keep on and they were quitters. Some of them have "gone white" and blame Geronimo for everything. I don't respect them. They were cowards. I won't name them. I am ashamed that they are Apaches.

And don't forget that Geronimo knew that it was hopeless. But that did not stop him. I admire him for that. He was a great leader of men, and it ill becomes the cowardly to find fault with the man who was trying to keep them free. And don't forget that he was fighting against enormous odds, or that nobody ever captured him.

Jasper Kanseah, nephew of Geronimo, also gave an account.

Kanseah

My father died before I was born, and my mother died when they drove us like cattle from Cochise's reservation to San Carlos. I had nobody but my grandmother and she had to walk. I was little, and when I couldn't keep up she carried me. She told me that Geronimo was my uncle, but I didn't remember him till he came to San Carlos. When he came my grandmother had already gone to the Happy Place, and I had nobody. But Indian women were good to me, and even when they were hungry they gave me some of the food their own children needed. We never went hungry till we got to San Carlos; and there we almost died because there was no food.

I think that I was eleven when my uncle, Geronimo, came and took me with him. And he gave me to Yahnosha to be his orderly and learn to be a warrior. I stayed with Yahnosha and cooked his food, and got his horse and fed and watered it; and I never spoke unless somebody asked me a question. And I ate what was left. No matter what happened, I didn't complain. And even when I talked I had to say it differently. (On the warpath we don't talk as we do most of the time, but differently.) I had to think what Yahnosha wanted next and then get it for him before he told me. But I was proud to be taught by a great warrior and I tried to do everything right.

I knew Geronimo and I knew that he was the victim of liars. He was lied about by many of his own people for whom he was fighting. He was betrayed by them. He was betrayed by Miles. I am not sure but that he was betrayed by Crook, though some think not. But I know that he was lied to by Miles. That man did not do what he promised. Geronimo was a really great fighting man, and Miles was a coward. Everything he needed for his troops was provided for him and them, but Geronimo had to obtain food for his men, and for their women and children. When they were hungry, Geronimo got food. When they were cold he provided blankets and clothing. When they were afoot, he stole horses. When they had no bullets, he got ammunition. He was a good man. I think that you have desperados among you White Eyes today that are much worse men and are more cruel than Geronimo.

1960
from Back on the War Ponies

BY JOHN WOODEN LEGS

The General Allotment Act of 1887, which divided Native American reservation land into parcels, aimed to weaken tribal structures and encourage private ownership of farms among Native Americans. Land swindlers (including the U.S. government) exploited the Act to steal more than two-thirds of the land allocated to reservations.

I AM NOT proud of myself for anything. I am a humble man. But I am proud to be a Cheyenne.

In the old days my people fought hard to defend their homeland. The Cheyennes were a small tribe—but fast on horseback. They came and went like a tornado. That is why the soldiers shot down old people and children when defeat came. The soldiers did not stop until my people were helpless.

Sixty years my people stood looking down at the ground. Hope was running out of them the way blood runs. I heard an Indian Bureau employee say, "The Northern Cheyenne Tribe is in the process of dissolution." He said that in front of me. He thought I did not know what he meant. . . .

I will tell you what it means to be a Cheyenne. Then you will understand what it means to my people to be back on the war ponies—going somewhere.

The white people living near us call the Cheyennes "those poor devils over on the reservation." Sometimes they call us "no-good Indians" and say we do not know how to use our land and the sooner we sell it to white men the better. Even our Bureau Area Director thinks that about us. He wrote me a letter that said my people should not try to keep their land. He said we should let white men buy all over our reservation, so that the Cheyennes could live next door to these white men and learn to be just like them.

To us, to be Cheyenne means being one tribe—living on our own land—in America, where we are citizens.

Our land is everything to us. It is the only place in the world where Cheyennes talk the Cheyenne language to each other. It is the only place where Cheyennes remember the same things together.

I will tell you one of the things we remember on our land.

We remember our grandfathers paid for it—with their life. My people and the Sioux defeated General Custer at the Little Big Horn. There never was an Indian victory after that. But the Army hated us. I think they were a little afraid of us too. They took my people away from Montana. They took them to Oklahoma Indian Territory. The people were sick there in all that heat and dust. They asked to go home again, but they were locked up in a military prison instead. Then Little Wolf and Dull Knife broke out of the prison, and they led the people on the long walk home. Montana is far away from Oklahoma, and they had no horses. They had no warm clothes, and many froze to death in the snow. They had nothing to fight with, and most of them were shot by the soldiers. A whole Army hunted them all the way. My grandmother told me she walked holding a little girl by the hand on each side. She had to keep pulling them out of the line of the soldiers' bullets. 300 of my people left Oklahoma. 100 came home. After that the Government gave us the reservation we live on now.

Now you can understand why we are fighting to save our land today. This fight is not against soldiers. It is a fight to stop land sales.

The General Allotment Act was passed in 1887. It is said that the Government could take away any reservation, and give every member of the tribe a piece of it, with the right to sell it to white men in twenty five years. In the southwest the Apache and other tribes never had their land allotted. These tribes have good economic development programs today. Their people are not turning into landless gypsies. . . .

Our Cheyenne land is cattle country. Sensible people knew it would be wrong to take cattle land like ours and divide it up into little pieces—big enough for grazing rabbits, but not cattle. Allotment was held off for the Cheyennes until 1926. My people did not know what allotment was. 25 years had to go by before individual Cheyennes could sell their pieces of our homeland out of Cheyenne ownership. Nobody worried until 1955—except white ranchers and speculators. They were waiting to defeat my hungry people with dollars the way soldiers defeated them with bullets. Then in 1955 the life and death fight of our Northern Cheyenne Tribe started.

When I tell you about the fight remember this. Cheyennes don't sell pieces of our homeland because they want to take their land sale money and go away from the people to live. They spend their land sale money on food—clothes—old cars to get around in. . . .

In 1955 the first tracts of Northern Cheyenne land were put up for sale by the Indian Bureau. Our people told us, the tribal council, to save the reservation any way we could—by asking the Bureau to stop Cheyenne land sales, by having the tribe buy up any land that was going to be sold. The tribal council liquidated our tribal steer enterprise, and we wanted to use $40,000 from this to keep the first Cheyenne land from being sold. The Bureau would not release our money to us in time for us to bid on the land. And they refused to hold up the land sale until our money was released. The Bixby Tracts were 1,340 acres of our best grazing and with water, and they were sold to a Mr. Norris for $22,458. A year later Mr. Norris offered to sell the land back to us again—for $47,736, a $25,278 profit. By then the tribe couldn't afford to buy back the Bixby Tracts, because the Billings Area Office of the Bureau was putting other tracts of our land up for sale as fast as they could. We had to bid on those tracts with the money we had. So far—from 1958 to 1959—the tribal council managed to hold our reservation together by bidding on every piece of land that went up for sale. In 1959 we borrowed $50,000 from the Indian Revolving Loan Fund at 4% interest. We knew this money will not be enough to buy all the land that ever comes up for sale. We thought we could save our homeland for a little while longer—and then the end would come.

The tribal council remembered the people told us to save the reservation. We prayed and thought. Then we wrote a plan to save the land the Cheyennes came home to from the Oklahoma. The people approved the plan. The Keeper of the Sacred Hat blessed it, and he is our holiest man.

Our plan is the Northern Cheyenne 50-Year Unallotment Program. It is a plan to make our reservation unallotted again in 50 years. The plan asks the Bureau to make us a 50-year loan of $500,000 at 2 ½% interest for land purchase. We have proved that we can repay this loan in 50 years or less out of income from the land the tribe will be buying. In the 50 years that the plan will be going on, we asked the Bureau to stop all Cheyenne land sales except to the tribe, and the tribe obligates itself to buy all land that individual Cheyennes want to sell. We also asked the Bureau to stop the approval of all fee patents during the period of the plan—and we asked them to allow members of the tribe to buy, sell and trade land among themselves without being forced to take it out of trust.

That plan could save our land. It will not cost the Government anything. The Government divided up our land so that it could be sold to white men in pieces. Now we are willing to buy every piece back again out of our own money.

We took our plan to the Interior Department—to Assistant Secretary Roger Ernst. He congratulated us for planning for ourselves. He said the plan would be approved if we could show that we could repay the loan we asked for.

We asked the Indian Bureau to stop all land sales on our reservation immediately, so that our lands would not be slipping away while we waited to get our loan. The Interior Department said the Bureau would do that. Right after we heard this good news, the Billings Area Office of the Bureau advertised 13 tracts of land for sale. The Association on American Indian Affairs told us to trust the Interior Department because Secretary Seaton and Secretary Ernst were men of their word. The Association was right. My people will tell the story of a thing that happened for a long time.

The land sale was advertised. Certain white men were wheeling around like buzzards waiting for the bidding to start. The Cheyennes could not talk—they were so angry and sad. Then all at once the land sale was called off—by a telephone call from Washington. You would have to be a Cheyenne to know what it meant when the Government in Washington kept its word—helped us against the Bureau in Montana. At first the people whispered the news to each other. Then they said it out loud. I never saw the Cheyennes as happy as that. I was never as happy myself in my whole life. I think all of us had a picture of the Government helping us save our land, then helping us with a plan to make our Cheyenne community a good part of America.

It is good for us to have that picture of how life can be for us. It will keep us strong in the fight ahead. . . .

My people are fighting to save their land. They are not fighting Congress or the Interior Department. . . .

1879
from *Land of the Spotted Eagle*

BY LUTHER STANDING BEAR

The Carlisle Indian School, which opened its doors in 1879, aimed to help Indian boys adopt the ways of white America—from red flannel underwear to tight shoes. It served as a model for government Indian schools. Luther Standing Bear of the Sioux tribe was a member of the school's first class.

TODAY MY PEOPLE, and all native people of this continent, are changed—degraded by oppression and poverty into but a semblance of their former being; health is undermined by disease, and the moral and spiritual life of the people deadened by the loss of the great sustaining forces of their devotional ceremonies. Our Indian boys and girls are going to segregated schools, are there taught to scorn all tribal institutions, and, to add insult to injury, are discountenanced by the race that brought their decline. There is not a tribe but has been poisoned by oppression and the thwarting of the natural course of life.

From the very first, the white strangers, who came unbidden, yet remained to become usurpers, assumed an attitude of superiority toward us, and because of this attitude there arose many false ideas concerning the Indian race that endure to this day. Though these white people did not observe the same high principles which we observed, and though they violated all of our rights as natives in our own land and as humans, and even the rights of creatures that we had so long protected, they looked upon us with disdain. They did not try to understand us and did not consider the fact that though we were different from them, still we were living our destiny according to the plan of the Supreme Dictator of mankind. Being narrow in both mind and spirit, they could see no possible good in us.

So for nearly four centuries the American Indian has been misinterpreted as to character, customs, practices in marriage, home, family, and religion. He has become imaged in the minds and hearts of a whole public as a whooping, yelling, vicious person without moral conscience and ethical scruples engaged in but one pursuit, that of war.

Irreparable damage has been done by white writers who discredit the Indian. Books have been written of the native American, so distorting his true nature that he scarcely resembles the real man; his faults have been magnified and his virtues minimized; his wars, and his battles, which, if successful, the white man chooses to call 'massacres,' have been told and retold, but little attention has been given to his philosophy and ideals. Books, paintings, and pictures have all joined in glorifying the pioneer—the hunter, trapper, woodsman, cowboy, and soldiery—in their course of conquest across the country, a conquest that could only have been realized by committing untold offenses against the aboriginal people. But who proclaims that every battle by the American Indian was a holy fight for the protection of wives, little children, and homeland; that every 'massacre' was the frenzied expression of the right to exist? Lurid fiction, cheap magazines, motion pictures, and newspapers help to impart the wrong idea that a scalp and a war dance are counterparts of native American life, while the truth is but not recorded, that the white man was always first met with friendliness on the part of the native; that whole tribes of people were sedentary and agricultural in occupation engaging only in defensive warfare; that, according to Caucasian war records, it was the white man who made scalping a part of organized military operations and also turned it into a business for profit, and that the finest warwhoops are produced under the influence of 'firewater.'

So, through the very agencies that reach the mass of people, that purport to instruct, educate, and perpetuate true history—books, schools, and libraries all over the land—there have been graven false ideas in the hearts and minds of the people. Even the boys and girls throughout the country, whose sources of information are inadequate, have the thought that the Indian is a curious creature, something to be amused at, and as not having contributed worth-while things to the culture of this country. This in spite of the fact that history for this continent did not begin with the landing of the Pilgrims, and that many notable cultural events had taken place before the coming of the European; that some of the truest and greatest patriots have been American Indians, and that such names as Red Jacket, Tecumseh, and Crazy Horse would brighten the pages of any history, while the name of Sequoia not only lights the pages of American history, but the history of achievement of all mankind.

The mothers and fathers of this land do their children an injustice by not seeing that their offspring are taught the true history of this continent and its people: that the Indian fed and nourished the weary travelers from over the seas and made it possible for them to remain to enjoy life and freedom; that they were not warlike demons, but that their philosophy was one of kindness; that some of their governmental principles were unequaled for equity; that some of their crafts are even today unsurpassed; and that this country has native contributions in song, stories, music, pageantry, dance, poetry, and oratory worthy of perpetuation. True, some noteworthy scholars have done diligent work along the lines of preservation, but their works have not yet found popular recognition. True, that valuable data have been compiled and can be found in reference libraries, but these statistical works lack the human touch, and the Indian of the cheap magazine and the movie still remain as the best type of the First American. So it is the parents and the grade teachers of this land who may now fulfill the duty of demanding that true histories be placed in the hands of the young.

It is now nearly four hundred years since 'civilization' was brought to us, and this is the situation: All groups of public opinion and action, the schools, universities, men's and women's clubs, churches, and other organizations are apathetic toward the Indian and his situation. If but two organized groups, the schools and the Federated Women's Clubs, to whom Charles Lummis so naively left the solution of the question and who have done nothing, were to concentrate action for just one year, something would be done. Even the law has forsaken him, and the Indian today is not only unheard and unheeded, but robbed, pillaged, denied his heritage, and held in bondage. The greatest hoax ever perpetrated upon him was the supposed citizenship of 1924 when President Coolidge signed a bill that freed the Indian. The signing of that bill changed not in the slightest measure the condition of the Indian. Not one agent was removed from office, Indian boys and girls are still segregated in school life, and the reservation and reservation rule still exist.

I grew up leading the traditional life of my people, learning the crafts of hunter, scout, and warrior from father, kindness to the old and feeble from mother, respect for wisdom and council from our wise men, and was trained by grandfather and older boys in the devotional rites to the Great Mystery. This was the scheme of existence as followed by my forefathers for many centuries, and more centuries might have come and gone in much the same way had it not been for a strange people who came from a far land to change and reshape our world.

At the age of eleven years, ancestral life for me and my people was most abruptly ended without regard for our wishes, comforts, or rights in the matter. At once I was thrust into an alien world, into an environment as different from the one into which I had been born as it is possible to imagine, to remake myself, if I could, into the likeness of the invader.

By 1879, my people were no longer free, but were subjects confined on reservations under the rule of agents. One day there came to the agency a party of white people from the East. Their presence aroused considerable excitement when it became known that these people were school teachers who wanted some Indian boys and girls to take away with them to train as were white boys and girls.

Now, father was a 'blanket Indian,' but he was wise. He listened to the white strangers, their offers and promises that if they took his son they would care well for him, teach him how to read and write, and how to wear white man's clothes. But to father all this was just 'sweet talk,' and I know that it was with great misgivings that he left the decision to me and asked if I cared to go with these people. I, of course, shared with the rest of my tribe a distrust of the white people, so I know that for all my dear father's anxiety he was proud to hear me say 'Yes.' That meant that I was brave.

I could think of no reason why white people wanted Indian boys and girls except to kill them, and not having the remotest idea of what a school was, I thought we were going East to die. But so well had courage and bravery been trained into us that it became a part of our unconscious thinking and acting, and personal life was nothing when it came time to do something for the tribe. Even in our play and games we voluntarily put ourselves to various tests in the effort to grow brave and fearless, for it was most discrediting to be called *can'l wanka,* or a coward. Accordingly there were few cowards, most Lakota men preferring to die in the performance of some act of bravery than to die of old age. Thus, in giving myself up to go East, I was proving to my father that he was honored with a brave son. In my decision to go, I gave up many things dear to the heart of a little Indian boy, and one of the things over which my child mind grieved was the thought of saying good-bye to my pony. I rode him as far as I could on the journey, which was to the Missouri River, where we took the boat. There we parted from our parents, and it was a heart-breaking scene, women and children weeping. Some of the children changed their minds and were unable to go on the boat, but for many who did go it was a final parting.

On our way to school we saw many white people, more than we ever dreamed existed, and the manner in which they acted when they saw us quite indicated their opinion of us. It was only about three years after the Custer battle, and the general opinion was that the Plains people merely infested the earth as nuisances, and our being there simply evidenced misjudgment on the part of Wakan Tanka. Whenever our train stopped at the railway stations, it was met by great numbers of white people who came to gaze upon the little Indian 'savages.' The shy little ones sat quietly at the car windows looking at the people who swarmed on the platform. Some of the children wrapped themselves in their blankets, covering all but their eyes. At one place we were taken off the train and marched a distance down the street to a restaurant. We walked down the street between two rows of uniformed men whom we called soldiers, though I suppose they were policemen. This must have been done to protect us, for it was surely known that we boys and girls could do no harm. Back of the rows of uniformed men stood the white people craning their necks, talking, laughing, and making a great noise. They yelled and tried to mimic us by giving what they thought were war-whoops. We did not like this, and some of the children were naturally very much frightened. I remember how I tried to crowd into the protecting midst of the jostling boys and girls. But we were all trying to be brave, yet going to what we thought would end in death at the hands of the white people whom we knew had no love for us. Back on the train the older boys sang brave songs in an effort to keep up their spirits and ours too. In my mind I often recall that scene—eighty-odd blanketed boys and girls marching down the street surrounded by a jeering, unsympathetic people whose only emotions were those of hate and fear; the conquerors looking upon the conquered. And no more understanding us than if we had suddenly been dropped from the moon.

At last at Carlisle the transforming, the 'civilizing' process began. It began with clothes. Never, no matter what our philosophy or spiritual quality, could we be civilized while wearing the moccasin and blanket. The task before us was not only that of accepting new ideas and adopting new manners, but actual physical changes and discomfort had to be borne uncomplainingly until the body adjusted itself to new tastes and habits. Our accustomed dress was taken and replaced with clothing that felt cumbersome and awkward. Against trousers and handkerchiefs we had a distinct feeling—they were unsanitary and the trousers kept us from breathing well. High collars, stiff-bosomed shirts, and suspenders fully three inches in width were uncomfortable, while leather boots caused actual suffering. We longed to go barefoot, but were told that the dew on the grass would give us colds. That was a new warning for us, for our mothers had never told us to beware of colds, and I remember as a child coming into the tipi with moccasins full of snow. Unconcernedly I would take them off my feet, pour out the snow, and put them on my feet again without any thought of sickness, for in that time colds, catarrh, bronchitis, and *la grippe* were unknown. But we were soon to know them. Then, red flannel undergarments were given us for winter wear, and for me, at least, discomfort grew into actual torture. I used to endure it as long as possible, then run upstairs and quickly take off the flannel garments and hide them. When inspection time came, I ran and put them on again, for I knew that if I were found disobeying the orders of the school I should be punished. My niece once asked me what it was that I disliked the most during those first bewildering days, and I said, 'red flannel.' Not knowing what I meant, she laughed, but I still remember those horrid, sticky garments which we had to wear next to the skin, and I still squirm and itch when I think of them. Of course, our hair was cut, and then there was much disapproval. But that was part of the transformation process and in some mysterious way long hair stood in the path of our development.

For all the grumbling among the bigger boys, we soon had our heads shaven. How strange I felt! Involuntarily, time and time again, my hands went to my head, and that night it was a long time before I went to sleep. If we did not learn much at first, it will not be wondered at, I think. Everything was queer, and it took a few months to get adjusted to the new surroundings.

Almost immediately our names were changed to those in common use in the English language. Instead of translating our names into English and calling Zinkcaziwin, Yellow Bird, and Wanbli K'leska, Spotted Eagle, which in itself would have been educational, we were just John, Henry, or Maggie, as the case might be. I was told to take a pointer and select a name for myself from the list written on the blackboard. I did, and since one was just as good as another, and as I could not distinguish any difference in them, I placed the pointer on the name Luther. I then learned to call myself by that name and got used to hearing others call me by it, too. By that time we had been forbidden to speak our mother tongue, which is the rule in all boarding-schools. This rule is uncalled for, and today is not only robbing the Indian, but America of a rich heritage. The language of a people is part of their history. Today we should be perpetuating history instead of destroying it, and this can only be effectively done by allowing and encouraging the young to keep it alive. A language, unused, embalmed, and reposing only in a book, is a dead language. Only the people themselves, and never the scholars, can nourish it into life.

Of all the changes we were forced to make, that of diet was doubtless the most injurious, for it was immediate and drastic. White bread we had for the first meal and thereafter, as well as coffee and sugar. Had we been allowed our own simple diet of meat, either boiled with soup or dried, and fruit, with perhaps a few vegetables, we should have thrived. But the change in clothing, housing, food, and confinement combined with lonesomeness was too much, and in three years nearly one half of the children from the Plains were dead and through with all earthly schools. In the graveyard at Carlisle most of the graves are those of little ones.

I am now going to confess that I had been at Carlisle a full year before I decided to learn all I could of the white man's ways, and then the inspiration was furnished by my father, the man who has been the greatest influence in all my life. When I had been in school a year, father made his first trip to see me. After I had received permission to speak to him, he told me that on his journey he had seen that the land was full of 'Long Knives.' 'They greatly outnumber us and are here to stay,' he said, and advised me, 'Son, learn all you can of the white man's ways and try to be like him,' From that day on I tried. Those few words of my father I remember as if we talked but yesterday, and in the maturity of my mind I have thought of what he said. He did not say that he thought the white man's ways better than our own; neither did he say that I could be like a white man. He said, 'Son, try to be like a white man.' So, in two more years I had been 'made over.' I was Luther Standing Bear wearing the blue uniform of the school, shorn of my hair, and trying hard to walk naturally and easily in stiff-soled cowhide boots. I was now 'civilized' enough to go to work in John Wanamaker's fine store in Philadelphia.

I returned from the East at about the age of sixteen, after five years' contact with the white people, to resume life upon the reservation. But I returned, to spend some thirty years before again leaving, just as I had gone—a Lakota.

Outwardly I lived the life of the white man, yet all the while I kept in direct contact with tribal life. While I had learned all that I could of the white man's culture, I never forgot that of my people. I kept the language, tribal manners and usages, sang the songs and danced the dances. I still listened to and respected the advice of the older people of the tribe. I did not come home so 'progressive' that I could not speak the language of my father and mother. I did not learn the vices of chewing tobacco, smoking, drinking, and swearing, and for all this I am grateful. I have never, in fact, 'progressed' that far.

But I soon began to see the sad sight, so common today, of returned students who could not speak their native tongue, or, worse yet, some who pretended they could no longer converse in the mother tongue. They had become ashamed and this led them into deception and trickery. The boys came home wearing stiff paper collars, tight patent-leather boots, and derby hats on heads that were meant to be clothed in the long hair of the Lakota brave. The girls came home wearing muslin dresses and long ribbon sashes in bright hues which were very pretty. But they were trying to squeeze their feet into heeled shoes of factory make and their waists into binding apparatuses that were not garments—at least they served no purpose of a garment, but bordered on some mechanical device. However, the wearing of them was part of the 'civilization' received from those who were doing the same thing. So we went to school to copy, to imitate; not to exchange languages and ideas, and not to develop the best traits that had come out of uncountable experiences of hundreds and thousands of years living upon this continent. Our annals, all happenings of human import, were stored in our song and dance rituals, our history differing in that it was not stored in books, but in the living memory. So, while the white people had much to teach us, we had much to teach them, and what a school could have been established upon that idea! However, this was not the attitude of the day, though the teachers were sympathetic and kind, and some came to be my lifelong friends. But in the main, Indian qualities were undivined and Indian virtues not conceded. And I can well remember when Indians in those days were stoned upon the streets as were the dogs that roamed them. We were 'savages,' and all who had not come under the influence of the missionary were 'heathen,' and Wakan Tanka, who had since the beginning watched over the Lakota and his land, was denied by these men of God. Should we not have been justified in thinking them heathen? And so the 'civilizing' process went on, killing us as it went.

When I came back to the reservation to resume life there, it was too late to go on the warpath to prove, as I had always hoped to prove to my people, that I was a real brave. However, there came the battle of my life—the battle with agents to retain my individuality and my life as a Lakota. I wanted to take part in the tribal dances, sing the songs I had heard since I was born, and repeat and cherish the tales that had been the delight of my boyhood. It was in these things and through these things that my people lived and could continue to live, so it was up to me to keep them alive in my mind.

Now and then the Lakotas were holding their tribal dances in the old way, and I attended. Though my hair had been cut and I wore civilian clothes, I never forsook the blanket. For convenience, no coat I have ever worn can take the place of the blanket robe; and the same with the moccasins, which are sensible, comfortable, and beautiful. Besides, they were devised by people who danced—not for pastime, excitement, or fashion—but because it was an innate urge. Even when studying under the missionary, I went to the dances of my tribe.

All the while the agent or white rule became harder and stricter. The missionary oftentimes was an ally to the agent in trying to stop everything the Indian naturally did either in the pursuit of living or pleasure. A rule would come out forbidding something to be done, and in a short while another order would be issued forbidding something else to be done, until gradually and slowly rights began to disappear. On the commissary door and in the trader's store there one day appeared a printed notice, by order of the agent, that no returned student would thereafter be permitted to attend any tribal dance. This was done in an effort to make young people turn away from things traditional. In a short while there came another order which allowed the old people to hold but one dance a week, and no more.

Soon another rule followed, stating that whenever a horse or present was given away, it must be done silently. Though there was nothing to disturb but the endless ether, there must be no glad announcing and no shouts of joy. The singing of praise songs by old men and the calling of gift-givers to some poor person were not to the liking of the white rulers. Cursing and yelling at football and baseball games were all to their liking and most certainly in order. But ceremonial gift-making was not to the order of their doing.

1998

from Whose History Do We Celebrate?

BY CHARLENE TETERS

Charlene Teters, a member of the Spokane Nation, is an artist, teacher, writer and activist. This article originally appeared in *Indian Artist*.

> "We took the liberty of removing Don Juan de Oñate's right foot on behalf of our brothers and sisters at Acoma Pueblo."
> —Anonymous letter to the Albuquerque Journal, *Jan. 8, 1998*

THIS YEAR MARKS the Cuartocentenario, the 400th anniversary of the incursion of the Spanish conquistador Don Juan de Oñate from Mexico into what is now Texas, Arizona, and New Mexico. Recently, however, New Mexicans on the verge of a year-long series of celebrations were shocked by the action of an unidentified group whose members sawed off the right foot of a bronze statue of Oñate in the Española Valley north of Santa Fe.

New Mexico, home to one of the largest contemporary American Indian populations, was quickly reminded that Indian people are still here—and that we are not always docile. The disfiguring of the statue also resulted in a quick and powerful history lesson for mainstream America. One of many brutal truths selectively omitted from most history books is this: in 1599, Oñate attacked Acoma Pueblo in retaliation for the death of his nephew, ordering that the right feet of all men in the pueblo above the age of twenty-five be chopped off.

History is very powerful. The manner in which it is presented has the ability to inspire or deflate, to move nations to love, joy, anger, or hatred. The vast majority of Americans know very little about how this continent—originally peopled by thousands of diverse Indian nations—came to be what is now the United States. This ignorance serves to perpetuate the doctrine of Manifest Destiny, the supposedly inevitable conquest of North America and the islands of the Pacific and the Caribbean. Twenty-five years ago, from Wounded Knee, South Dakota, the American Indian Movement decried the absence of American Indian history in the nation's classrooms. Even today, many remain willfully ignorant of it.

I embrace the concept of personal destiny. I am a survivor, not a victim. And yet during my public school experience, the presentation of American history deeply influenced my self-esteem, as it did for many Native children. I remember trying to become invisible as teachers told stories of brave settlers, untamed lands, and savage, uncivilized Indians. Washington State history simply did not include American Indian history. To this day, it remains largely ignored or distorted in most American schools.

While growing up in Washington State, I also felt the impact of a powerful mural portraying the explorers Lewis and Clark pointing to the western horizon in the direction of my homeland in Washington State. That same mural depicts Indians and other people of color bowed in an all-too-typical posture of servitude before the two glorified travelers. The caption beneath it reads, "The first civilized men to look upon the Inland Empire."

Now, many year later, I still feel the sting of ethnocentric propaganda in public art. As an artist, I know the power of art used to reinforce heroes, icons, and political ideology. All across the United States, bronze statues, monuments, and murals celebrate conquests and commemorate the fulfillment of Manifest Destiny.

Art also has a history of effective use in social activism. As the nation celebrates numerous anniversaries—the Quincentennial of Columbus's landing in America, the Oklahoma Land Rush, the California Gold Rush, and the Cuartocentenario—the question is: how do we Indians find appropriate ways to mark these events in our collective history? How do we reconcile that some of America's heroes are not *our* heroes? Glorifying Indian killers feels to us like glorifying Hitler.

Cutting the foot off the Oñate statue in the face of public celebrations forces the issue that there is another side to the notion of conquest. Native artists have often used art to express their own reactions to historical events. But such expression often appears in subversive forms, as our dissenting voices are still largely unwelcome in such national festivities.

Another dissenting voice is Edgar Heap of Birds, a Cheyenne-Arapaho conceptual artist, who responded to Oklahoma's 1989 Land Rush celebrations with a series of five billboards that spelled out the words, "RUN OVER INDIAN NATIONS, APARTHEID OKLAHOMA." Like the sawing off of Oñate's foot, Heap of Birds's caustic message didn't stand in the way of reenactments, parades, and speeches, but it gave voice to a strong and widespread sentiment that was missing in the state-sanctioned celebrations.

Art also provides more mainstream ways of expressing dissent. In a break from tradition this year, the Oakland Museum in California is presenting a series of programs giving expression to California's untold stories. With the museum's blessing, Maidu artist Harry Fonseca has created a body of work entitled *The Discovery of Gold in California,* which explores the impact of the Gold Rush on California's Indian population. Similarly, the American Indian House Gallery in New York City is planning a summer exhibition that will express two histories simultaneously: that of the Indians and that of the colonizers.

These two exhibitions are steps in the right direction, because our history is very different from that of the colonizers. For Indians to celebrate many events in American history requires either that we have historical amnesia or that we grant amnesty for the atrocities committed on our populations. The cost of either of these alternatives is too great to pay. It is time we all began acknowledging a more balanced history than that provided by schoolbooks and supermarket tabloids. Together, let us find more ways to honor the victims and survivors of the legacy of conquest, who are also American citizens.

1998
Transcript from a Class Action Suit Against the U.S. Government

The Bureau of Indian Affairs (BIA) has acted as a trustee for the American Indians since the 1880s. Five plaintiffs in 1996 sued the government on behalf of 500,000 Indians. The plaintiffs hoped to reclaim an estimated $10 billion loss of income. Defending attorney Lewis Wiener in this transcript makes excuses for having failed to comply with court-ordered requests for documents related to the case. U.S. District Court Judge Royce C. Lamberth presides, and attorneys Thaddeus Holt and Dennis M. Gingold represent the plaintiffs.

LEWIS WIENER: Your Honor, we are here to discuss how we are going to bring ourselves into compliance with the Court's order. Let me state that it was never the government's intent to willfully disregard that order. We have spent considerable time thinking about and in fact putting into motion the elements that need to be in place to allow us to produce documents for the five named plaintiffs.

We met with the plaintiffs on November 10. It was a very candid meeting. It was—I hope plaintiffs will agree—very beneficial. We cleared the air on several issues, and, more than anything else, we agreed that the kinds of disputes that led us down the wrong path last time will not recur. We discussed a great many issues, including the production of BIA documents.

It has been discovered, however, that the potential for hantavirus disease exists at the Albuquerque site [where some of the BIA documents are stored]. Hantavirus has a 50 percent mortality rate. Half the people who get it die. It's an enormously serious disease. The office cannot get to any of the documents until the facilities are cleaned up. But as soon as the facilities are accessible, the government plans to put this at the top of the list.

I'd like to call to testify Dr. Terry Yates. Good afternoon, Dr. Yates. Would you please review for the Court what you were asked to do in this case?

TERRY YATES: I was basically asked to assess the nature and extent of potential hantavirus infection in two warehouses in Albuquerque.

Wiener: What did you find?

YATES: The two facilities in Albuquerque are clearly contaminated with rodent feces. Dead mice were even found in some of the boxes. There are approximately 20,000 boxes in these warehouses, and, in my judgment, they certainly represent a potential danger. Let me point out that this kind of hantavirus is a BioSafety Level 4 virus. By comparison, AIDS is Level 2. This virus goes directly from rodents to humans, and we think the most common route is through inhalation of dust particles. The best analogy I can think of is if you ever sit in your house on a cold winter day and you see these little dust particles suspended in the air coming in with the sunlight—this virus can do that.

So what we'll have to do is send a team wearing HEPA filter respirators into the warehouse, have them open every box, clean those boxes appropriately, transfer the material to new boxes if it's soiled or contaminated with urine or something, then shrink-wrap all those boxes with heavy plastic and put them into a hantavirus holding facility for fourteen days, just as an extra precaution to make sure that any virus particles are killed.

Wiener: As far as the individuals who would be doing this—can you just go out and get some part-time high school students to come in?

YATES: No. You have to have people that are specifically trained for doing this kind of work.

Wiener: Dr. Yates, bottom line: how long will it take to clean up the Albuquerque facilities based on the protocol you have suggested?

YATES: Well, being unaware of everything that's in all of the boxes, there may be some variation in this estimate—but we can probably take care of those facilities in two and a half to three months.

Wiener: Your Honor, if it please the Court, our next witness is Mr. Charlie Janes. Please state your name and title for the record.

CHARLES JANES: Charles Janes. I'm chief of the Division of Safety Management for the Bureau of Indian Affairs.

Wiener: Mr. Janes, have any of the other BIA document-storage facilities been inspected?

JANES: Yes. So far we've screened Crow Creek, Rosebud, Yankton, Fort Berthold, Fort Totten, Turtle Mountain. All were free of infestation, and we've let the records folks know that record retrieval could commence at those sites.

Wiener: Do you have a timetable by which at least an initial screening of the approximately seventy offices could be completed?

JANES: Thirty days or so would be a reasonable estimate.

Wiener: How long would it take to clean up any sites where infestation is identified?

JANES: Cleanup is a completely separate issue. We don't have people out there who are capable of this. There are a handful at CDC, Dr. Yates has a handful. I think there are some researchers in Bozeman, Montana, and maybe some at Yavapai College in Arizona. I just don't know what resources we can bring to the cleanup issue.

Wiener: Yield to Mr. Holt, Your Honor.

THADDEUS HOLT: Your Honor, Mr. Gingold will address briefly the question of compliance up till now with the Court's outstanding production orders.

LAMBERTH: All right.

DENNIS M. GINGOLD: Your Honor, not a single document-production order, scheduling order, or document-production request has been satisfied. On December 24, 1996, plaintiffs served the first formal request for production of documents. No documents have been provided. On June 5, 1998, a second formal request was issued. Most of these documents have been withheld as privileged. And we've received nothing with regard to our third and fourth requests of June 11 and October 19, and the original closing date for document production was November 17.

We recognize that there is a serious problem in Albuquerque, New Mexico, but not one of our named plaintiffs is in Albuquerque, New Mexico. Our clients are waiting and waiting for their money. One of our named plaintiffs has died since the beginning of this litigation. What has been done? I mean, we're talking a year, two years ago this Court issued the first order of production, and today we are not much further ahead than we were back then. How many more years are we going to go?

Wiener: Your Honor, I just have to throw up my hands. I don't know why plaintiffs need these documents. They don't need the documents of the five named plaintiffs for purposes of conducting their analysis on how to fix the system. They agreed—

LAMBERTH: No, no, no. I ordered it, and you can't raise the question whether they need it.

Wiener: But that's why we came here today with a plan on how we were going to produce documents for the five named plaintiffs.

LAMBERTH: I understand.

Wiener: And we said—

LAMBERTH: And an answer for why you haven't produced things that I ordered two years ago? You can't answer that.

Wiener: Your Honor, all that I can tell you is that the department has used its best efforts.

LAMBERTH: Well, they're pretty poor, aren't they?

Wiener: Your Honor, I—that is for you to say, not me.

slavery

from *The Life of Olaudah Equiano*

BY OLAUDAH EQUIANO

Olaudah Equiano (Gustavus Vassa), kidnapped from his
African village at the age of eleven, made the notorious
"Middle Passage" across the Atlantic and spent ten years as
a slave before buying his freedom. He was forty-four when
he wrote his best-selling autobiography, which went
through nine editions before his death eight years later.

MY FATHER, BESIDES many slaves, had a numerous family, of which
seven lived to grow up, including myself and a sister, who was the
only daughter. As I was the youngest of the sons, I became, of course,
the greatest favourite with my mother, and was always with her; and
she used to take particular pains to form my mind. I was trained up
from my earliest years in the art of war; my daily exercise was
shooting and throwing javelins; and my mother adorned me with
emblems, after the manner of our greatest warriors. In this way I
grew up till I was turned the age of eleven, when an end was put to
my happiness in the following manner:—Generally when the grown
people in the neighbourhood were gone far in the fields to labour, the
children assembled together in some of the neighbours' premises to
play; and commonly some of us used to get up a tree to look out for
any assailant, or kidnapper, that might come upon us; for they sometimes took those opportunities of our parents' absence to attack and
carry off as many as they could seize. One day, as I was watching at
the top of a tree in our yard, I saw one of those people come into the
yard of our next neighbour but one, to kidnap, there being many

stout young people in it. Immediately on this I gave the alarm of the rogue, and he was surrounded by the stoutest of them, who entangled him with cords, so that he could not escape till some of the grown people came and secured him. But alas! ere long it was my fate to be thus attacked, and to be carried off, when none of the grown people were nigh. One day, when all our people were gone out to their works as usual, and only I and my dear sister were left to mind the house, two men and a woman got over our walls, and in a moment seized us both, and, without giving us time to cry out, or make resistance, they stopped our mouths, and ran off with us into the nearest wood. Here they tied our hands, and continued to carry us as far as they could, till night came on, when we reached a small house, where the robbers halted for refreshment, and spent the night. We were then unbound, but were unable to take any food; and, being quite overpowered by fatigue and grief, our only relief was some sleep, which allayed our misfortune for a short time. The next morning we left the house, and continued travelling all the day. For a long time we had kept the woods, but at last we came into a road which I believed I knew. I had now some hopes of being delivered; for we had advanced but a little way before I discovered some people at a distance, on which I began to cry out for their assistance: but my cries had no other effect than to make them tie me faster and stop my mouth, and then they put me into a large sack. They also stopped my sister's mouth, and tied her hands; and in this manner we proceeded till we were out of the sight of these people. When we went to rest the following night they offered us some victuals; but we refused it; and the only comfort we had was in being in one another's arms all that night, and bathing each other with our tears. But alas! we were soon deprived of even the small comfort of weeping together. The next day proved a day of greater sorrow than I had yet experienced; for my sister and I were then separated, while we lay clasped in each other's arms. It was in vain that we besought them not to part us; she was torn from me, and immediately carried away, while I was left in a state of distraction not to be described. I cried and grieved continually; and for several days I did not eat any thing but what they forced into my mouth. At length, after many days travelling, during which I had often changed masters, I got into the hands of a chieftain, in a very pleasant country. This man had two wives and some children, and they all used me extremely well, and did all they could to comfort me; particularly the first wife, who was something like my mother. Although I was a great many days journey from my father's house, yet these people spoke exactly the same language with us. This first master of mine, as I may call him, was a smith, and my principal employment was working his bellows, which were the same kind as I had seen in my vicinity. They were in some respects not unlike the stoves here in gentlemen's kitchens; and were covered over with leather; and in the middle of that leather a stick was fixed, and a person stood up, and worked it, in the same manner as is done to pump water out of a cask with a hand pump. I believe it was gold he worked, for it was of a lovely bright yellow colour, and was worn by the women on their wrists and ankles. I was there I suppose about a month, and they at last used to trust me some little distance from the house. This liberty I used in embracing every opportunity to inquire the way to my own home: and I also sometimes, for the same purpose, went with the maidens, in the cool of the evenings, to bring pitchers of water from the springs for the use of the house. I had also remarked where the sun rose in the morning, and set in the evening, as I had travelled along; and I had observed that my father's house was towards the rising of the sun. I therefore determined to seize the first opportunity of making my escape, and to shape my course for that quarter; for I was quite oppressed and weighed down by grief after my mother and friends; and my love of liberty, ever great, was strengthened by the mortifying circumstance of not daring to eat with the free-born children, although I was mostly their companion.

While I was projecting my escape, one day an unlucky event happened, which quite disconcerted my plan, and put an end to my hopes. I used to be sometimes employed in assisting an elderly woman slave to cook and take care of the poultry; and one morning, while I was feeding some chickens, I happened to toss a small pebble at one of them, which hit it on the middle and directly killed it. The old slave, having soon after missed the chicken, inquired after it; and on my relating the accident (for I told her the truth, because my mother would never suffer me to tell a lie) she flew into a violent passion, threatened that I should suffer for it; and, my master being out, she immediately went and told her mistress what I had done. This alarmed me very much, and I expected an instant flogging, which to me was uncommonly dreadful; for I had seldom been beaten at home. I therefore resolved to fly; and accordingly I ran into a thicket that was hard by, and hid myself in the bushes. Soon afterwards my mistress and the slave returned, and, not seeing me, they searched all the house, but not finding me, and I not making answer when they called to me, they thought I had run away, and the whole neighbourhood was raised in the pursuit of me. In that part of the country (as in ours) the houses and villages were skirted with woods, or shrubberies, and the bushes were so thick that a man could readily conceal himself in them, so as to elude the strictest search. The neighbours continued the whole day looking for me, and several times many of them came within a few yards of the place where I lay hid. I then gave myself up for lost entirely, and expected every moment, when I heard a rustling among the trees, to be found out, and punished by my master: but they never discovered me, though they were often so near that I even heard their conjectures as they were looking about for me; and I now learned from them, that any attempt to return home would be hopeless. Most of them supposed I had fled towards home; but the distance was so great, and the way so intricate, that they thought I could never reach it, and that I should be lost in the woods. When I heard this I was seized with a violent panic, and abandoned myself to despair. Night too began to approach, and aggravated all my fears. I had before entertained hopes of getting home, and I had determined when it should be dark to make the attempt; but I was now convinced it was fruitless, and I began to consider that, if possibly I could escape all other animals, I could not those of the human kind; and that, not knowing the way, I must perish in the woods. Thus was I like the hunted deer:

> —Ev'ry leaf and ev'ry whisp'ring breath
> Convey'd a foe, and ev'ry foe a death.

I heard frequent rustlings among the leaves; and being pretty sure they were snakes I expected every instant to be stung by them. This increased my anguish, and the horror of my situation became now quite insupportable. I at length quitted the thicket, very faint and hungry, for I had not eaten or drank any thing all the day; and crept to my master's kitchen, from whence I set out at first, and which was an open shed, and laid myself down in the ashes with an anxious wish for death to relieve me from all my pains. I was scarcely awake in the morning when the old woman slave, who was the first up, came to light the fire, and saw me in the fire place. She was very much surprised to see me, and could scarcely believe her own eyes. She now promised to intercede for me, and went for her master, who soon after came, and, having slightly reprimanded me, ordered me to be taken care of, and not to be ill-treated.

Soon after this my master's only daughter, and child by his first wife, sickened and died, which affected him so much that for some time he was almost frantic, and really would have killed himself, had he not been watched and prevented. However, in a small time afterwards he recovered, and I was again sold. I was now carried to the left of the sun's rising, through many different countries, and a number of large woods. The people I was sold to used to carry me very often, when I was tired, either on their shoulders or on their backs. I saw many convenient well-built sheds along the roads, at proper distances, to accommodate the merchants and travellers, who lay in those buildings along with their wives, who often accompany them; and they always go well armed.

From the time I left my own nation I always found somebody that understood me till I came to the sea coast. The languages of different nations did not totally differ, nor were they so copious as those of the Europeans, particularly the English. They were therefore easily learned; and, while I was journeying thus through Africa, I acquired two or three different tongues. In this manner I had been travelling for a considerable time, when one evening, to my great surprise, whom should I see brought to the house where I was but my dear sister! As soon as she saw me she gave a loud shriek, and ran into my arms—I was quite overpowered: neither of us could speak; but, for a considerable time, clung to each other in mutual embraces, unable to do any thing but weep. Our meeting affected all who saw us; and indeed I must acknowledge, in honour of those sable destroyers of human rights, that I never met with any ill treatment, or saw any offered to their slaves, except tying them, when necessary, to keep them from running away. When these people knew we were brother and sister they indulged us together; and the man, to whom I supposed we belonged, lay with us, he in the middle, while she and I held one another by the hands across his breast all night; and thus for a while we forgot our misfortunes in the joy of being together: but even this small comfort was soon to have an end; for scarcely had the fatal morning appeared, when she was again torn from me for ever! I was now more miserable, if possible, than before. The small relief which her presence gave me from pain was gone, and the wretchedness of my situation was redoubled by my anxiety after her fate, and my apprehensions lest her sufferings should be greater than mine, when I could not be with her to alleviate them. Yes, thou dear partner of all my childish sports! thou sharer of my joys and sorrows! happy should I have ever esteemed myself to encounter every misery for you, and to procure your freedom by the sacrifice of my own. Though you were early forced from my arms, your image has been always riveted in my heart, from which neither *time nor fortune* have been able to remove it; so that, while the thoughts of your sufferings have damped my prosperity, they have mingled with adversity and increased its bitterness. To that Heaven which protects the weak from the strong, I commit the care of your innocence and virtues, if they have not already received their full reward, and if your youth and delicacy have not long since fallen victims to the violence of the African trader, the pestilential stench of a Guinea ship, the seasoning in the European colonies, or the lash and lust of a brutal and unrelenting overseer.

I did not long remain after my sister. I was again sold, and carried through a number of places, till, after travelling a considerable time, I came to a town called Tinmah, in the most beautiful country I had yet seen in Africa. It was extremely rich, and there were many rivulets which flowed through it, and supplied a large pond in the centre of the town, where the people washed. Here I first saw and tasted cocoanuts, which I thought superior to any nuts I had ever tasted before; and the trees, which were loaded, were also interspersed amongst the houses, which had commodious shades adjoining, and were in the same manner as ours, the insides being neatly plastered and whitewashed. Here I also saw and tasted for the first time sugar-cane. Their money consisted of little white shells, the size of the finger nail. I was sold here for one hundred and seventy-two of them by a merchant who lived and brought me there. I had been about two or three days at his house, when a wealthy widow, a neighbour of his, came there one evening, and brought with her an only son, a young gentleman about my own age and size. Here they saw me; and, having taken a fancy to me, I was bought of the merchant, and went home with them. Her house and premises were situated close to one of those rivulets I have mentioned, and were the finest I ever saw in Africa: they were very extensive, and she had a number of slaves to attend her. The next day I was washed and perfumed, and when meal-time came I was led into the presence of my mistress, and ate and drank before her with her son. This filled me with astonishment; and I could scarce help expressing my surprise that the young gentleman should suffer me, who was bound, to eat with him who was free; and not only so, but that he would not at any time either eat or drink till I had taken first, because I was the eldest, which was agreeable to our custom. Indeed every thing here, and all their treatment of me, made me forget that I was a slave. The language of these people resembled ours so nearly, that we understood each other perfectly. They had also the very same customs as we. There were likewise slaves daily to attend us, while my young master and I with other boys sported with our darts and bows and arrows, as I had been used to do at home. In this resemblance to my former happy state I passed about two months; and I now began to think I was to be adopted into the family, and was beginning to be rereconciled to my situation, and to forget by degrees my misfortunes, when all at once the delusion vanished; for, without the least previous knowledge, one morning early, while my dear master and companion was still asleep, I was wakened out of my reverie to fresh sorrow, and hurried away even amongst the uncircumcised.

Thus, at the very moment I dreamed of the greatest happiness, I found myself most miserable; and it seemed as if fortune wished to give me this taste of joy, only to render the reverse more poignant. The change I now experienced was as painful as it was sudden and unexpected. It was a change indeed from a state of bliss to a scene which is inexpressible by me, as it discovered to me an element I had never before beheld, and till then had no idea of, and wherein such instances of hardship and cruelty continually occurred as I can never reflect on but with horror.

All the nations and people I had hitherto passed through resembled our own in their manners, customs, and language: but I came at length to a country, the inhabitants of which differed from us in all those particulars. I was very much struck with this difference, especially when I came among a people who did not circumcise, and ate without washing their hands. They cooked also in iron pots, and had European cutlasses and cross bows, which were unknown to us, and fought with their fists amongst themselves. Their women were not so modest as ours, for they ate, and drank, and slept, with their men. But, above all, I was amazed to see no sacrifices or offerings among them. In some of those places the people ornamented themselves with scars, and likewise filed their teeth very sharp. They wanted sometimes to ornament me in the same manner, but I would not suffer them; hoping that I might some time be among a people who did not thus disfigure themselves, as I thought they did. At last I came to the banks of a large river, which was covered with canoes, in which the people appeared to live with their household utensils and provisions of all kinds. I was beyond measure astonished at this, as I had never before seen any water larger than a pond or a rivulet: and my surprise was mingled with no small fear when I was put into one of these canoes, and we began to paddle and move along the river. We continued going on thus till night; and when we came to land, and made fires on the banks, each family by themselves, some dragged their canoes on shore, others stayed and cooked in theirs, and laid in them all night. Those on the land had mats, of which they made tents, some in the shape of little houses: in these we slept; and after the morning meal we embarked again and proceeded as before. I was often very much astonished to see some of the women, as well as the men, jump into the water, dive to the bottom, come up again, and swim about. Thus I continued to travel, sometimes by land, sometimes by water, through different countries and various nations, till, at the end of six or seven months after I had been kidnapped, I arrived at the sea coast. It would be tedious and uninteresting to relate all the incidents which befell me during this journey, and which I have not yet forgotten; of the various hands I passed through, and the manners and customs of all the different people among whom I lived: I shall therefore only observe, that in all the places where I was the soil was exceedingly rich; the pomkins, eadas, plantains, yams, &c. &c. were in great abundance, and of incredible size. There were also vast quantities of different gums, though not used for any purpose; and every where a great deal of tobacco. The cotton even grew quite wild; and there was plenty of redwood. I saw no mechanics whatever in all the way, except such as I have mentioned. The chief employment in all these countries was agriculture, and both the males and females, as with us, were brought up to it, and trained in the arts of war.

The first object which saluted my eyes when I arrived on the coast was the sea, and a slave ship, which was then riding at anchor, and waiting for its cargo. These filled me with astonishment, which was soon converted into terror when I was carried on board. I was immediately handled and tossed up to see if I were sound by some of the crew; and I was now persuaded that I had gotten into a world of bad spirits, and that they were going to kill me. Their complexions too differing so much from ours, their long hair, and the language they spoke, (which was very different from any I had ever heard) united to confirm me in this belief. Indeed such were the horrors of my views and fears at the moment, that, if ten thousand worlds had been my own, I would have freely parted with them all to have exchanged my condition with that of the meanest slave in my own country. When I looked round the ship too and saw a large furnace or copper boiling, and a multitude of black people of every description chained together, every one of their countenances expressing dejection and sorrow, I no longer doubted of my fate; and, quite overpowered with horror and anguish, I fell motionless on the deck and fainted. When I recovered a little I found some black people about me, who I believed were some of those who brought me on board, and had been receiving their pay; they talked to me in order to cheer me, but all in vain. I asked them if we were not to be eaten by those white men with horrible looks, red faces, and loose hair. They told me I was not; and one of the crew brought me a small portion of spirituous liquor in a wine glass; but, being afraid of him, I would not take it out of his hand. One of the blacks therefore took it from him and gave it to me, and I took a little down my palate, which, instead of reviving me, as they thought it would, threw me into the greatest consternation at the strange feeling it produced, having never tasted any such liquor before. Soon after this the blacks who brought me on board went off, and left me abandoned to despair. I now saw myself deprived of all chance of returning to my native country, or even the least glimpse of hope of gaining the shore, which I now considered as friendly; and I even wished for my former slavery in preference to my present situation, which was filled with horrors of every kind, still heightened by my ignorance of what I was to undergo. I was not long suffered to indulge my grief; I was soon put down under the decks, and there I received such a salutation in my nostrils as I had never experienced in my life: so that, with the loathsomeness of the stench, and crying together, I became so sick and low that I was not able to eat, nor had I the least desire to taste any thing. I now wished for the last friend, death, to relieve me; but soon, to my grief, two of the white men offered me eatables; and, on my refusing to eat, one of them held me fast by the hands, and laid me across I think the windlass, and tied my feet, while the other flogged me severely. I had never experienced any thing of this kind before; and although, not being used to the water, I naturally feared that element the first time I saw it, yet nevertheless, could I have got over the nettings, I would have jumped over the side, but I could not; and, besides, the crew used to watch us very closely who were not chained down to the decks, lest we should leap into the water: and I have seen some of these poor African prisoners most severely cut for attempting to do so, and hourly whipped for not eating. This indeed was often the case with myself. In a little time after, amongst the poor chained men, I found some of my own nation, which in a small degree gave ease to my mind. I inquired of these what was to be done with us; they gave me to understand we were to be carried to these white people's country to work for them. I then was a little revived, and thought, if it were no worse than working, my situation was not so desperate: but still I feared I should be put to death, the white people looked and acted, as I thought, in so savage a manner; for I had never seen among any people such instances of brutal cruelty; and this not only shewn towards us blacks, but also to some of the whites themselves. One white man in particular I saw, when we were permitted to be on deck, flogged so unmercifully with a large rope near the foremast, that he died in consequence of it; and they tossed him over the side as they would have done a brute. This made me fear these people the more; and I expected nothing less than to be treated in the same manner. I could not help expressing my fears and apprehensions to some of my countrymen: I asked them if these people had no country, but lived in this hollow place (the ship): they told me they did not, but came from a distant one. 'Then,' said I, 'how comes it in all our country we never heard of them?' They told me because they lived so very far off. I then asked where were their women? had they any like themselves? I was told they had: 'and why,' said I, 'do we not see them?' they answered, because they were left behind. I asked how the vessel could go? they told me they could not tell; but that there were cloths put upon the masts by the help of the ropes I saw, and then the vessel went on; and the white men had some spell or magic they put in the water when they liked in order to stop the vessel. I was exceedingly amazed at this account, and really thought they were spirits. I therefore wished much to be from amongst them, for I expected they would sacrifice me: but my wishes were vain; for we were so quartered that it was impossible for any of us to make our escape. While we stayed on the coast I was mostly on deck; and one day, to my great astonishment, I saw one of these vessels coming in with the sails up. As soon as the whites saw it, they gave a great shout, at which we were amazed; and the more so as the vessel appeared larger by approaching nearer. At last she came to an anchor in my sight, and when the anchor was let go I and my countrymen who saw it were lost in astonishment to observe the vessel stop; and were now convinced it was done by magic. Soon after this the other ship got her boats out, and they came on board of us, and the people of both ships seemed very glad to see each other. Several of the strangers also shook hands with us black people, and made motions with their hands, signifying I suppose we were to go to their country; but we did not understand them. At last, when the ship we were in had got in all her cargo, they made ready with many fearful noises, and we were all put under deck, so that we could not see how they managed the vessel. But this disappointment was the least of my sorrow. The stench of the hold while we were on the coast was so intolerably loathsome, that it was dangerous to remain there for any time, and some of us had been permitted to stay on the deck for the fresh air; but now that the whole ship's cargo were confined together, it became absolutely pestilential. The closeness of the place, and the heat of the climate, added to the number in the ship, which was so crowded that each had scarcely room to turn himself, almost suffocated us. This produced copious perspirations, so that the air soon became unfit for respiration, from a variety of loathsome smells, and brought on a sickness among the slaves, of which many died, thus falling victims to the improvident avarice, as I may call it, of their purchasers. This wretched situation was again aggravated by the galling of the chains, now become insupportable; and the filth of the necessary tubs, into which the children often fell, and were almost suffocated. The shrieks of the women, and the groans of the dying, rendered the whole a scene of horror almost inconceivable. Happily perhaps for myself I was soon reduced so low here that it was thought necessary to keep me almost always on deck; and from my extreme youth I was not put in fetters. In this situation I expected every hour to share the fate of my companions, some of whom were almost daily brought upon deck at the point of death, which I began to hope would soon put an end to my miseries. Often did I think many of the inhabitants of the deep much more happy than myself. I envied them the freedom they enjoyed, and as often wished I could change my condition for theirs. Every circumstance I met with served only to render my state more painful, and heighten my apprehensions, and my opinion of the cruelty of the whites. One day they had taken a number of fishes; and when they had killed and satisfied themselves with as many as they thought fit, to our astonishment who were on the deck, rather than give any of them to us to eat as we expected, they tossed the remaining fish into the sea again, although we begged and prayed for some as well as we could, but in vain; and some of my countrymen, being pressed by hunger, took an opportunity, when they thought no one saw them, of trying to get a little privately; but they were discovered, and the attempt procured them some very severe floggings. One day, when we had a smooth sea and moderate wind, two of my wearied countrymen who were chained together (I was near them at the time), preferring death to such a life of misery, somehow made through the nettings and jumped into the sea: immediately another quite dejected fellow, who, on account of his illness, was suffered to be out of irons, also followed their example; and I believe many more would very soon have done the same if they had not been prevented by the ship's crew, who were instantly alarmed. Those of us that were the most active were in a moment put down under the deck, and there was such a noise and confusion amongst the people of the ship as I never heard before, to stop her, and get the boat out to go after the slaves. However two of the wretches were drowned, but they got the other, and afterwards flogged him unmercifully for thus attempting to prefer death to slavery. In this manner we continued to undergo more hardships than I can now relate, hardships which are inseparable from this accursed trade. Many a time we were near suffocation from the want of fresh air, which we were often without for whole days together. This, and the stench of the necessary tubs, carried off many. During our passage I first saw flying fishes, which surprised me very much: they used frequently to fly across the ship, and many of them fell on the deck. I also now first saw the use of the quadrant; I had often with astonishment seen the mariners make observations with it, and I could not think what it meant. They at last took notice of my surprise; and one of them, willing to increase it, as well as to gratify my curiosity, made me one day look through it. The clouds appeared to me to be land, which disappeared as they passed along. This heightened my wonder; and I was now more persuaded than ever that I was in another world, and that every thing about me was magic. At last we came in sight of the island of Barbadoes, at which the whites on board gave a great shout, and made many signs of joy to us. We did not know what to think of this; but as the vessel drew nearer we plainly saw the harbour, and other ships of different kinds and sizes; and we soon anchored amongst them off Bridge Town. Many merchants and planters now came on board, though it was in the evening. They put us in separate parcels, and examined us attentively. They also made us jump, and pointed to the land, signifying we were to go there. We thought by this we should be eaten by these ugly men, as they appeared to us; and, when soon after we were all put down under the deck again, there was much dread and trembling among us, and nothing but bitter cries to be heard all the night from these apprehensions, insomuch that at last the white people got some old slaves from the land to pacify us. They told us we were not to be eaten, but to work, and were soon to go on land, where we should see many of our country people. This report eased us much; and sure enough, soon after we were landed, there came to us Africans of all languages. We were conducted immediately to the merchant's yard, where we were all pent up together like so many sheep in a fold, without regard to sex or age. As every object was new to me every thing I saw filled me with surprise. What struck me first was that the houses were built with stories, and in every other respect different from those in Africa: but I was still more astonished on seeing people on horseback. I did not know what this could mean; and indeed I thought these people were full of nothing but magical arts. While I was in this astonishment one of my fellow prisoners spoke to a countryman of his about the horses, who said they were the same kind they had in their country. I understood them, though they were from a distant part of Africa, and I thought it odd I had not seen any horses there; but afterwards, when I came to converse with different Africans, I found they had many horses amongst them, and much larger than those I then saw. We were not many days in the merchant's custody before we were sold after their usual manner, which is this:—On a signal given, (as the beat of a drum) the buyers rush at once into the yard where the slaves are confined, and make choice of that parcel they like best. The noise and clamour with which this is attended, and the eagerness visible in the countenances of the buyers, serve not a little to increase the apprehensions of the terrified Africans, who may well be supposed to consider them as the ministers of that destruction to which they think themselves devoted. In this manner, without scruple, are relations and friends separated, most of them never to see each other again. I remember in the vessel in which I was brought over, in the men's apartment, there were several brothers, who, in the sale, were sold in different lots; and it was very moving on this occasion to see and hear their cries at parting. O, ye nominal Christians! might not an African ask you, learned you this from your God, who says unto you, Do unto all men as you would men should do unto you? Is it not enough that we are torn from our country and friends to toil for your luxury and lust of gain? Must every tender feeling be likewise sacrificed to your avarice? Are the dearest friends and relations, now rendered more dear by their separation from their kindred, still to be parted from each other, and thus prevented from cheering the gloom of slavery with the small comfort of being together and mingling their sufferings and sorrows? Why are parents to lose their children, brothers their sisters, or husbands their wives? Surely this is a new refinement in cruelty, which, while it has no advantage to atone for it, thus aggravates distress, and adds fresh horrors even to the wretchedness of slavery.

1847

from *The Narrative of William W. Brown, A Fugitive Slave*

BY WILLIAM W. BROWN

William Wells Brown (1814-1884) was the son of a slave woman and a white man related to her owner. Brown escaped to freedom in January 1834, joined the abolitionist movement, and worked as a lecturer and writer (his books include *Clotel,* the first novel published by an African-American).

MY MASTER BEING a political demagogue, soon found those who were ready to put him into office, for the favors he could render them; and a few years after his arrival in Missouri, he was elected to a seat in the Legislature. In his absence from home, everything was left in charge of Mr. Cook, the overseer, and he soon became more tyrannical and cruel. Among the slaves on the plantation, was one by the name of Randall. He was a man about six feet high, and well-proportioned, and known as a man of great strength and power. He was considered the most valuable and able-bodied slave on the plantation; but no matter how good or useful a slave may be, he seldom escapes the lash. But it was not so with Randall. He had been on the plantation since my earliest recollection, and I had never known of his being flogged. No thanks were due to the master or overseer for this. I have often heard him declare, that no white man should ever whip him—that he would die first.

Cook, from the time that he came upon the plantation, had frequently declared, that he could and would flog any nigger that was put into the field to work under him. My master had repeatedly told him not to attempt to whip Randall, but he was determined to try it. As soon as he was left sole dictator, he thought the time had come to put his threats into execution. He soon began to find fault with Randall, and threatened to whip him, if he did not do better. One day he gave him a very hard task,—more than he could possibly do; and at night, the task not being performed, he told Randall that he should remember him the next morning. On the following morning, after the hands had taken breakfast, Cook called out to Randall, and told him that he intended to whip him, and ordered him to cross his hands and be tied. Randall asked why he wished to whip him. He answered, because he had not finished his task the day before. Randall said that the task was too great, or he should have done it. Cook said it made no difference,—he should whip him. Randall stood silent for a moment, and then said, "Mr. Cook, I have always tried to please you since you have been on the plantation, and I find you are determined not to be satisfied with my work, let me do as well as I may. No man has laid hands on me, to whip me, for the last ten years, and I have long since come to the conclusion not to be whipped by any man living." Cook, finding by Randall's determined look and gestures, that he would resist, called three of the hands from their work, and commanded them to seize Randall, and tie him. The hands stood still;—they knew Randall—and they also knew him to be a powerful man, and were afraid to grapple with him. As soon as Cook had ordered the men to seize him, Randall turned to them, and said—"Boys, you all know me; you know that I can handle any three of you, and the man that lays hands on me shall die. This white man can't whip me himself, and therefore he has called you to help him." The overseer was unable to prevail upon them to seize and secure Randall, and finally ordered them all to go to their work together.

Nothing was said to Randall by the overseer, for more than a week. One morning, however, while the hands were at work in the field, he came into it, accompanied by three friends of his, Thompson, Woodbridge and Jones. They came up to where Randall was at work, and Cook ordered him to leave his work, and go with them to the barn. He refused to go; whereupon he was attacked by the overseer and his companions, when he turned upon them, and laid them, one after another, prostrate on the ground. Woodbridge drew out his pistol, and fired at him, and brought him to the ground by a pistol ball. The others rushed upon him with their clubs, and beat him over the head and face, until they succeeded in tying him. He was then taken to the barn, and tied to a beam. Cook gave him over one hundred lashes with a heavy cowhide, had him washed with salt and water, and left him tied during the day. The next day he was untied, and taken to a blacksmith's shop, and had a ball and chain attached to his leg. He was compelled to labor in the field, and perform the same amount of work that the other hands did. When his master returned home, he was much pleased to find that Randall had been subdued in his absence.

from a July 4, 1852 Speech

BY FREDERICK DOUGLASS

Frederick Douglass, on July 4, 1852, gave a speech in Rochester, New York (where he lived at the time) at an event to commemorate the signing of the Declaration of Independence.

FELLOW-CITIZENS, PARDON me, allow me to ask, why am I called upon to speak here to-day? What have I, or those I represent, to do with your national independence? Are the great principles of political freedom and of natural justice, embodied in that Declaration of Independence, extended to us? and am I, therefore, called upon to bring our humble offering to the national altar, and to confess the benefits and express devout gratitude for the blessings resulting from your independence to us?

Would to God, both for your sakes and ours, that an affirmative answer could be truthfully returned to these questions! Then would my task be light, and my burden easy and delightful. For who is there so cold, that a nation's sympathy could not warm him? Who so obdurate and dead to the claims of gratitude, that would not thankfully acknowledge such priceless benefits? Who so stolid and selfish, that would not give his voice to swell the hallelujahs of a nation's jubilee, when the chains of servitude had been torn from his limbs? I am not that man. In a case like that, the dumb might eloquently speak, and the "lame man leap as an hart."

But, such is not the state of the case. I say it with a sad sense of the disparity between us. I am not included within the pale of this glorious anniversary! Your high independence only reveals the immeasurable distance between us. The blessings in which you, this day, rejoice, are not enjoyed in common. The rich inheritance of justice, liberty, prosperity and independence, bequeathed by your fathers, is shared by you, not by me. The sunlight that brought life and healing to you, has brought stripes and death to me. This Fourth [of] July is yours, not mine. You may rejoice, I must mourn. To drag a man in fetters into the grand illuminated temple of liberty, and call upon him to join you in joyous anthems, were inhuman mockery and sacrilegious irony. Do you mean, citizens, to mock me, by asking me to speak to-day? If so, there is a parallel to your conduct. And let me warn you that it is dangerous to copy the example of a nation whose crimes, lowering up to heaven, were thrown down by the breath of the Almighty, burying that nation in irrecoverable ruin! I can to-day take up the plaintive lament of a peeled and woe-smitten people!

"By the rivers of Babylon, there we sat down. Yea! we wept when we remembered Zion. We hanged our harps upon the willows in the midst thereof. For there, they that carried us away captive, required of us a song; and they who wasted us required of us mirth, saying, Sing us one of the songs of Zion. How can we sing the Lord's song in a strange land? If I forget thee, O Jerusalem, let my right hand forget her cunning. If I do not remember thee, let my tongue cleave to the roof of my mouth."

Fellow-citizens; above your national, tumultous joy, I hear the

mournful wail of millions! whose chains, heavy and grievous yesterday, are, to-day, rendered more intolerable by the jubilee shouts
that reach them. If I do forget, if I do not faithfully remember those
bleeding children of sorrow this day, "may my right hand forget her
cunning, and may my tongue cleave to the roof of my mouth!" To
forget them, to pass lightly over their wrongs, and to chime in with
the popular theme, would be treason most scandalous and shocking,
and would make me a reproach before God and the world. My subject, then fellow-citizens, is AMERICAN SLAVERY. I shall see, this
day, and its popular characteristics, from the slave's point of view.
Standing, there, identified with the American bondman, making his
wrongs mine, I do not hesitate to declare, with all my soul, that the
character and conduct of this nation never looked blacker to me than
on this 4th of July! Whether we turn to the declarations of the past,
or to the professions of the present, the conduct of the nation seems
equally hideous and revolting. America is false to the past, false to the
present, and solemnly binds herself to be false to the future. Standing
with God and the crushed and bleeding slave on this occasion, I will,
in the name of humanity which is outraged, in the name of liberty
which is fettered, in the name of the constitution and the Bible,
which are disregarded and trampled upon, dare to call in question
and to denounce, with all the emphasis I can command, everything
that serves to perpetuate slavery—the great sin and shame of America!
"I will not equivocate; I will not excuse;" I will use the severest language I can command; and yet not one word shall escape me that any
man, whose judgement is not blinded by prejudice, or who is not at
heart a slaveholder, shall not confess to be right and just.

But I fancy I hear some one of my audience say, it is just in this
circumstance that you and your brother abolitionists fail to make a
favorable impression on the public mind. Would you argue more,
and denounce less, would you persuade more, and rebuke less, your
cause would be much more likely to succeed. But, I submit, where

all is plain there is nothing to be argued. What point in the anti-slavery creed would you have me argue? On what branch of the subject do the people of this country need light? Must I undertake to prove that the slave is a man? That point is conceded already. Nobody doubts it. The slaveholders themselves acknowledge it in the enactment of laws for their government. They acknowledge it when they punish disobedience on the part of the slave. There are seventy-two crimes in the State of Virginia, which, if committed by a black man, (no matter how ignorant he be), subject him to the punishment of death; while only two of the same crimes will subject a white man to the like punishment. What is this but the acknowledgement that the slave is a moral, intellectual and responsible being? The manhood of the slave is conceded. It is admitted in the fact that Southern statute books are covered with enactments forbidding, under severe fines and penalties, the teaching of the slave to read or to write. When you can point to any such laws, in reference to the beasts of the field, then I may consent to argue the manhood of the slave. When the dogs in your streets, when the fowls of the air, when the cattle on your hills, when the fish of the sea, and the reptiles that crawl, shall be unable to distinguish the slave from a brute, there will I argue with you that the slave is a man!

For the present, it is enough to affirm the equal manhood of the negro race. Is it not astonishing that, while we are ploughing, planting and reaping, using all kinds of mechanical tools, erecting houses, constructing bridges, building ships, working in metals of brass, iron, copper, silver and gold; that, while we are reading, writing and cyphering, acting as clerks, merchants and secretaries, having among us lawyers, doctors, ministers, poets, authors, editors, orators and teachers; that, while we are engaged in all manner of enterprises common to other men, digging gold in California, capturing the whale in the Pacific, feeding sheep and cattle on the hill-side, living, moving, acting, thinking, planning, living in families as husbands, wives and children, and, above all, confessing and worshipping the Christian's God, and looking hopefully for life and immortality beyond the grave, we are called upon to prove that we are men!

Would you have me argue that man is entitled to liberty? that he is the rightful owner of his own body? You have already declared it. Must I argue the wrongfulness of slavery? Is that a question for Republicans? Is it to be settled by the rules of logic and argumentation, as a matter beset with great difficulty, involving a doubtful application of the principle of justice, hard to be understood? How should I look to-day, in the presence of Americans, dividing, and subdividing a discourse, to show that men have a natural right to freedom? speaking of it relatively, and positively, negatively, and affirmatively. To do so, would be to make myself ridiculous, and to offer an insult to your understanding. There is not a man beneath the canopy of heaven, that does not know that slavery is wrong for him.

What, am I to argue that it is wrong to make men brutes, to rob them of their liberty, to work them without wages, to keep them ignorant of their relations to their fellow men, to beat them with sticks, to flay their flesh with the lash, to load their limbs with irons, to hunt them with dogs, to sell them at auction, to sunder their families, to knock out their teeth, to burn their flesh, to starve them into obedience and submission to their masters? Must I argue that a system thus marked with blood, and stained with pollution, is wrong? No! I will not. I have better employments for my time and strength, than such arguments would imply.

What, then, remains to be argued? Is it that slavery is not divine; that God did not establish it; that our doctors of divinity are mistaken? There is blasphemy in the thought. That which is inhuman, cannot be divine! Who can reason on such a proposition? They that can, may; I cannot. The time for such argument is past.

At a time like this, scorching irony, not convincing argument, is needed. O! had I the ability, and could I reach the nation's ear, I would, to-day, pour out a fiery stream of biting ridicule, blasting reproach, withering sarcasm and stern rebuke. For it is not light that is needed, but fire; it is not the gentle shower, but thunder. We need the storm, the whirlwind and the earthquake. The feeling of the nation must be quickened; the conscience of the nation must be roused; the propriety of the nation must be startled; the hypocrisy of the nation must be exposed; and its crimes against God and man must be proclaimed and denounced.

What, to the American slave, is your 4th of July? I answer: a day that reveals to him, more than all other days in the year, the gross injustice and cruelty to which he is the constant victim. To him, your celebration is a sham; your boasted liberty, an unholy license; your national greatness, swelling vanity; your sounds of rejoicing are empty and heartless; your denunciations of tyrants, brass fronted impudence; your shouts of liberty and equality, hollow mockery; your prayers and hymns, your sermons and thanksgivings, with all your religious parade, and solemnity, are, to him, mere bombast, fraud, deception, impiety and hypocrisy—a thin veil to cover up crimes which would disgrace a nation of savages. There is not a nation on the earth guilty of practices, more shocking and bloody, than are the people of these United States, at this very hour.

Go where you may, search where you will, roam through all the monarchies and despotisms of the old world, travel through South America, search out every abuse, and when you have found the last, lay your facts by the side of the everyday practices of this nation, and you will say with me, that, for revolting barbarity and shameless hypocrisy, America reigns without a rival.

1901
from *Up from Slavery*

by Booker T. Washington

Booker T. Washington built the Tuskegee Institute into a
leading facility for black education. By the 1890s, he was
the country's most prominent African American. Here is
his recollection of his early years as a slave.

I WAS BORN a slave on a plantation in Franklin County, Virginia. I
am not quite sure of the exact place or exact date of my birth, but at
any rate I suspect I must have been born somewhere and at some
time. As nearly as I have been able to learn, I was born near a cross-
roads post-office called Hale's Ford, and the year was 1858 or 1859.
I do not know the month or the day. The earliest impressions I can
now recall are of the plantation and the slave quarters—the latter
being the part of the plantation where the slaves had their cabins.

My life had its beginning in the midst of the most miserable, deso-
late, and discouraging surroundings. This was so, however, not because
my owners were especially cruel, for they were not, as compared with
many others. I was born in a typical log cabin, about fourteen by sixteen feet square. In this cabin I lived with my mother and a brother and
sister till after the Civil War, when we were all declared free.

Of my ancestry I know almost nothing. In the slave quarters, and
even later, I heard whispered conversations among the coloured
people of the tortures which the slaves, including, no doubt, my
ancestors on my mother's side, suffered in the middle passage of the
slave ship while being conveyed from Africa to America. I have been

unsuccessful in securing any information that would throw any accurate light upon the history of my family beyond my mother. She, I remember, had a half-brother and a half-sister. In the days of slavery not very much attention was given to family history and family records—that is, black family records. My mother, I suppose, attracted the attention of a purchaser who was afterward my owner and hers. Her addition to the slave family attracted about as much attention as the purchase of a new horse or cow. Of my father I know even less than of my mother. I do not even know his name. I have heard reports to the effect that he was a white man who lived on one of the near-by plantations. Whoever he was, I never heard of his taking the least interest in me or providing in any way for my rearing. But I do not find especial fault with him. He was simply another unfortunate victim of the institution which the Nation unhappily had engrafted upon it at that time.

The cabin was not only our living-place, but was also used as the kitchen for the plantation. My mother was the plantation cook. The cabin was without glass windows; it had only openings in the side which let in the light, and also the cold, chilly air of winter. There was a door to the cabin—that is, something that was called a door—but the uncertain hinges by which it was hung, and the large cracks in it, to say nothing of the fact that it was too small, made the room a very uncomfortable one. In addition to these openings there was, in the lower right-hand corner of the room, the "cat-hole,"—a contrivance which almost every mansion or cabin in Virginia possessed during the ante-bellum period. The "cat-hole" was a square opening, about seven by eight inches, provided for the purpose of letting the cat pass in and out of the house at will during the night. In the case of our particular cabin I could never understand the necessity for this convenience, since there were at least a half-dozen other places in the cabin that would have accommodated the cats. There was no wooden floor in our cabin, the naked earth being used as a floor. In the centre of the earthen floor there was a large, deep opening covered with boards, which was used as a place in which to store sweet potatoes during the winter. An impression of this potato-hole is very distinctly engraved upon my memory, because I recall that during the process of putting the potatoes in or taking them out I would often come into possession of one or two, which I roasted and thoroughly enjoyed. There was no cooking-stove on our plantation, and all the cooking for the whites and slaves my mother had to do over an open fireplace, mostly in pots and "skillets." While the poorly built cabin caused us to suffer with cold in the winter, the heat from the open fireplace in summer was equally trying.

The early years of my life, which were spent in the little cabin, were not very different from those of thousands of other slaves. My mother, of course, had little time in which to give attention to the training of her children during the day. She snatched a few moments for our care in the early morning before her work began, and at night after the day's work was done. One of my earliest recollections is that of my mother cooking a chicken late at night, and awakening her children for the purpose of feeding them. How or where she got it I do not know. I presume, however, it was procured from our owner's farm. Some people may call this theft. If such a thing were to happen now, I should condemn it as theft myself. But taking place at the time it did, and for the reason that it did, no one could ever make me believe that my mother was guilty of thieving. She was simply a victim of the system of slavery. I cannot remember having slept in a bed until after our family was declared free by the Emancipation Proclamation. Three children—John, my older brother, Amanda, my sister, and myself—had a pallet on the dirt floor, or, to be more correct, we slept in and on a bundle of filthy rags laid upon the dirt floor.

I was asked not long ago to tell something about the sports and pastimes that I engaged in during my youth. Until that question was asked it had never occurred to me that there was no period of my life that was devoted to play. From the time that I can remember anything, almost every day of my life has been occupied in some kind of labour; though I think I would now be a more useful man if I had had time for sports. During the period that I spent in slavery I was not large enough to be of much service, still I was occupied most of the time in cleaning the yards, carrying water to the men in the fields, or going to the mill, to which I used to take the corn, once a week, to be ground. The mill was about three miles from the plantation. This work I always dreaded. The heavy bag of corn would be thrown across the back of the horse, and the corn divided about evenly on each side; but in some way, almost without exception, on these trips, the corn would so shift as to become unbalanced and would fall off the horse, and often I would fall with it. As I was not strong enough to reload the corn upon the horse, I would have to wait, sometimes for many hours, till a chance passer-by came along who would help me out of my trouble. The hours while waiting for some one were usually spent in crying. The time consumed in this way made me late in reaching the mill, and by the time I got my corn ground and reached home it would be far into the night. The road was a lonely one, and often led through dense forests. I was always frightened. The woods were said to be full of soldiers who had deserted from the army, and I had been told that the first thing a deserter did to a Negro boy when he found him alone was to cut off his ears. Besides, when I was late in getting home I knew I would always get a severe scolding or a flogging.

I had no schooling whatever while I was a slave, though I remember on several occasions I went as far as the schoolhouse door with one of my young mistresses to carry her books. The picture of several dozen boys and girls in a schoolroom engaged in study made a deep impression upon me, and I had the feeling that to get into a schoolhouse and study in this way would be about the same as getting into paradise.

So far as I can now recall, the first knowledge that I got of the fact that we were slaves, and that freedom of the slaves was being discussed, was early one morning before day, when I was awakened by my mother kneeling over her children and fervently praying that Lincoln and his armies might be successful, and that one day she and her children might be free. In this connection I have never been able to understand how the slaves throughout the South, completely ignorant as were the masses so far as books or newspapers were concerned, were able to keep themselves so accurately and completely informed about the great National questions that were agitating the country. From the time that Garrison, Lovejoy, and others began to agitate for freedom, the slaves throughout the South kept in close touch with the progress of the movement. Though I was a mere child during the preparation for the Civil War and during the war itself, I now recall the many late-at-night whispered discussions that I heard my mother and the other slaves on the plantation indulge in. These discussions showed that they understood the situation, and that they kept themselves informed of events by what was termed the "grapevine" telegraph.

During the campaign when Lincoln was first a candidate for the Presidency, the slaves on our far-off plantation, miles from any railroad or large city or daily newspaper, knew what the issues involved were. When war was begun between the North and the South, every slave on our plantation felt and knew that, though other issues were discussed, the primal one was that of slavery. Even the most ignorant members of my race on the remote plantations felt in their hearts, with a certainty that admitted of no doubt, that the freedom of the slaves would be the one great result of the war, if the Northern armies conquered. Every success of the Federal armies and every defeat of the Confederate forces was watched with the keenest and most intense interest. Often the slaves got knowledge of the results of great battles before the white people received it. This news was usually gotten from the coloured man who was sent to the post-office for the mail. In our case post-office was about three miles from the plantation and the mail came once or twice a week. The man who was sent to the office would linger about the place long enough to get the drift of the conversation from the group of white people who naturally congregated there, after receiving their mail, to discuss the latest news. The mail-carrier on his way back to our master's house would as naturally retail the news that he had secured among the slaves, and in this way they often heard of important events before the white people at the "big house," as the master's house was called.

I cannot remember a single instance during my childhood or early boyhood when our entire family sat down to the table together, and God's blessing was asked, and the family ate a meal in a civilized manner. On the plantation in Virginia, and even later, meals were gotten by the children very much as dumb animals get theirs. It was a piece of bread here and a scrap of meat there. It was a cup of milk at one time and some potatoes at another. Sometimes a portion of our family would eat out of the skillet or pot, while some one else would eat from a tin plate held on the knees, and often using nothing but the hands with which to hold the food. When I had grown to sufficient size, I was required to go to the "big house" at meal-times to fan the flies from the table by means of a large set of paper fans operated by a pulley. Naturally much of the conversation of the white people turned upon the subject of freedom and the war, and I absorbed a good deal of it. I remember that at one time I saw two of my young mistresses and some lady visitors eating ginger-cakes, in the yard. At that time those cakes seemed to me to be absolutely the most tempting and desirable things that I had ever seen; and I then and there resolved that, if I ever got free, the height of my ambition would be reached if I could get to the point where I could secure and eat ginger-cakes in the way that I saw those ladies doing.

Of course as the war was prolonged the white people, in many cases, often found it difficult to secure food for themselves. I think the slaves felt the deprivation less than the whites, because the usual diet for the slaves was corn bread and pork, and these could be raised on the plantation; but coffee, tea, sugar, and other articles which the whites had been accustomed to use could not be raised on the plantation, and the conditions brought about by the war frequently made it impossible to secure these things. The whites were often in great straits. Parched corn was used for coffee, and a kind of black molasses was used instead of sugar. Many times nothing was used to sweeten the so-called tea and coffee.

The first pair of shoes that I recall wearing were wooden ones. They had rough leather on the top, but the bottoms, which were about an inch thick, were of wood. When I walked they made a fearful noise, and besides this they were very inconvenient since there was no yielding to the natural pressure of the foot. In wearing them one presented an exceedingly awkward appearance. The most trying ordeal that I was forced to endure as a slave boy, however, was the wearing of a flax shirt. In the portion of Virginia where I lived it was common to use flax as part of the clothing for the slaves. That part of the flax from which our clothing was made was largely the refuse, which of course was the cheapest and roughest part. I can scarcely imagine any torture, except, perhaps, the pulling of a tooth, that is equal to that caused by putting on a new flax shirt for the first time. It is almost equal to the feeling that one would experience if he had a dozen or more chestnut burrs, or a hundred small pin-points, in contact with his flesh. Even to this day I can recall accurately the tortures that I underwent when putting on one of these garments. The fact that my flesh was soft and tender added to the pain. But I had no choice. I had to wear the flax shirt or none; and had it been left to me to choose, I should have chosen to wear no covering. In connection with the flax shirt, my brother John, who is several years older than I am, performed one of the most generous acts that I ever heard of one slave relative doing for another. On several occasions when I was being forced to wear a new flax shirt, he generously agreed to put it on in my stead and wear it for several days, till it was "broken in." Until I had grown to be quite a youth this single garment was all that I wore.

One may get the idea, from what I have said, that there was bitter feeling toward the white people on the part of my race, because of the fact that most of the white population was away fighting in a war which would result in keeping the Negro in slavery if the South was successful. In the case of the slaves on our place this was not true, and it was not true of any large portion of the slave population in the South where the Negro was treated with anything like decency. During the Civil War one of my young masters was killed, and two were severely wounded. I recall the feeling of sorrow which existed among the slaves when they heard of the death of "Mars' Billy." It was no sham sorrow, but real. Some of the slaves had nursed "Mars' Billy"; others had played with him when he was a child. "Mars' Billy" had begged for mercy in the case of others when the overseer or master was thrashing them. The sorrow in the slave quarter was only second to that in the "big house." When the two young masters were brought home wounded the sympathy of the slaves was shown in many ways. They were just as anxious to assist in the nursing as the family relatives of the wounded. Some of the slaves would even beg for the privilege of sitting up at night to nurse their wounded masters. This tenderness and sympathy on the part of those held in bondage was a result of their kindly and generous nature. In order to defend and protect the women and children who were left on the plantations when the white males went to war, the slaves would have laid down their lives. The slave who was selected to sleep in the "big house" during the absence of the males was considered to have the place of honour. Any one attempting to harm "young Mistress" or "old Mistress" during the night would have had to cross the dead body of the slave to do so. I do not know how many have noticed it, but I think that it will be found to be true that there are few instances, either in slavery or freedom, in which a member of my race has been known to betray a specific trust.

As a rule, not only did the members of my race entertain no feelings of bitterness against the whites before and during the war, but there are many instances of Negroes tenderly caring for their former masters and mistresses who for some reason have become poor and dependent since the war. I know of instances where the former masters of slaves have for years been supplied with money by their former slaves to keep them from suffering. I have known of still other cases in which the former slaves have assisted in the education of the descendants of their former owners. I know of a case on a large plantation in the South in which a young white man, the son of the former owner of the estate, has become so reduced in purse and self-control by reason of drink that he is a pitiable creature; and yet, notwithstanding the poverty of the coloured people themselves on this plantation, they have for years supplied this young white man with the necessities of life. One sends him a little coffee or sugar, another a little meat, and so on. Nothing that the coloured people possess is too good for the son of "old Mars' Tom," who will perhaps never be permitted to suffer while any remain on the place who knew directly or indirectly of "old Mars' Tom."

I have said that there are few instances of a member of my race betraying a specific trust. One of the best illustrations of this which I know of is in the case of an ex-slave from Virginia whom I met not long ago in a little town in the state of Ohio. I found that this man had made a contract with his master, two or three years previous to the Emancipation Proclamation, to the effect that the slave was to be permitted to buy himself, by paying so much per year for his body; and while he was paying for himself, he was to be permitted to labour where and for whom he pleased. Finding that he could secure better wages in Ohio, he went there. When freedom came, he was still in debt to his master some three hundred dollars. Notwithstanding that the Emancipation Proclamation freed him from any obligation to his master, this black man walked the greater portion of the distance back to where his old master lived in Virginia, and placed the last dollar, with interest, in his hands. In talking to me about this, the man told me that he knew that he did not have to pay the debt, but that he had given his word to his master, and his word he had never broken. He felt that he could not enjoy his freedom till he had fulfilled his promise.

From some things that I have said one may get the idea that some of the slaves did not want freedom. This is not true. I have never seen one who did not want to be free, or one who would return to slavery.

I pity from the bottom of my heart any nation or body of people that is so unfortunate as to get entangled in the net of slavery. I have long since ceased to cherish any spirit of bitterness against the Southern white people on account of the enslavement of my race. No one section of our country was wholly responsible for its introduction, and, besides, it was recognized and protected for years by the General Government. Having once got its tentacles fastened on to the economic and social life of the Republic, it was no easy matter for the country to relieve itself of the institution. Then, when we rid ourselves of prejudice, or racial feeling, and look facts in the face, we must acknowledge that, notwithstanding the cruelty and moral wrong of slavery, the ten million Negroes inhabiting this country, who themselves or whose ancestors went through the school of American slavery, are in a stronger and more hopeful condition, materially, intellectually, morally, and religiously, than is true of an equal number of black people in any other portion of the globe. This is so to such an extent that Negroes in this country, who themselves or whose forefathers went through the school of slavery, are constantly returning to Africa as missionaries to enlighten those who remained in the fatherland. This I say, not to justify slavery—on the other hand, I condemn it as an institution, as we all know that in America it was established for selfish and financial reasons, and not from a missionary motive—but to call attention to a fact, and to show how Providence so often uses men and institutions to accomplish a purpose. When persons ask me in these days how, in the midst of what sometimes seem hopelessly discouraging conditions, I can have such faith in the future of my race in this country, I remind them of the wilderness through which and out of which, a good Providence has already led us.

Ever since I have been old enough to think for myself, I have entertained the idea that, notwithstanding the cruel wrongs inflicted upon us, the black man got nearly as much out of slavery as the white man did. The hurtful influences of the institution were not by any means confined to the Negro. This was fully illustrated by the life upon our own plantation. The whole machinery of slavery was so constructed as to cause labour, as a rule, to be looked upon as a badge of degradation, of inferiority. Hence labour was something that both races on the slave plantation sought to escape. The slave system on our place, in a large measure, took the spirit of self-reliance and self-help out of the white people. My old master had many boys and girls, but not one, so far as I know, ever mastered a single trade or special line of productive industry. The girls were not taught to cook, sew, or to take care of the house. All of this was left to the slaves. The slaves, of course, had little personal interest in the life of the plantation, and their ignorance prevented them from learning how to do things in the most improved and thorough manner. As a result of the system, fences were out of repair, gates were hanging half off the hinges, doors creaked, window-panes were out, plastering had fallen but was not replaced, weeds grew in the yard. As a rule, there was food for whites and blacks, but inside the house, and on the dining room table, there was wanting that delicacy and refinement of touch and finish which can make a home the most convenient, comfortable, and attractive place in the world. Withal there was a waste of food and other materials which was sad. When freedom came, the slaves were almost as well fitted to begin life anew as the master, except in the matter of book-learning and ownership of property. The slave owner and his sons had mastered no special industry. They unconsciously had imbibed the feeling that manual labour was not the proper thing for them. On the other hand, the slaves, in many cases, had mastered some handicraft, and none were ashamed, and few unwilling, to labour.

Finally the war closed, and the day of freedom came. It was a momentous and eventful day to all upon our plantation. We had been expecting it. Freedom was in the air, and had been for months. Deserting soldiers returning to their homes were to be seen every day. Others who had been discharged, or whose regiments had been paroled, were constantly passing near our place. The "grape-vine telegraph" was kept busy night and day. The news and mutterings of great events were swiftly carried from one plantation to another. In the fear of "Yankee" invasions, the silverware and other valuables were taken from the "big house," buried in the woods, and guarded by trusted slaves. Woe be to any one who would have attempted to disturb the buried treasure. The slaves would give the Yankee soldiers food, drink, clothing—anything but that which had been specifically intrusted to their care and honour. As the great day drew nearer, there was more singing in the slave quarters than usual. It was bolder, had more ring, and lasted later into the night. Most of the verses of the plantation songs had some reference to freedom. True, they had sung those same verses before, but they had been careful to explain that the "freedom" in these songs referred to the next world, and had no connection with life in this world. Now they gradually threw off the mask, and were not afraid to let it be known that the "freedom" in their songs meant freedom of the body in this world. The night before the eventful day, word was sent to the slave quarters to the effect that something unusual was going to take place at the "big house" the next morning. There was little, if any, sleep that night. All was excitement and expectancy. Early the next morning word was sent to all the slaves, old and young, to gather at the house. In company with my mother, brother, and sister, and a large number of other slaves, I went to the master's house. All of our master's family were either standing or seated on the veranda of the house, where they could see what was to take place and hear what was said. There was a feeling of deep interest, or perhaps sadness, on their faces, but not bitterness. As I now recall the impression they made upon me, they did not at the moment seem to be sad because of the loss of property, but rather because of parting with those whom they had reared and who were in many ways very close to them. The most distinct thing that I now recall in connection with the scene was that some man who seemed to be a stranger (a United States officer, I presume) made a little speech and then read a rather long paper—the Emancipation Proclamation, I think. After the reading we were told that we were all free, and could go when and where we pleased. My mother, who was standing by my side, leaned over and kissed her children, while tears of joy ran down her cheeks. She explained to us what it all meant, that this was the day for which she had been so long praying, but fearing that she would never live to see.

For some minutes there was great rejoicing, and thanksgiving, and wild scenes of ecstasy. But there was no feeling of bitterness. In fact, there was pity among the slaves for our former owners. The wild rejoicing on the part of the emancipated coloured people lasted but for a brief period, for I noticed that by the time they returned to their cabins there was a change in their feelings. The great responsibility of being free, of having charge of themselves, of having to think and plan for themselves and their children, seemed to take possession of them. It was very much like suddenly turning a youth of ten or twelve years out into the world to provide for himself. In a few hours the great questions with which the Anglo-Saxon race had been grappling for centuries had been thrown upon these people to be solved. These were the questions of a home, a living, the rearing of children, education, citizenship, and the establishment and support of churches. Was it any wonder that within a few hours the wild rejoicing ceased and a feeling of deep gloom seemed to pervade the slave quarters? To some it seemed that, now that they were in actual possession of it, freedom was a more serious thing than they had expected to find it. Some of the slaves were seventy or eighty years old; their best days were gone. They had no strength with which to earn a living in a strange place and among strange people, even if they had been sure where to find a new place of abode. To this class the problem seemed especially hard. Besides, deep down in their hearts there was a strange and peculiar attachment to "old Marster" and "old Missus," and to their children, which they found it hard to think of breaking off. With these they had spent in some cases nearly a half-century, and it was no light thing to think of parting. Gradually, one by one, stealthily at first, the older slaves began to wander from the slave quarters back to the "big house" to have a whispered conversation with their former owners as to the future.

peace

1825

from *Address to the Massachusetts Peace Society*

BY WILLIAM LADD

William Ladd (1778-1841) was at various times was a merchant ship captain, the owner of a slave-free cotton plantation, and an activist and writer for peace.

IN ANCIENT TIMES, differences were settled by judicial combat. Public opinion sanctioned the practice, and the conqueror was honoured, while the vanquished was consigned to contempt and ignominy. Unfortunately, this savage custom is not entirely obliterated, but public opinion is so far corrected, that the vanquished are sometimes buried with military honours.

Slavery is so intimately connected with war, that it fairly comes within the range of my subject. The present generation has witnessed a wonderful change in this particular. Fifty years ago, the slave trade was as honourable, as it was lucrative. Now it is made piracy, by law, and is viewed with horror and disgust, by every virtuous member of society.

Formerly, prisoners of war were put to the torture, or murdered in cold blood, or enslaved. Now, the moment an enemy lays down his arms, he ceases to be a foe, and is treated with all the hospitality, which is due to a stranger. So great is our detestation of a contrary line of conduct, that, notwithstanding our sympathy for the suffering Greeks, we are shocked at their barbarities, and lament that they have inherited the cruelty, along with the bravery of their pagan ancestors;

regardless of the precepts of that benign religion, by the sacred name of which they are called.

The time was, when women and children were carried into captivity and sold for slaves; now, not only they, but, all other non-combatants, except seamen in the merchant service, are unmolested.

But I need not take up your time, to enumerate customs, which have long since, and forever, passed away; but which were once as strenuously advocated, as the custom of war is now, or ever has been;—for your memory will furnish you with changes in public opinion, as great as any I have mentioned. We may therefore safely conclude, from the experience of the past, that, as mankind advance in knowledge and refinement, other changes, ameliorating the condition of the human species, may be effected; and that, among other evils, the custom of war, the most direful scourge that has ever afflicted mankind, may cease.

What gives us the greatest encouragement in this hope, is the fact, that society itself has the supreme control over that passion, which above all others, is a cause of war,—*a love of military glory.* And what is this glory? A bubble,—"a puff of noisy breath," which every individual in society, however low his station, can increase or diminish;— a *vampyre,* which lives on the breath of the people, and starves the living, to feed the dead.

So long as mankind continue to elevate invaders and conquerors,— those scourges of their race,—to the highest pinnacle of renown, so long must they expect to smart beneath their lash. What induced Alexander to depopulate his paternal dominions, to enable him to conquer Persia? The love of glory. What induced Charles the Twelfth to draw, from his iron hills, "the soldier and his sword," and impoverish a country already poor? It was the example of Alexander, which fired his mind, with the love of military glory. What induced Frederick of Prussia to make war on the young, defenceless, orphan Queen of Hungary? He tells you himself,—"the hope of acquiring *renown.*" In what do these characters differ from the marauder, who robs the sheepfold and butchers the flock, for sport;—from the highwayman, who plunders the traveller of a jewel, that he may give it away;—from the bully, who waylays, robs and insults a defenceless woman, that he may boast of it;—in what do they differ, except in the magnitude of their crimes, and the multitude of their offences? As such men are influenced by public opinion, if they met the same contempt in one case as in the other; if, instead of being entitled "the great," they were branded as infamous,—there would be no such characters.

It is evident, that the continuance of the custom of war depends on *the voice of the people,* not only in republican governments, where it is the supreme law, but also in the most absolute monarchies; for even despots bow to the "Queen of the world" and acknowledge her power. Public opinion can not only prevent those wars which originate in a love of glory, which are by far the greater part,—but it can also overawe the love of power, of wealth, of revenge, and say to the angry passions, "peace, be still."

There is not probably in this assembly, nor in all our happy country, a man so hardened, as to assert, that war is a blessing,—that it is not a curse,—a most direful calamity. War's greatest apologists universally agree to call it an evil; a tremendous evil.

Since then, all acknowledge war to be an evil of enormous magnitude, it is unnecessary for me to descant on its horrors and atrocities. Unfortunately, they have been too well exemplified, in our day. What pencil can paint, what language can describe, the horrors of Borodino, Moscow, Berezina and Waterloo?—horrors which have not been equalled since the sack of Jerusalem. Nor are these miseries confined to the wounded soldier, consumed, alive, in the burning hospital, amid the shrieks and groans of twelve thousand others, as wretched as himself; (*a*) nor to him who, overcome with hunger and fatigue, and pierced by the northern blast, falls, unheeded by his companions in misery, among the drifted snow, which soon covers him; (*b*) nor to him who, benumbed with cold, seated on the dead body of his fellow-soldier, gnaws a half wasted human limb, or the remains of a scanty pittance of horse flesh, of which he has just robbed his dying comrade; too happy, if the excess of his sufferings has brought on a delirium, which causes his hysteric laugh to prevail over the dying groans of his companions; (*c*) nor to him who, having escaped these dangers, is tumbled, by a fellow-soldier's arm, from the bridge, into the freezing current of the Berezina, or is trampled to death, beneath the hoofs of the flying cavalry, or is crushed beneath the ponderous wheels of the retreating artillery; (*d*) nor to him, who lay fourteen nights and days,—oh how long those nights and days!—expiring on the field of Waterloo. (*e*) Nor is this all,—no, nor trampled harvests,—nor burning cottages,—nor plundered villages,—nor sacked cities;—no, nor houseless age, nor starving childhood, nor even the shrieks of virgin beauty, flying, in vain, from the hot pursuit of lust;—no, these do not fill up the picture. In the background, obscured from vulgar gaze, the aged parent, robbed, by the conscription or impressment, of his last earthly hope,—the widowed mother, with her defenceless orphans,—the betrothed virgin, with all her fond anticipations blasted, and the cup of connubial felicity dashed untasted from her lips,—and the thousand ramifications of misery, wherever there are hearts to bleed or bosoms to heave,—all these are necessary to make up the scene. And when all these well authenticated facts, and ten thousand others, are collected together, and there is added to them, all that the most vivid imagination can conceive, still the picture falls far, very far, short of the original. Now what is the cause of all this intensity of suffering? Ambition. And who feeds this insatiable monster with applause, without which it must die? We, the people.

• • •

But, without war, what should we do for materials for history? What! shall we encourage highway robbery and murder, lest the annals of Newgate and the newspapers of the day should lack interest? Are mankind such vultures, that nothing will suit their appetite but blood and carnage. Are not tornadoes, inundations, earthquakes and pestilence, sufficient to satisfy our longings for the miseries of our fellow-creatures? What prevents us from taking an interest in the march of intellect, the progress of science, improvements in the arts, the spread of the Gospel and the increasing comforts of all classes of men at home and abroad. But, our moral taste is vitiated, in our youth—even in our infancy. Almost the first sounds we hear are martial, the first playthings we handle are military, the first pictures and spectacles we see are warlike, and the first books we read exalt valour over every other virtue, and conquerors above all other men. Were it not for this, a safety lamp would interest us more than a Congreve rocket, the tunnel under the Thames more than the trophy at Waterloo; the canals from Portsmouth to London, and from Havre to Paris, more than the battle of the Nile, which, to say nothing of the loss of lives and limbs, cost more money than both; and, to come back to our own country, had not our taste been thus vitiated, our grand canal, which, like most other great and noble enterprises, was at its commencement sneered at by little minds, but by the completion of which, the stupendous genius, that planned the gigantic work, has covered himself with unfading laurels, and erected a monument, infinitely surpassing the trophies of Alexander or Caesar, of Tamerlane or Napoleon; I say, were it not for prejudices imbibed in our youth, this splendid and bloodless victory of art over nature, would be a greater cause of exultation than all the glory of the late war, though purchased at less than a twentieth part of the expense.

But war is an interesting spectacle. So is a city on fire; but what modern Nero would set fire to this city, or rejoice in the conflagration, that he might witness the grandeur of the scene? The view of a volcano is grand and majestic, but who would wish to see the vineyards, villas and villages, which adorn the base of Vesuvius, inundated by a flood of burning lava, and Naples, like Herculaneum and Pompeii, buried under a shower of cinders, that he might gratify his admiration of the sublime.

But, say our opponents, war is necessary to drain off the refuse of society, and cleanse the body politic of its peccant humors; a fine compliment to the dignity of human nature in general, and to the army and navy in particular! But fact speaks a contrary doctrine, and assures us that where one vagabond is disposed of in war, ten others are made; to say nothing of the brave, the generous and humane, who, infatuated by a love of fame, rush blindly into the same destructive vortex. That war corrupts the public morals and lowers the standard of morality is proverbial; so that a nation that engages in war, for the purpose of mending its morals, acts as wisely as the man, who subjects himself to a loathsome disease, in order to purify his blood.

But, say the friends of war,—allowing all your arguments to be correct, still it is necessary to keep up a martial spirit for the purpose of self-defence. In the reign of Queen Elizabeth, every man in England wore a sword. History does not inform us who first laid it aside, nor is the time of the change distinctly marked, but the fashion altered, and the citizen of London is now infinitely less exposed to insult, than when he went armed. What protects the unarmed citizen? Public opinion; and public opinion, when well informed, will equally protect the state, that seeks for peace. Besides, the progress of the principles of peace will, like all other great changes, be gradual and general, though they may prevail more in one country than in another; and experience has shewn, that where they have been adopted, they have not invited aggression.

Our opponents also join our lukewarm friends and say, however good your motive, your object is chimerical and utopian, and your hopes will never be realized, wars will continue so long as the world stands. The same objections were made against the early reformers, the opposers of the slave trade and the advocates for religious toleration. Yet, these causes have succeeded in a measure, are still in progress, and will advance until the most sanguine expectations of their first movers shall be realized. The greatest changes must have a beginning. All the great moral revolutions, which the world has witnessed, have each been commenced by one or two individuals. Luther and Calvin began the reformation; Clarkson and Wilberforce undertook the abolition of the slave trade. Had not individuals made the attempt, the Roman Catholic superstition and the slave trade would have continued to this day undiminished.

But were it always peace, we should have none of the "pomp and circumstance of glorious war." We should miss our triumphs, our illuminations, our military reviews and balls, our anniversaries of battles and all that display of beauty, eloquence, glitter and parade, which are so captivating to the fancy of the young, and which renew the youthful vigor of the hoary veteran. These are fine flowers, it must be confessed, but they are manured with the blood of the brave, and watered with the tears of widows and orphans, and their fruits are often "the grapes of Sodom and the clusters of Gomorrah." Instead of a triumphal procession, after a victory, should the livid and disfigured corses of the dead be borne along, followed by litters filled with the wounded, and surrounded by widows and orphans;—if, instead of martial music, were heard the loud groans of the wounded, and the shrieks of the bereaved, one *such* triumph would forever sicken us of war.

1863
from The Record of a Quaker Conscience

BY CYRUS PRINGLE

The Union army drafted Cyrus Pringle and two of his
fellow Quakers on July 13, 1863. The Quakers refused to
bear arms. These passages from Pringle's diary are taken
from the February, 1913 issue of the *Atlantic Monthly*.

AT BURLINGTON, VT., on the 13th of the seventh month, 1863, I
was drafted. . . . I was to report on the 27th. . . .

We were urged by our acquaintances to pay our commutation
money; by some through well-meant kindness and sympathy; by
others through interest in the war; and by others still through a belief
they entertained it was our duty. But we confess a higher duty than
that to country; and, asking no military protection of our Government and grateful for none, deny any obligation to support so
unlawful a system, as we hold a war to be even when waged in opposition to an evil and oppressive power and ostensibly in defense of
liberty, virtue, and free institutions; and, though touched by the kind
interest of friends, we could not relieve their distress by a means we
hold even more sinful than that of serving ourselves, as by supplying
money to hire a substitute we would not only be responsible for the
result, but be the agents in bringing others into evil.

L.M.M. and I addressed the following letter to Governor Holbrook
and hired a corporal to forward it to him.

Brattleboro, Vt., *26th, 8th* month, 1863.

Frederick Holbrook,

Governor of Vermont:—

We, the undersigned members of the Society of Friends, beg leave to represent to thee, that we were lately drafted in the 3d Dist. of Vermont, have been forced into the army and reached the camp near this town yesterday.

That in the language of the elders of our New York Yearly Meeting, 'We love our country and acknowledge with gratitude to our Heavenly Father the many blessings we have been favored with under the government; and can feel no sympathy with any who seek its overthrow.'

But that, true to well-known principles of our society, we cannot violate our religious convictions either by complying with military requisitions or by the equivalents of this compliance,— the furnishing of a substitute or payment of commutation money. That, therefore, we are brought into suffering and exposed to insult and contempt from those who have us in charge, as well as to the penalties of insubordination, though liberty of conscience is *denied* us by the Constitution of Vermont as well as that of the United States.

Therefore, we beg of thee as Governor of our State any assistance thou may be able to render, should it be no more than the influence of thy position interceding in our behalf.

Truly Thy Friend,

Cyrus G. Pringle.

P.S.—We are informed we are to be sent to the vicinity of Boston tomorrow.

31st., 8th month, 1863. In Guard House.—Yesterday morning L.M.M. and I were called upon to do fatigue duty. The day before we were asked to do some cleaning about camp and to bring water. We wished to be obliging, to appear willing to bear a hand toward that which would promote our own and our fellows' health and convenience; but as we worked we did not feel easy. Suspecting we had beeen assigned to such work, the more we discussed in our minds the subject, the more clearly the right way seemed opened to us; and we separately came to the judgment that we must not conform to this requirement. So when the sergeant bade us 'Police the streets,' we asked him if he had received instructions with regard to us, and he replied we had been assigned to 'Fatigue Duty.' L.M.M. answered him that we could not obey. He left us immediately for the Major (Jarvis of Weathersfield, Vt.). He came back and ordered us to the Major's tent. The latter met us outside and inquired concerning the complaint he had heard of us. Upon our statement of our position, he apparently undertook to argue our whimsies, as he probably looked upon our principles, out of our heads. We replied to his points as we had ability; but he soon turned to bullying us rather than arguing with us, and would hardly let us proceed with a whole sentence. 'I make some pretension to religion myself,' he said; and quoted the Old Testament freely in support of war. Our terms were, submission or the guard-house. We replied we could not obey.

This island was formerly occupied by a company, who carried on the large farm it comprises and opened a great hotel as a summer resort.

The subjects of all misdemeanors, grave and small, are here confined. Those who have deserted or attempted it; those who have insulted officers and those guilty of theft, fighting, drunkenness, etc. In *most,* as in the camps, there are traces yet of manhood and of the Divine Spark, but some are abandoned, dissolute. There are many here among the substitutes who were actors in the late New York riots. They show unmistakably the characteristics and sentiments of those rioters, and, especially, hatred to the blacks drafted and about camp, and exhibit this in foul and profane jeers heaped upon these unoffending men at every opportunity. In justice to the blacks I must say they are superior to the whites in all their behavior.

31*st*. p.m.—Several of us were a little time ago called out one by one to answer inquiries with regard to our offenses. We replied we could not comply with military requisitions. P. D., being last, was asked if he would die first, and replied promptly but mildly, *Yes.*

Here we are in prison in our own land for no crimes, no offense to God nor man; nay, more: we are here for obeying the commands of the Son of God and the influences of his Holy Spirit. I must look for patience in this dark day. I am troubled too much and excited and perplexed.

Camp Near Culpeper. *25th*.—My distress is too great for words; but I must overcome my disinclination to write, or this record will remain unfinished. So, with aching head and heart, I proceed.

Yesterday morning we were roused early for breakfast and for preparation for starting. After marching out of the barracks, we were first taken to the armory, where each man received a gun and its equipments and a piece of tent. We stood in line, waiting for our turn with apprehensions of coming trouble. Though we had felt free to keep with those among whom we had been placed, we could not consent to carry a gun, even though we did not intend to use it; and, from our previous experience, we knew it would go harder with us, if we took the first step in the wrong direction, though it might seem an unimportant one, and an easy and not very wrong way to avoid difficulty. So we felt decided we must decline receiving the guns. In the hurry and bustle of equipping a detachment of soldiers, one attempting to explain a position and the grounds therefor so peculiar as ours to junior, petty officers, possessing liberally the characteristics of these: pride, vanity, conceit, and an arbitrary spirit, impatience, profanity, and contempt for holy things, must needs find the opportunity a very favorable one.

We succeeded in giving these young officers a slight idea of what we were; and endeavored to answer their questions of why we did not pay our commutation, and avail ourselves of that provision made expressly for such; of why we had come as far as that place, etc. We realized then the unpleasant results of that practice, that had been employed with us by the successive officers into whose hands we had fallen,—of shirking any responsibility, and of passing us on to the next officer above.

A council was soon holden to decide what to do with us. One proposed to place us under arrest, a sentiment we rather hoped might prevail, as it might prevent our being sent on to the front; but another, in some spite and impatience, insisted, as it was their duty to supply a gun to every man and forward him, that the guns should be put upon us, and we be made to carry them. Accordingly the equipment was buckled about us, and the straps of the guns being loosened, they were thrust over our heads and hung upon our shoulders. In this way we were urged forward through the streets of Alexandria; and, having been put upon a long train of dirt cars, were started for Culpeper. We came over a long stretch of desolated and deserted country, through battlefields of previous summers, and through many camps now lively with the work of this present campaign. Seeing, for the first time, a country made dreary by the war-blight, a country once adorned with graves and green pastures and meadows and fields of waving grain, and happy with a thousand homes, now laid with the ground, one realizes as he can in no other way something of the ruin that lies in the trail of a war. But upon these fields of Virginia, once so fair, there rests a two-fold blight, first that of slavery, now that of war. When one contrasts the face of this country with the smiling hillsides and vales of New England, he sees stamped upon it in characters so marked, none but a blind man can fail to read, the great irrefutable arguments against slavery and against war, too; and must be filled with loathing for these twin relics of barbarism, so awful in the potency of their consequences that they can change even the face of the country.

Through the heat of this long ride, we felt our total lack of water and the meagreness of our supply of food. Our thirst became so oppressive as we were marched here from Culpeper, some four miles with scarcely a halt to rest, under our heavy loads, and through the heat and deep dust of the road, that we drank water and dipped in the brooks we passed, though it was discolored with the soap the soldiers had used in washing. The guns interfered with our walking, and, slipping down, dragged with painful weight upon our shoulders. Poor P. D. fell out from exhaustion and did not come in till we had been some little time at the camp. We were taken to the 4th Vermont regiment and soon apportioned to companies. Though we waited upon the officer commanding the company in which we were placed, and endeavored to explain our situation, we were required immediately after to be present at inspection of arms. We declined, but an attempt was made to force us to obedience, first, by the officers of the company, then, by those of the regiment; but, failing to exact obedience of us, we were ordered by the colonel to be tied, and, if we made outcry, to be gagged also, and to be kept so till he gave orders for our release. After two or three hours we were relieved and left under guard; lying down on the ground in the open air, and covering ourselves with our blankets, we soon fell asleep from exhaustion, and the fatigue of the day.

This morning the officers told us we must yield. We must obey and serve. We were threatened great severities and even death. We seem perfectly at the mercy of the military power, and, more, in the hands of the inferior officers, who, from their being far removed from Washington, feel less restraint from those Regulations of the Army, which are for the protection of privates from personal abuse.

Regimental Hospital, 4th Vermont. *29th*. [*9th* month.]—On the evening of the 26th the Colonel came to us apologizing for the roughness with which he treated us at first, which was, as he insisted, through ignorance of our real character and position. He told us if we persisted in our course, death would probably follow; though at another time he confessed to P.D. that this would only be the extreme sentence of court-martial.

He urged us to go into the hospital, stating that this course was advised by Friends about New York. We were too well aware of such a fact to make any denial, though it was a subject of surprise to us that he should be informed of it. He pleaded with us long and earnestly, urging us with many promises of indulgence and favor and attentions we found afterwards to be untrue. He gave us till the next morning to consider the question and report our decision. In our discussion of the subject among ourselves, we were very much perplexed. If all his statements concerning the ground taken by our Society were true, we seemed to be liable, if we persisted in the course which alone seemed to us to be in accordance with Truth, to be exposed to the charge of over-zeal and fanaticism even among our own brethren. Regarding the work to be done in hospital as one of mercy and benevolence, we asked if we had any right to refuse its performance; and questioned whether we could do more good by endeavoring to bear to the end a clear testimony against war, than by laboring by word and deed among the needy in the hospitals and camps. We saw around us a rich field for usefulness in which there were scarce any laborers, and toward whose work our hands had often started involuntarily and unbidden. At last we consented to a trial, at least till we could make inquiries concerning the Colonel's allegations, and ask the counsel of our friends, reserving the privilege of returning to our former position.

6*th.* At Washinqton.—At first, after being informed of our declining to serve in his hospital, Colonel Foster did not appear altered in his kind regard for us. But his spleen soon became evident. At the time we asked for a trial by court-martial, and it was his duty to place us under arrest and proceed with the preferring of his charges against us. For a while he seemed to hesitate and consult his inferior officers, and among them his Chaplain. The result of the conference was our being ordered into our companies, that, separated, and with the force of the officers of a company bearing upon us, we might the more likely be subdued. Yet the Colonel assured L. M. M., interceding in my behalf, when the lieutenant commanding my company threatened force upon me, that he should not allow any personal injury. When we marched next day I was compelled to bear a gun and equipments. My associates were more fortunate, for, being asked if they would carry their guns, declined and saw no more trouble from them. The captain of the company in which P. D. was placed told him he did not believe he was ugly about it, and that he could only put him under arrest and prefer charges against him. He accordingly was taken under guard, where he lay till we left for here.

The next morning the men were busy in burnishing their arms. When I looked toward the one I had borne, yellow with rust, I trembled in the weakness of the flesh at the trial I felt impending over me. Before the Colonel was up I knocked at his tent, but was told he was asleep, though, through the opening, I saw him lying gazing at me. Although I felt I should gain no relief from him, I applied again soon after. He admitted me and, lying on his bed, inquired with cold heartlessness what I wanted. I stated to him, that I could never consent to serve, and, being under the war-power, was resigned to suffer instead all the just penalties of the law. I begged of him release from the attempts by violence to compel my obedience and service, and a trial, though likely to be made by those having no sympathy with me, yet probably in a manner comfortable to law.

He replied that he had shown us all the favor he should; that he had, now, turned us over to the military power and was going to let that take its course; that is, henceforth we were to be at the mercy of the inferior officers, without appeal to law, justice, or mercy. He said he had placed us in a pleasant position, against which we could have no reasonable objection, and that we had failed to perform our agreement. He wished to deny that our consent was only temporary and conditional. He declared, furthermore, his belief, that a man who would not fight for his country did not deserve to live. I was glad to withdraw from his presence as soon as I could.

I went back to my tent and laid down for a season of retirement, endeavoring to gain resignation to any event. I dreaded torture and desired strength of flesh and spirit. My trial soon came. The lieutenant called me out, and pointing to the gun that lay near by, asked if I was going to clean it. I replied to him, that I could not comply with military requisitions, and felt resigned to the consequences. 'I do not ask about your feelings; I want to know if you are going to clean that gun.' 'I cannot do it,' was my answer. He went away, saying, 'Very well,' and I crawled into the tent again. Two sergeants soon called for me, and taking me a little aside, bid me lie down on my back, and stretching my limbs apart tied cords to my wrists and ankles and these to four stakes driven in the ground somewhat in the form of an X.

I was very quiet in my mind as I lay there on the ground [soaked] with the rain of the previous day, exposed to the heat of the sun, and suffering keenly from the cords binding my wrists and straining my muscles. And, if I dared the presumption, I should say that I caught a glimpse of heavenly pity. I wept, not so much from my own suffering as from sorrow that such things should be in our own country, where Justice and Freedom and Liberty of Conscience have been the annual boast of Fourth-of-July orators so many years. It seemed that our forefathers in the faith had wrought and suffered in vain, when the privileges they so dearly bought were so soon set aside. And I was sad, that one endeavoring to follow our dear Master should be so generally regarded as a despicable and stubborn culprit.

After something like an hour had passed, the lieutenant came with his orderly to ask me if I was ready to clean the gun. I replied to the orderly asking the question, that it could but give me pain to be asked or required to do anything I believed wrong. He repeated it to the lieutenant just behind him, who advanced and addressed me. I was favored to improve the opportunity to say to him a few things I wished. He said little; and, when I had finished, he withdrew with the others who had gathered around. About the end of another hour his orderly came and released me.

I arose and sat on the ground. I did not rise to go away. I had not where to go, nothing to do. As I sat there my heart swelled with joy from above. The consolation and sweet fruit of tribulation patiently endured. But I also grieved, that the world was so far gone astray, so cruel and blind. It seemed as if the gospel of Christ had never been preached upon earth, and the beautiful example of his life had been utterly lost sight of.

Some of the men came about me, advising me to yield, and among them one of those who had tied me down, telling me what I had already suffered was nothing to what I must yet suffer unless I yielded; that human flesh could not endure what they would put upon me. I wondered if it could be that they could force me to obedience by torture, and examined myself closely to see if they had advanced yet one step toward the accomplishment of their purposes. Though weaker in body, I believed I found myself, through divine strength, as firm in my resolution to maintain my allegiance to my Master.

The relaxation of my nerves and muscles after having been so tensely strained left me that afternoon so weak that I could hardly walk or perform any mental exertion.

I had not yet eaten the mean and scanty breakfast I had prepared, when I was ordered to pack up my things and report myself at the lieutenant's tent. I was accustomed to such orders and complied, little moved.

The lieutenant received me politely with, 'Good-morning, Mr. Pringle,' and desiring me to be seated, proceeded with the writing with which he was engaged. I sat down in some wonderment and sought to be quiet and prepared for any event.

'You are ordered to report to Washington,' said he; 'I do not know what it is for.' I assured him that neither did I know. We were gathered before the Major's tent for preparation for departure. The regimental officers were there manifesting surprise and chagrin; for they could not but show both as they looked upon us, whom the day before they were threatening to crush into submission, and attempting also to execute their threats that morning, standing out of their power and under orders from one superior to their Major Commanding E.M. As the bird uncaged, so were our hearts that morning. Short and uncertain at first were the flights of Hope. As the slave many times before us, leaving his yoke behind him, turned from the plantations of Virginia and set his face toward the far North, so we from out a grasp as close and as abundant in suffering and severity, and from without the line of bayonets that had so many weeks surrounded us, turned our backs upon the camp of the 4th Vermont and took our way over the turnpike that ran through the tented fields of Culpeper.

At the War Office we were soon admitted to an audience with the Adjutant General, Colonel Townsend, whom we found to be a very fine man, mild and kind. He referred our cases to the Secretary of War, Stanton, by whom we were ordered to report for service to Surgeon General Hammond. Here we met Isaac Newton, Commissioner of Agriculture, waiting for our arrival, and James Austin of Nantucket, expecting his son, Charles L. Austin, and Edward W. Holway of Sandwich, Mass., conscripted Friends like ourselves, and ordered here from the 22nd Massachusetts.

We understand it is through the influence of Isaac Newton that Friends have been able to approach the heads of Government in our behalf and to prevail with them to so great an extent. He explained to us the circumstance in which we are placed. That the Secretary of War and President sympathized with Friends in their present suffering, and would grant them full release, but that they felt themselves bound by their oaths that they would execute the laws, to carry out to its full extent the Conscription Act. That there appeared but one door of relief open,—that was to parole us and allow us to go home, but subject to their call again ostensibly, though this they neither wished nor proposed to do. That the fact of Friends in the Army and refusing service had attracted public attention so that it was not expedient to parole us at present. That, therefore, we were to be sent to one of the hospitals for a short time, where it was hoped and expressly requested that we would consent to remain quiet and acquiesce, if possible, in whatever might be required of us. That our work there would be quite free from objection, being for the direct relief of the sick; and that there he would release none for active service in the field, as the nurses were hired civilians.

9th.—We all went, thinking to do the whole city in a day, but before the time of our passes expired, we were glad to drag ourselves back to the rest and quiet of D. H. During the day we called upon our friend I.N. in the Patent Office. When he came to see us on the 7th, he stated he had called upon the President that afternoon to request him to release us and let us go home to our friends. The President promised to consider it over-night. Accordingly yesterday morning, as I.N. told us, he waited upon him again. He found there a woman in the greatest distress. Her son, only a boy of fifteen years and four months, having been enticed into the Army, had deserted and been sentenced to be shot the next day. As the clerks were telling her, the President was in the War Office and could not be seen, nor did they think he could attend to her case that day. I.N. found her almost wild with grief. 'Do not despair, my good woman,' said he, 'I guess the President can be seen after a bit.' He soon presented her case to the President, who exclaimed at once, 'That must not be, I must look into that case, before they shoot that boy'; and telegraphed at once to have the order suspended.

I.N. judged it was not a fit time to urge our case. We feel we can afford to wait, that a life may be saved. But we long for release. We do not feel easy to remain here.

21*st*—I.N. has not called yet; our situation is becoming almost intolerable. I query if patience is justified under the circumstances. My distress of mind may be enhanced by my feeble condition of health, for to-day I am confined to my bed, almost too weak to get downstairs. This is owing to exposure after being heated over furnaces.

6*th*—Last evening E.W.H. saw I.N. particularly on my behalf, I suppose. He left at once for the President. This morning he called to inform us of his interview at the White House. The President was moved to sympathy in my behalf, when I.N. gave him a letter from one of our Friends in New York. After its perusal he exclaimed to our friend, 'I want you to go and tell Stanton, that it is my wish all those young men be sent home at once.' He was on his way to the Secretary this morning as he called.

Later. I.N. has just called again informing us in joy that we are free. At the War Office he was urging the Secretary to consent to our paroles, when the President entered. 'It is my urgent wish,' said he.

The Secretary yielded; the order was given, and we were released. What we had waited for so many weeks was accomplished in a few moments by a Providential ordering of circumstances.

1898

1898
My Country Right or Wrong

BY MARK TWAIN

Mark Twain wrote this brief diatribe in response to the Spanish-American War.

I PRAY YOU to pause and consider. Against our traditions we are now entering upon an unjust and trivial war, a war against a helpless people, and for a base object—robbery. At first our citizens spoke out against this thing, by an impulse natural to their training. Today they have turned, and their voice is the other way. What caused the change? Merely a politician's trick—a high-sounding phrase, a blood stirring phrase which turned their uncritical heads: Our Country, right or wrong! An empty phrase, a silly phrase. It was shouted by every newspaper, it was thundered from the pulpit, the Superintendent of Public Instruction placarded it in every schoolhouse in the land, the War Department inscribed it upon the flag. And every man who failed to shout it or who was silent, was proclaimed a traitor—none but those others were patriots. To be a patriot, one had to say, and keep on saying, "Our Country, right or wrong," and urge on the little war. Have you not perceived that that phrase is an insult to the nation?

For in a republic, who is "the Country"? Is it the Government which is for the moment in the saddle? Why, the Government is merely a servant—merely a temporary servant; it cannot be its prerogative to determine what is right and what is wrong, and decide who is a patriot and who isn't. Its function is to obey orders, not originate them. Who, then, is "the Country"? Is it the newspaper? Is it the pulpit? Is it the school superintendent? Why, these are mere parts of the country, not the whole of it; they have not command, they have only their little share in the command. They are but one in the thousand; it is in the thousand that command is lodged; they must determine what is right and what is wrong; they must decide who is a patriot and who isn't.

Who are the thousand—that is to say, who are "the Country"? In a monarchy, the king and his family are the country; in a republic it is the common voice of the people. Each of you, for himself, by himself and on his own responsibility, must speak. And it is a solemn and weighty responsibility, and not lightly to be flung aside at the bullying of pulpit, press, government, or the empty catch-phrases of politicians. Each must for himself alone decide what is right and what is wrong, and which course is patriotic and which isn't. You cannot shirk this and be a man. To decide it against your convictions is to be an unqualified and inexcusible traitor, both to yourself and to your country, let men label you as they may. If you alone of all the nation shall decide one way, and that way be the right way according to your convictions of the right, you have done your duty by yourself and by your country—hold up your head! You have nothing to be ashamed of.

Only when a republic's life is in danger should a man uphold his government when it is in the wrong. There is no other time.

This Republic's life is not in peril. The nation has sold its honor for a phrase. It has swung itself loose from its safe anchorage and is drifting, its helm is in private hands. The stupid phrase needed help, and it got another one: "Even if the war be wrong we are in it and must fight it out: *we cannot retire from it without dishonor.*" Why, not even a burglar could have said it better. We cannot withdraw from this sordid raid because to grant peace to those little people under their terms—independence—would dishonor us. You have flung away Adam's phrase—you should take it up and examine it again. He said, *"An inglorious peace is better than a dishonorable war."*

You have planted a seed, and it will grow.

1987
from *The Great Divide*
by Studs Terkel

Oral historian Studs Terkel's "Great Divide" referred to the cultural, financial and political gap opening between various groups of Americans.

It is August 18, 1987. It is thirteen days after his arrest. His voice, long-distance, sounds high-spirited, buoyant. "It is now my turn to do a little hammering," he had written in a letter received after his arrest.

He, together with a young Catholic pacifist, Jerry Ebner, is at the Wyandotte County Jail, Kansas City, Kansas. "The charge against us is destruction of government property. Helen Woodson was, in spirit, part of this action. She's doing twelve years up in Shakopee, Minnesota, at the state prison."

In the letter, Joe said: "There is no group more suited to work toward the total elimination of these weapons than my generation. We went to school, spent time in military service, married, had families, and worked toward achieving the American dream. We were either silent or cheered when the Bomb was dropped, paid taxes to develop more and better bombs. . . . I am not prepared to leave this legacy to my children or yours. With Jean, I am saying NO, no longer in my name.

"Please forgive me for not sharing my plans with you, dear friends. My silence in this regard was essential for your protection. . . . It also saved us from saying good-bye in a less casual way when we were last together."

On August 5, 1987, at approximately 5:15 p.m., Jerry and I entered the silo. They call them missile launch facilities. It's near Butler, Missouri, about fifty miles south of Kansas City. The time corresponds to 8:15, August 6, in Hiroshima, when the bomb exploded.

August 6 also happens to celebrate the Feast of Transfiguration. Christ and His apostles Peter, James, and John went to the mountain to pray. He became transfigured and His divinity was revealed. So we took the name Transfiguration Plowshares.

Jean chose silo M-10. About a year and a half later, I chose silo K-9. We had a lot of choices (laughs). There are eleven groups of silos, and 150 warheads in this field. We carried our tools and banners in socks. This was recovered property that Jean and her friends had used on Good Friday. We were recycling (laughs).

We added a banner that had pictures of our two grandsons, who were born since Jean's action. It said: DISARMAMENT INSURES A FUTURE FOR THE CHILDREN. We hung them on the cyclone fence that surrounded the silo. Very ordinary. When you drive past these places, they're hardly noticeable.

We had all sorts of hammers: sledge, ball peen, pick. We chiseled a cross. On top of the cover, I poured three baby bottles of blood, Jerry's and mine, and made a cross out of it. We had brought our Bibles along, and after we had finished what we planned to do we sat on top of the silo, prayed, and sang songs. We drank a lot of ice water. It was about 100 degrees out there.

About forty-two minutes later, an air force station wagon came up the road. We were covered by three guys with automatic rifles. They had us raise our hands. We called out to them that we were unarmed and nonviolent and walked to the gate.

We lay face down on the ground, spread-eagled. They didn't even attempt to frisk us. They were real young kids and seemed rather nervous. They weren't quite sure they knew what they were doing, and a guy on the hill was giving them instructions. We were turned over to the county sheriff and handcuffed. By the time we left, there were about eight cars around.

So we were in a cell. About one-thirty in the morning, a guy from the air force special investigations came in. We refused to answer any of his questions. He was the one from whom we recovered the banners used in the previous Plowshare actions.

The grand jury reconvened yesterday. The charge, destruction of government property, carries a ten years' jail sentence, maximum, and a fine of $250,000. They'll most likely add a conspiracy charge. And possibly, sabotage.

Dan Stewart, the assistant to the U.S. Attorney, who handled Jean's case, will probably do the major trial work. We keep running into familiar faces. It's unlikely Jean's judge, Elmo Hunter, will handle this one. He recently made some statements in the paper that Jean's sentence wasn't severe enough, because it apparently didn't deter me.

We're going *pro se*. We will be our own attorneys. We will have a lawyer advising us, but he won't represent us in court.

Our defense is that we haven't committed a crime; that the crime really is the existence of these weapons of indiscriminate destruction that are violations of the Nuremburg principles, United Nations principles—that the crime would be for us to sit idly by. It's the necessity defense: the imminent danger posed by these weapons justifies what the law considers an illegal act.

I'm a chemical engineer, with an M.B.A. degree from the University of Chicago. For the past few years, I've worked as a salesman of food process equipment. You become a questionable commodity in the market at my age. The company I worked for had gone out of business, so I took up a new career: a resister to the military buildup. It's a real career change (laughs).

The first thing I did was to go to Alderson and visit Jean for five days. It will be the last time that we will be able to see each other for quite some time now. Actually, Jean will probably visit me in prison the next time.

I didn't tell the kids what I had in mind. They all suspected something, because they observed the way I was behaving over the past year or so. This is not something you just decide to do.

I feel great. This is a happy time right now. It was something I felt increasingly strongly about since Jean was in jail. We've made our statement and I feel good.

I'm sure her example had a lot to do with getting me interested. It's a time of real adjustment: reorientation of things you considered to be important from your earliest days. I guess you'd call it resetting your priorities.

Because our family was raised, I had no strong obligations that prevented me from doing something that would separate me from normal society for a number of years. We're at the point now where we can enjoy some of the free time, enjoy our grandchildren. But it's at this time that we have the freedom to make a statement like this. Ultimately it's going to benefit our grandchildren far more than anything we could do in a more normal course of events. If we're silent, there may be no planet for them to enjoy.

I'm not saying that people should go out and bang on a silo. There are so many other ways to resist. Once you cut through the obfuscation they throw at you, you realize our fate is being determined by pseudo-experts.

I'm going to be someone who questions. I will satisfy my own sense of understanding before I believe anything that is told to me. If I hear something said by the government that is blatantly false, I will speak out against it, I will resist it and I will suffer the consequences.

This feeling of happiness is something that has been acquired. It gives you such delight to be able to just feel this way, it's hard to describe.

Postscript: On December 11, 1987, Joe Gump and Jerry Ebner were sentenced to prison terms of thirty and forty months, respectively, and were ordered to make restitution for damages they caused August 5 (Chicago Sun-Times, December 12, 1987).

#03789-045, A.K.A. JEAN GUMP

August 15, 1987. It is a long-distance call from the Correctional Institution for Women, Alderson, West Virginia.

She is chuckling: "They don't do much correcting here. Heaven knows, they try, but it doesn't seem to be effective." She appears amused during much of the conversation.

Our conversation is being taped.

Yes, I've got the machine working—

I mean, by others. It's good. I've always believed in education. Of course all my letters are read. I like that. I usually put something in there that I would like the staff to see. If some of the staff are lazy and choose not to read the mail, I usually write on the envelope "Legal Mail." This way it will surely be read. It's important that we educate everybody as we go along.

It's exactly eleven months to this day that I've been here. I think this is the place for me at this time in my life. The feds probably think it's a good place for me for the rest of my life.

There are things here called contraband. Eighty percent of the inmates are here on drug-related charges. Drugs are of course contraband. But another real no-no is a brown paper bag. I'm not sure why. It might be a fire hazard, you think? A real awful thing is bubble gum. A person can go in the hole for that—solitary confinement. It's a funny thing, I haven't been there yet. I'm a kind of law-and-order freak. I follow rules extremely well.

I enjoy the compound and especially enjoy my sister inmates. As for the staff, the system is geared for them to do things they probably wouldn't do on the outside. Most of us would find reading other people's mail detestable. But that's part of the job. Lying is part of the job, too.

I have to think of my guards as individuals. We have to have strip searches. I find it so vulgar, so demeaning, so intrusive, it makes me cringe. But that guard is trying to feed her family—we have male guards here, too. Maybe if there were no other jobs, I'd be doing that, too.

As inmates, we're property. We belong to Mr. Meese, we belong to the Bureau of Prisons. A month ago, a young woman had come here from another federal institution. She had been locked up for fourteen months without seeing the light of day. On arriving here, she was so happy to be out in the sunlight, she lay down and got herself a sunburn. They wrote a shot—that's an incident report. The shot read: Destruction of government property. Her skin, okay?

What did she destroy?

Her skin. She got a sunburn.

You're putting me on.

I wouldn't tease you about a thing like that. That is a fact, okay? Her sunburn deterred her from working. Her skin, her being, is the property of the United States government.

How do the other inmates feel about me? I feel I'm respected, though they may think I'm kind of a ding-a-ling. But nice. I like them, too, though our backgrounds are very different. After eight and a half months, I'm finally in a double room. I'm on the bottom bunk. Unfortunately, my roommate was just put in the hole.

I wake up quite early in the morning and I meditate and read Scripture for an hour. I have to be at work at 7:45. I work in the greenhouse and it's delightful. We're with living plants and we have National Public Radio on all day long. We listen to symphony music and the news. It's a peaceful place.

I get home about 3:45.

Home?

This is home, kid. Every inmate has to be in her room at 4:00. We have a count. They don't like to lose people. By 4:30, they've been able to count the 62 women in this cottage. There's something like 15 cottages, housing from 62 to 70 each. The facility was built to accommodate 300.

So many women here have experienced long separation from families. It hasn't been so with me. I think we're closer now, although I'm not present. When my son, Joey, graduated from law school, they had a big party at the house. They sent me a videotape. It was wonderful.

I'd like to have been there. I said to the warden, "Hey, listen, my son is gonna graduate. I think it would be nice if you gave me a furlough, so I could be there." He said I have to be eligible for release in two years and in community custody. That means the government trusts you enough to go home and say hello. I have what they call out-custody.

Let's say there was a death in the family. I would have to go home with federal marshals. They would take me to the wake in handcuffs to view the body. Then they'd put me in jail for overnight. They'd be staying at a hotel, which I would pay for. I'd pay for their meals as well. The next morning, they'd pick me up for the funeral, which I would attend in handcuffs. They play hard ball here, kid.

In addition to her six-year sentence, there is a five-year probation period, following release.

I owe the government $424.28 for the repair of the damage done to the nuclear missile. Plus $100 assessment. I chose not to pay this.

I don't think nuclear weapons should be repaired. They should be abolished. The government will have to pay it itself, I'm sorry.

I've wondered what would happen, if after I've served my six years and I'm on probation, will I still owe the government the five hundred bucks? The fact of the matter is, I will.* I've written to my judge and told him I won't pay the money. If after I go back for five more years and have served eleven years, will I still owe them the $524.28? I think I will.

You could be in forever. **

I suggested an alternative in a letter to the U.S. Probation Office. I'm always interested in saving money for American taxpayers. It costs taxpayers $28,000 per year per inmate. If my arithmetic is correct, my confinement for eleven years will cost around $308,000. If the government should pay the $524.28, it will save the taxpayers $307,457.52. Not a bad deal, eh?

Did Joe surprise you doing what he did?

Oh, no. I don't know how to explain it. All the things we had most of our lives thought important were no longer that important. He asked me one time, "What would you think if I sat on a missile?" I

---

* In an exchange of letters with the supervising probation officer, it was determined that her refusal of restitution would constitute violation of parole and she would be subject to further imprisonment.

** A remembrance of a Willie and Eugene Howard sketch is evoked. They were two celebrated vaudeville comics whose most memorable routine dealt with a two-dollar fine and a refusal to pay and years and years in prison.

said, "Joe, I wouldn't advise you on something like that. It's so very personal. It's your entire life we're talking about." I don't think anyone can make that kind of a decision for anyone else.

Each individual brings a certain difference to it. None of us is the same. There was a funny reaction here. I had called my sister at the time of Joe's arrest. I'd been fasting. With the news, it was a time of celebration. My sister inmates couldn't understand why one should celebrate a husband's imprisonment.

We were celebrating because someone whom I love very much had decided to take this stand. Oh, it's a hard spot to be in, but it's not an impossible one. It is saying to the people of the world that we have to give up a little of our comfort now, in a critical time, to point up the horrendous errors of a government. I always thought Joe and I had a lovely love affair when we were young. It's only gotten better. We're not going to see each other for a while—that's hard.

My health? Funny you should ask that. I had a little problem with blood pressure prior to coming here. The other day I had it taken and it was 110 over 80. This is what a stressless life will bring you. I'm very much at peace here.

I never viewed myself as a troublemaker. I like things nice and easy, I really do. But I don't want the goodies that the government has to offer at the expense of my grandchildren's future here. Oh, God, I have a tremendous hope. I figure if somebody like me can put aside her selfish interests and do something, anybody in the United States can. When Eisenhower was leaving office, he said, Someday people are going to want peace so bad, the government had better step aside and let them have it. I think that's coming to pass.

(Suddenly) Can you remember your number?

Certainly. It's like my toothbrush. (Rattles it off) 03789-045 (laughs).

1990
from *Peacework*
BY JUDITH PORTER ADAMS

Beth Robinson Coats (born 1916) became involved in the peace movement through the Unitarian church in 1958.

As A CHILD I was given the feeling that people all over the world were friends of mine. I remember that mother got me books about twins; oh, there were the Swiss twins and the Indian twins, and so on. I was learning about the home life of children in other parts of the world. That gave me a feeling of interest in the world. My mother had a humanistic point of view. She conveyed to us the feeling that we should understand people and help them.

As far as political activity, I didn't get started until very late. My family was very conservative. When World War II came along, I thought it was necessary. We were told to save fat because we needed it for armaments. So I saved every little bit of fat, which is quite a lot of work to do. You have to clarify it and all of that. I would save this fat, and somehow or another I never did get it turned in. I'd save it and save it, and then I'd set it out on the back porch, and dogs would come and get it or something. All the time I kept saving it because I felt I had to. But I didn't turn any of it in. As soon as the war was over, we were told to go on saving fat because it was needed for soap in Europe. From that time on I turned all the fat in. That made me realize that subconsciously I was a pacifist, but I hadn't admitted it to myself. I simply couldn't turn it in for armaments. But it wasn't until about 1958 that I actually became interested in politics and in making changes and began to really understand what changes were needed.

I had four children, and when the first two were in grammar school, I was active in the PTA. They didn't have any kind of United Nations committee or any kind of world policy committee, and I felt it was really important for us to support the United Nations. So I remember getting up and saying that we should have a U.N. committee. I was very shy and hated to talk in public, so for me it was a very brave thing to do. But it was necessary that I do this because of a conversation I'd had with my child that day. He had asked me, "Are we going to get killed in a war?" He had been hearing on television about bombs. This was after the war, in the late forties. There was a lot of talk about atomic bombs. I said, "No, I don't think we will, because there are people working to make sure we don't have another war. They're working in the U.N. and trying to bring peace around the world." And then he said, "What are you doing, Mommy?" That really hit me on the head. So I went to the PTA meeting that night and told them the story. They set up a U.N. committee, and it became fairly active.

Aside from a few things like that, it wasn't until the late fifties that what amounted to a religious conversion happened to me. I hadn't taken much interest in politics up to that time. I went to a meeting on the Nuclear Test Ban Treaty. At that time I didn't know whether we should have one or not; I was certainly not in the peace movement or even acquainted with it. Oh, I was interested in the subject; I was concerned about it. But I wasn't at all sure that we didn't need to test bombs. I just knew that it was a very dangerous thing and was worried about it. At this meeting they had two very good speakers, one of whom was a scientist from the Lawrence Livermore Labs, who was very knowledgeable about our weapons and a very honest man. He was completely convinced that we had to build up our weapons as fast as we could. He told us exactly what the weapons situation was—what the Russians had and why he thought we had to keep building more. Well, that was so scary. I hadn't really faced it before, and it terrified me.

Then a man from the American Friends Service Committee in San Francisco got up and said, "Well, obviously that way is madness. The only thing we can do is turn around and go in the opposite direction." And I felt as if I'd been hit on the head. I just realized that, well, he's right. That's all you can do; there's no alternative. Well, at the end of the meeting I felt as if I had the flu, it had affected me so strongly. I felt I could hardly walk; I was very weak. It was just like a religious conversion—that powerful. So I went home and thought to myself, "What can I do?" I figured that every day I would do something for peace. Every day I'll think about it and see if I can think of one thing I can do. The first day I wrote a letter to the president saying how much I thought we ought to have a test ban treaty, and after a few days, each day I could think of a few more things. About the end of the first week, I volunteered to be the chair of the World Concern Committee at the Unitarian church. Like I say, I just made a complete change.

About a month after that, I joined the Women's International League for Peace and Freedom. I told them at the time that I was busy with other committees and that it would be about a year before I could be active. I asked them not to urge me because I had all that I could handle. I had four kids. So they were all very nice about it. They didn't urge me for a year. Then at the end of the year they asked me if I'd be president. It was ridiculous because I'd had no experience with the WILPF, and it was simply because they were desperate for a president and didn't know who to ask. They'd tried everybody they could think of. But I accepted in the end because at that time in the WILPF almost all the women were very old. It seemed to me that the organization was a very worthwhile one, and if someone didn't do something quickly, it was going to die out. So I decided that I didn't have anything to offer except being younger than most of them, but I figured maybe that would help. They were all boasting about their brown-haired president!

Many of the women in WILPF had been active for their whole lifetimes, working for peace just years and years before I was born. It was a marvelous experience to get acquainted with these women and learn about what they'd done and how they felt about things. We were concerned, for example, about the Vietnam War before most people knew there was anything going on out there. Kennedy was sending so-called advisors over there. We were trying to alert people at that early time that there was danger. The country got into the war, of course, and the WILPF worked against it by counseling war resisters.

My son was a war resister. I have three sons. The oldest one became a conscientious objector before we really went into the Vietnam War. I had never talked to him about conscientious objector status. He did it on his own initiative. The second son became a C.O. during the Vietnam War; he knew very well that he wasn't going to fight that war. He was against war; it was the most logical position for him. Our third son during the early seventies decided that rather than being a C.O. he'd be a resister. He asked the Quaker meeting in Palo Alto if they would accept his draft card and send it to the district attorney for him. The Friends had a meeting to support him, which was a very marvelous thing, so helpful to my husband and me because we didn't want him to go to prison. He was young, and we felt it would really mar his life. We wanted very much for him to be a C.O. instead. But he felt that he couldn't do that. To see all the community support for him was very helpful to us, to help us accept it. We hadn't fought it, but we certainly hadn't felt comfortable with it until then. After that, I felt comfortable with it, and my husband accepted it. Then I started helping draft resisters.

We had an organization called Draft Refuser Support here in this area. Groups started here and in San Francisco and Berkeley. We had potlucks, and we'd invite all the draft refusers to come to dinner and conversation. Then we helped them to get jobs and homes and that sort of thing, and we worked with those in prison. Around this time, there was a big project in the whole San Francisco Bay area of people going to jail for sitting in front of induction centers. We went too. There was a big WILPF group that went to jail. In fact, our branch president was one of them, and she said that they could have a board meeting there, since most of the board was in jail. They were in for ten days.

My daughter Kitty was in junior high school then, I think. My son Tom sat in, too, as a resister. Kitty wanted to, but I urged her not to since she was underage. So she didn't. We sat in at the induction center just before Christmas and were in jail over Christmas, which was quite an experience. I was very glad I did it. We had twenty-one days in jail. I haven't gone to jail in protest since then. I may do it again. A number of times, I've wanted to join the farmworkers, but something comes up each time, and I haven't been able to.

The Vietnam War ended a month after my son Tom was killed in a canoeing accident. He was training in Philadelphia to be an activist in the Movement for a New Society. He'd had one year of training, and he was going to have one more, and then he was going to come out here and form a branch in this area. I heard about his death on a day when I was on a march for the farm workers union. It was a beautiful march, a beautiful day, a large crowd. It was a very short time after that that the war ended. I was numb at the time, and I felt very sorry that Tom couldn't know that the war had ended. He worked so hard. Of course it was a tremendous relief that the war ended.

I wasn't really politically active again until about 1978, when I got involved in working for solar energy. Curiously, right after I heard about Tom, my feeling was that I wasn't going to let this make me stop; I'm going to work all the harder. I thought, I'm going to work twice as hard because Tom was a peace activist, and I'll have to do his part as well as mine. That was my feeling.

Right after we heard he'd died, I went to the Social Concerns Committee of the church—I was chairman of it—and I went on and conducted the meeting as if nothing had happened. I guess I was really just suffering shock and didn't know it. I just felt that I was going to keep right on doing things, but it didn't work that way right after his death. For a few weeks I went into a state of nothingness. Then I started talking art classes. That's what finally took me out of the house. It was something I'd wanted to do all my life and never had time for. Later I got involved in my WILPF committees again, like with the Energy Task Force, but for a while I just took art classes.

When you're suddenly confronted with a death that way, it gives you a very dear understanding of your own mortality. You realize that you don't have forever in this world. Anything you're going to do, you'd better darn do it.

2003
Senate Speech

by Robert C. Byrd

Robert C. Byrd delivered this speech on the floor of the
United States Senate on February 12, 2003. The United
States attacked Iraq thirty-five days later.

To CONTEMPLATE WAr is to think about the most horrible of human
experiences. On this February day, as this nation stands at the brink
of battle, every American on some level must be contemplating the
horrors of war.

Yet, this Chamber is, for the most part, silent—ominously, dread-
fully silent. There is no debate, no discussion, no attempt to lay out
for the nation the pros and cons of this particular war. There is
nothing.

We stand passively mute in the United States Senate, paralyzed by
our own uncertainty, seemingly stunned by the sheer turmoil of
events. Only on the editorial pages of our newspapers is there much
substantive discussion of the prudence or imprudence of engaging in
this particular war.

And this is no small conflagration we contemplate. This is no
simple attempt to defang a villain. No. This coming battle, if it mate-
rializes, represents a turning point in U.S. foreign policy and possibly
a turning point in the recent history of the world.

This nation is about to embark upon the first test of a revolutionary doctrine applied in an extraordinary way at an unfortunate
time. The doctrine of preemption—the idea that the United States or
any other nation can legitimately attack a nation that is not immi-
nently threatening but may be threatening in the future—is a radical

new twist on the traditional idea of self defense. It appears to be in contravention of international law and the U.N. Charter. And it is being tested at a time of world-wide terrorism, making many countries around the globe wonder if they will soon be on our—or some other nation's—hit list.

High-level administration figures recently refused to take nuclear weapons off of the table when discussing a possible attack against Iraq. What could be more destabilizing and unwise than this type of uncertainty, particularly in a world where globalism has tied the vital economic and security interests of many nations so closely together? There are huge cracks emerging in our time-honored alliances, and U.S. intentions are suddenly subject to damaging worldwide speculation. Anti-Americanism based on mistrust, misinformation, suspicion and alarming rhetoric from U.S. leaders is fracturing the once solid alliance against global terrorism which existed after 9/11.

Here at home, people are warned of imminent terrorist attacks with little guidance as to when or where such attacks might occur. Family members are being called to active military duty, with no idea of the duration of their stay or what horrors they may face. Communities are being left with less than adequate police and fire protection. Other essential services are also short-staffed. The mood of the nation is grim. The economy is stumbling. Fuel prices are rising and may soon spike higher.

This administration, now in power for a little over two years, must be judged on its record. I believe that that record is dismal.

In that scant two years, this administration has squandered a large projected surplus of some $5.6 trillion over the next decade and taken us to projected deficits as far as the eye can see. This administration's domestic policy has put many of our states in dire financial condition, underfunding scores of essential programs for our people. This administration has fostered policies which have slowed economic growth. This administration has ignored urgent matters such as the crisis in health care for our elderly. This administration has been slow to provide adequate funding for homeland security. This administration has been reluctant to better protect our long and porous borders.

In foreign policy, this administration has failed to find Osama bin Laden. In fact, just yesterday we heard from him again marshaling his forces and urging them to kill. This administration has split traditional alliances, possibly crippling, for all time, international order-keeping entities like the United Nations and NATO. This administration has called into question the traditional worldwide perception of the United States as well-intentioned peacekeeper. This administration has turned the patient art of diplomacy into threats, labeling and name calling of the sort that reflects quite poorly on the intelligence and sensitivity of our leaders, and which will have consequences for years to come.

Calling heads of state pygmies, labeling whole countries as evil, denigrating powerful European allies as irrelevant—these types of crude insensitivities can do our great nation no good. We may have massive military might, but we cannot fight a global war on terrorism alone. We need the cooperation and friendship of our time-honored allies as well as the newer-found friends whom we can attract with our wealth. Our awesome military machine will do us little good if we suffer another devastating attack on our homeland that would severely damage our economy. Our military manpower is already stretched thin and we will need the augmenting support of those nations who can supply troop strength, not just sign letters cheering us on.

The war in Afghanistan has cost us $37 billion so far, yet there is evidence that terrorism may already be starting to regain its hold in that region. We have not found bin Laden, and unless we secure the peace in Afghanistan, the dark dens of terrorism may yet again flourish in that remote and devastated land.

Pakistan as well is at risk of destabilizing forces. This administration has not finished the first war against terrorism and yet it is eager to embark on another conflict with perils much greater than those in Afghanistan. Is our attention span that short? Have we not learned that after winning the war one must always secure the peace?

And yet we hear little about the aftermath of war in Iraq. In the absence of plans, speculation abroad is rife. Will we seize Iraq's oil fields, becoming an occupying power which controls the price and supply of that nation's oil for the foreseeable future? To whom do we propose to hand the reigns of power after Saddam Hussein?

Will our war inflame the Muslim world resulting in devastating attacks on Israel? Will Israel retaliate with its own nuclear arsenal? Will the Jordanian and Saudi Arabian governments be toppled by radicals, bolstered by Iran which has much closer ties to terrorism than Iraq?

Could a disruption of the world's oil supply lead to a world-wide recession? Has our senselessly bellicose language and our callous disregard of the interests and opinions of other nations increased the global race to join the nuclear club and made proliferation an even more lucrative practice for nations which need the income?

In only the space of two short years this reckless and arrogant administration has initiated policies which may reap disastrous consequences for years.

One can understand the anger and shock of any president after the savage attacks of 9/11. One can appreciate the frustration of having only a shadow to chase and an amorphous, fleeting enemy on which it is nearly impossible to exact retribution.

But to turn one's frustration and anger into the kind of extremely destabilizing and dangerous foreign policy debacle that the world is currently witnessing is inexcusable from any administration charged with the awesome power and responsibility of guiding the destiny of the greatest superpower on the planet. Frankly many of the pronouncements made by this administration are outrageous. There is no other word.

Yet this chamber is hauntingly silent. On what is possibly the eve of horrific infliction of death and destruction on the population of the nation of Iraq—a population, I might add, of which over 50 percent is under age 15—this chamber is silent. On what is possibly only days before we send thousands of our own citizens to face unimagined horrors of chemical and biological warfare—this chamber is silent. On the eve of what could possibly be a vicious terrorist attack in retaliation for our attack on Iraq, it is business as usual in the United States Senate.

We are truly "sleepwalking through history." In my heart of hearts I pray that this great nation and its good and trusting citizens are not in for a rudest of awakenings.

To engage in war is always to pick a wild card. And war must always be a last resort, not a first choice. I truly must question the judgment of any president who can say that a massive unprovoked military attack on a nation which is over 50 percent children is "in the highest moral traditions of our country." This war is not necessary at this time. Pressure appears to be having a good result in Iraq. Our mistake was to put ourselves in a corner so quickly. Our challenge is to now find a graceful way out of a box of our own making. Perhaps there is still a way if we allow more time.

2003
Dispatch from Rafah, Occupied Palestine

BY RACHEL CORRIE

Rachel Corrie, twenty-three, was crushed by a bulldozer on March 16, 2003. She was acting as a human shield to prevent the destruction of Palestinian homes. These emails were among her last correspondence.

FEBRUARY 7 2003

Hi friends and family, and others,

I have been in Palestine for two weeks and one hour now, and I still have very few words to describe what I see. It is most difficult for me to think about what's going on here when I sit down to write back to the United States. Something about the virtual portal into luxury. I don't know if many of the children here have ever existed without tank-shell holes in their walls and the towers of an occupying army surveying them constantly from the near horizons. I think, although I'm not entirely sure, that even the smallest of these children understand that life is not like this everywhere. An eight-year-old was shot and killed by an Israeli tank two days before I got here, and many of the children murmur his name to me—Ali—or point at the posters of him on the walls. The children also love to get me to practice my limited Arabic by asking me, "Kaif Sharon?" "Kaif Bush?" and they laugh when I say, "Bush Majnoon", "Sharon Majnoon" back in my limited arabic. (How is Sharon? How is Bush? Bush is crazy. Sharon is crazy.) Of course this isn't quite what I believe, and some of the adults who have the English correct me: "Bush mish Majnoon" . . . Bush is a businessman. Today

I tried to learn to say, "Bush is a tool", but I don't think it translated quite right. But anyway, there are eight-year-olds here much more aware of the workings of the global power structure than I was just a few years ago.

Nevertheless, no amount of reading, attendance at conferences, documentary viewing and word of mouth could have prepared me for the reality of the situation here. You just can't imagine it unless you see it—and even then you are always well aware that your experience of it is not at all the reality: what with the difficulties the Israeli army would face if they shot an unarmed US citizen, and with the fact that I have money to buy water when the army destroys wells, and the fact, of course, that I have the option of leaving. Nobody in my family has been shot, driving in their car, by a rocket launcher from a tower at the end of a major street in my hometown. I have a home. I am allowed to go see the ocean. When I leave for school or work I can be relatively certain that there will not be a heavily armed soldier waiting halfway between Mud Bay and downtown Olympia at a checkpoint with the power to decide whether I can go about my business, and whether I can get home again when I'm done. As an afterthought to all this rambling, I am in Rafah: a city of about 140,000 people, approximately 60% of whom are refugees—many of whom are twice or three times refugees. Today, as I walked on top of the rubble where homes once stood, Egyptian soldiers called to me from the other side of the border, "Go! Go!" because a tank was coming. And then waving and "What's your name?". Something disturbing about this friendly curiosity. It reminded me of how much, to some degree, we are all kids curious about other kids. Egyptian kids shouting at strange women wandering into the path of tanks. Palestinian kids shot from the tanks when they peek out from behind walls to see what's going on. International kids standing in front of tanks with banners. Israeli kids in the tanks anonymously—occasionally shouting and also occasionally waving—many forced to be here, many just aggressive—shooting into the houses as we wander away.

I've been having trouble accessing news about the outside world here, but I hear an escalation of war on Iraq is inevitable. There is a great deal of concern here about the "reoccupation of Gaza". Gaza is reoccupied every day to various extents but I think the fear is that the tanks will enter all the streets and remain here instead of entering some of the streets and then withdrawing after some hours or days to observe and shoot from the edges of the communities. If people aren't already thinking about the consequences of this war for the people of the entire region then I hope you will start.

My love to everyone. My love to my mom. My love to smooch. My love to fg and barnhair and sesamees and Lincoln School. My love to Olympia.

Rachel

FEBRUARY 20 2003

Mama,

Now the Israeli army has actually dug up the road to Gaza, and both of the major checkpoints are closed. This means that Palestinians who want to go and register for their next quarter at university can't. People can't get to their jobs and those who are trapped on the other side can't get home; and internationals, who have a meeting tomorrow in the West Bank, won't make it. We could probably make it through if we made serious use of our international white person privilege, but that would also mean some risk of arrest and deportation, even though none of us has done anything illegal.

The Gaza Strip is divided in thirds now. There is some talk about the "reoccupation of Gaza", but I seriously doubt this will happen, because I think it would be a geopolitically stupid move for Israel right now. I think the more likely thing is an increase in smaller below-the-international-outcry-radar incursions and possibly the oft-hinted "population transfer".

I am staying put in Rafah for now, no plans to head north. I still feel like I'm relatively safe and think that my most likely risk in case of a larger-scale incursion is arrest. A move to reoccupy Gaza would generate a much larger outcry than Sharon's assassination-during-peace-negotiations/land grab strategy, which is working very well now to create settlements all over, slowly but surely eliminating any meaningful possibility for Palestinian self-determination. Know that I have a lot of very nice Palestinians looking after me. I have a small flu bug, and got some very nice lemony drinks to cure me. Also, the woman who keeps the key for the well where we still sleep keeps asking me about you. She doesn't speak a bit of English, but she asks about my mom pretty frequently—wants to make sure I'm calling you.

Love to you and Dad and Sarah and Chris and everybody.

Rachel

FEBRUARY 27 2003

(To her mother)

Love you. Really miss you. I have bad nightmares about tanks and bulldozers outside our house and you and me inside. Sometimes the adrenaline acts as an anesthetic for weeks and then in the evening or at night it just hits me again—a little bit of the reality of the situation. I am really scared for the people here. Yesterday, I watched a father lead his two tiny children, holding his hands, out into the sight of tanks and a sniper tower and bulldozers and Jeeps because he thought his house was going to be exploded. Jenny and I stayed in the house with several women and two small babies. It was our mistake in translation that caused him to think it was his house that was being exploded. In fact, the Israeli army was in the process of detonating an explosive in the ground nearby—one that appears to have been planted by Palestinian resistance.

This is in the area where Sunday about 150 men were rounded up and contained outside the settlement with gunfire over their heads and around them, while tanks and bulldozers destroyed 25 greenhouses—the livelihoods for 300 people. The explosive was right in front of the greenhouses—right in the point of entry for tanks that might come back again. I was terrified to think that this man felt it was less of a risk to walk out in view of the tanks with his kids than to stay in his house. I was really scared that they were all going to be shot and I tried to stand between them and the tank. This happens every day, but just this father walking out with his two little kids just looking very sad, just happened to get my attention more at this particular moment, probably because I felt it was our translation problems that made him leave.

I thought a lot about what you said on the phone about Palestinian violence not helping the situation. Sixty thousand workers from Rafah worked in Israel two years ago. Now only 600 can go to Israel for jobs. Of these 600, many have moved, because the three checkpoints between here and Ashkelon (the closest city in Israel) make what used to be a 40-minute drive, now a 12-hour or impassible journey. In addition, what Rafah identified in 1999 as sources of economic growth are all completely destroyed—the Gaza international airport (runways demolished, totally closed); the border for trade with Egypt (now with a giant Israeli sniper tower in the middle of the crossing); access to the ocean (completely cut off in the last two years by a checkpoint and the Gush Katif settlement). The count of homes destroyed in Rafah since the beginning of this intifada is up around 600, by and large people with no connection to the resistance but who happen to live along the border. I think it is maybe official now that Rafah is the poorest place in the world. There used to be a middle class here—recently. We also get reports that in the past, Gazan flower shipments to Europe were delayed for two weeks at the Erez crossing for security inspections. You can imagine the value of two-week-old cut flowers in the European market, so that market dried up. And then the bulldozers come and take out people's vegetable farms and gardens. What is left for people? Tell me if you can think of anything. I can't.

If any of us had our lives and welfare completely strangled, lived with children in a shrinking place where we knew, because of previous experience, that soldiers and tanks and bulldozers could come for us at any moment and destroy all the greenhouses that we had been cultivating for however long, and did this while some of us were beaten and held captive with 149 other people for several hours—do you think we might try to use somewhat violent means to protect whatever fragments remained? I think about this especially when I see orchards and greenhouses and fruit trees destroyed—just years of care and cultivation. I think about you and how long it takes to make things grow and what a labour of love it is. I really think, in a similar situation, most people would defend themselves as best they could. I think Uncle Craig would. I think probably Grandma would. I think I would.

You asked me about non-violent resistance.

When that explosive detonated yesterday it broke all the windows in the family's house. I was in the process of being served tea and playing with the two small babies. I'm having a hard time right now. Just feel sick to my stomach a lot from being doted on all the time, very sweetly, by people who are facing doom. I know that from the United States, it all sounds like hyperbole. Honestly, a lot of the time the sheer kindness of the people here, coupled with the overwhelming evidence of the willful destruction of their lives, makes it seem unreal to me. I really can't believe that something like this can happen in the world without a bigger outcry about it. It really hurts me, again, like it has hurt me in the past, to witness how awful we can allow the world to be. I felt after talking to you that maybe you didn't completely believe me. I think it's actually good if you don't, because I do believe pretty much above all else in the importance of independent critical thinking. And I also realise that with you I'm much less careful than usual about trying to source every assertion that I make. A lot of the reason for that is I know that you actually do go and do your own research. But it makes me worry about the job I'm doing. All of the situation that I tried to enumerate above—and a lot of other things—constitutes a some-what gradual—often hidden, but nevertheless massive—removal and destruction of the ability of a particular group of people to sur-vive. This is what I am seeing here. The assassinations, rocket attacks and shooting of children are atrocities—but in focusing on them I'm terrified of missing their context. The vast majority of people here—even if they had the economic means to escape, even if they actually wanted to give up resisting on their land and just leave (which appears to be maybe the less nefarious of Sharon's pos-sible goals), can't leave. Because they can't even get into Israel to apply for visas, and because their destination countries won't let them in (both our country and Arab countries). So I think when all means of survival is cut off in a pen (Gaza) which people can't get out of, I think that qualifies as genocide. Even if they could get out, I think it would still qualify as genocide. Maybe you could look up the definition of genocide according to international law. I don't remember it right now. I'm going to get better at illustrating this, hopefully. I don't like to use those charged words. I think you know this about me. I really value words. I really try to illustrate and let people draw their own conclusions.

Anyway, I'm rambling. Just want to write to my Mom and tell her that I'm witnessing this chronic, insidious genocide and I'm really scared, and questioning my fundamental belief in the goodness of human nature. This has to stop. I think it is a good idea for us all to drop everything and devote our lives to making this stop. I don't think it's an extremist thing to do anymore. I still really want to dance around to Pat Benatar and have boyfriends and make comics for my coworkers. But I also want this to stop. Disbelief and horror is what I feel. Disappointment. I am disappointed that this is the base reality of our world and that we, in fact, participate in it. This is not at all what I asked for when I came into this world. This is not at all what the people here asked for when they came into this world. This is not the world you and Dad wanted me to come into when you decided to have me. This is not what I meant when I looked at Capital Lake and said: "This is the wide world and I'm coming to it." I did not mean that I was coming into a world where I could live a comfortable life and possibly, with no effort at all, exist in complete unawareness of my participation in genocide. More big explosions somewhere in the distance outside.

When I come back from Palestine, I probably will have nightmares and constantly feel guilty for not being here, but I can channel that into more work. Coming here is one of the better things I've ever done. So when I sound crazy, or if the Israeli military should break with their racist tendency not to injure white people, please pin the reason squarely on the fact that I am in the midst of a genocide which I am also indirectly supporting, and for which my government is largely responsible.

I love you and Dad. Sorry for the diatribe. OK, some strange men next to me just gave me some peas, so I need to eat and thank them.

Rachel

February 28 2003

(To her mother)

Thanks, Mom, for your response to my email. It really helps me to get word from you, and from other people who care about me.

After I wrote to you I went incommunicado from the affinity group for about 10 hours which I spent with a family on the front line in Hi Salam—who fixed me dinner—and have cable TV. The two front rooms of their house are unusable because gunshots have been fired through the walls, so the whole family—three kids and two parents—sleep in the parents' bedroom. I sleep on the floor next to the youngest daughter, Iman, and we all shared blankets. I helped the son with his English homework a little, and we all watched Pet Sematary, which is a horrifying movie. I think they all thought it was pretty funny how much trouble I had watching it. Friday is the holiday, and when I woke up they were watching Gummy Bears dubbed into Arabic. So I ate breakfast with them and sat there for a while and just enjoyed being in this big puddle of blankets with this family watching what for me seemed like Saturday morning cartoons. Then I walked some way to B'razil, which is where Nidal and Mansur and Grandmother and Rafat and all the rest of the big family that has really wholeheartedly adopted me live. (The other day, by the way, Grandmother gave me a pantomimed lecture in Arabic that involved a lot of blowing and pointing to her black shawl. I got Nidal to tell her that my mother would appreciate knowing that someone here was giving me a lecture about smoking turning my lungs black.) I met their sister-in-law, who is visiting from Nusserat camp, and played with her small baby.

Nidal's English gets better every day. He's the one who calls me, "My sister." He started teaching Grandmother how to say, "Hello. How are you?" In English. You can always hear the tanks and bulldozers passing by, but all of these people are genuinely cheerful with each other, and with me. When I am with Palestinian friends I tend to be somewhat less horrified than when I am trying to act in a role of human rights observer, documenter, or direct-action resister. They are a good example of how to be in it for the long haul. I know that the situation gets to them—and may ultimately get them—on all kinds of levels, but I am nevertheless amazed at their strength in being able to defend such a large degree of their humanity—laughter, generosity, family-time—against the incredible horror occurring in their lives and against the constant presence of death. I felt much better after this morning. I spent a lot of time writing about the disappointment of discovering, somewhat first-hand, the degree of evil of which we are still capable. I should at least mention that I am also discovering a degree of strength and of basic ability for humans to remain human in the direst of circumstances—which I also haven't seen before. I think the word is dignity. I wish you could meet these people. Maybe, hopefully, someday you will.

women

Legal Disabilities of Women

BY SARAH MOORE GRIMKÉ

Sarah Moore Grimké was born in 1792 to an aristocratic family in Charleston, South Carolina. She discovered the Quaker faith during a trip to Philadelphia, and in 1832 moved North with her sister Angelina. The two sisters boldly spoke out for the rights of slaves—and later, for the rights of women. Sarah wrote this letter to her sister from Concord, Massachusetts.

CONCORD, 9TH MO., 6TH, 1837.

My dear sister,—There are few things which present greater obstacles to the improvement and elevation of woman to her appropriate sphere of usefulness and duty, than the laws which have been enacted to destroy her independence, and crush her individuality; laws which, although they are framed for her government, she has had no voice in establishing, and which rob her of some of her *essential rights*. Woman has no political existence. With the single exception of presenting a petition to the legislative body, she is a cipher in the nation; or, if not actually so in representative governments, she is only counted, like the slaves of the South, to swell the number of law-makers who form decrees for her government, with little reference to her benefit, except so far as her good may promote their own. I am not sufficiently acquainted with the laws respecting women on the continent of Europe, to say anything about them. But Prof. Follen, in his essay on

"The Cause of Freedom in our Country," says, "Woman, though fully possessed of that rational and moral nature which is the foundation of all rights, enjoys amongst us fewer legal rights than under the civil law of continental Europe." I shall confine myself to the laws of our country. These laws bear with peculiar rigor on married women. Blackstone, in the chapter entitled "Of husband and wife," says:—

> "By marriage, the husband and wife are one person in law; that is, *the very being, or legal existence of the woman* is suspended during the marriage, or at least is incorporated and consolidated into that of the husband under whose wing, protection and cover she performs everything." "For this reason, a man cannot grant anything to his wife, or enter into covenant with her; for the grant would be to suppose her separate existence, and to covenant with her would be to covenant with himself; and there-fore it is also generally true, that all compacts made between hus-band and wife when single, are voided by the intermarriage. A woman indeed may be attorney for her husband, but that implies no separation from, but is rather a representation of, her love."

Here now, the very being of a woman, like that of a slave, is absorbed in her master. All contracts made with her, like those made with slaves by their owners, are a mere nullity. Our kind defenders have legislated away almost all our legal rights, and in the true spirit of such injustice and oppression, have kept us in ignorance of those very laws by which we are governed. They have persuaded us, that we have no right to investigate the laws, and that, if we did, we could not comprehend them; they alone are capable of understanding the mys-teries of Blackstone, &c. But they are not backward to make us feel the practical operation of their power over our actions.

"The husband is bound to provide his wife with necessaries by law, as much himself; and if she contracts debts for them, he is obliged to pay for them; but for anything besides necessaries, he is not chargeable."

Yet a man may spend the property he has acquired by marriage at the ale-house, the gambling table, or in any other way that he pleases. Many instances of this kind have come to my knowledge; and women, who have brought their husbands handsome fortunes, have been left, in consequence of the wasteful and dissolute habits of their husbands, in straitened circumstances, and compelled to toil for the support of their families.

"If the wife be indebted before marriage, the husband is bound afterwards to pay the debt; for he has adopted her and her circumstances together."

The wife's property is, I believe, equally liable for her husband's debts contracted before marriage.

"If the wife be injured in her person or property, she can bring no action for redress without her husband's concurrence, and his name as well as her own: neither can she be sued, without making her husband a defendant."

This law that "a wife can bring no action," &c., is similar to the law respecting slaves. "A slave cannot bring a suit against his master, or any other person, for an injury—his master, must bring it." So if any damages are recovered for an injury committed on a wife, the husband pockets it; in the case of the slave, the master does the same.

"In criminal prosecutions, the wife may be indicted and punished separately, unless there be evidence of coercion from the fact that the offence was committed in the presence, or by the command of her husband. A wife is excused from punishment for theft committed in the presence, or by the command of her husband."

It would be difficult to frame a law better calculated to destroy the responsibility of woman as a moral being, or a free agent. Her husband is supposed to possess unlimited control over her; and if she can offer the flimsy excuse that he bade her steal, she may break the eighth commandment with impunity, as far as human laws are concerned.

"Our law, in general, considers man and wife as one person; yet there are some instances in which she is separately considered, as inferior to him and acting by his compulsion. Therefore, all deeds executed, and acts done by her during her coverture (i.e. marriage,) are void, except it be a fine, or like matter of record, in which case she must be solely and secretly examined, to learn if her act be voluntary."

Such a law speaks volumes of the abuse of that power which men have vested in their own hands. Still the private examination of a wife, to know whether she accedes to the disposition of property made by her husband is, in most cases, a mere form; a wife dares not do what will be disagreeable to one who is, in his own estimation, her superior, and who makes her feel, in the privacy of domestic life, that she has thwarted him. With respect to the nullity of deeds or acts done by a wife, I will mention one circumstance. A respectable woman borrowed of a female friend a sum of money to relieve her son from some distressing pecuniary embarrassment. Her husband was from home, and she assured the lender, that as soon as he returned, he would gratefully discharge the debt. She gave her note, and the lender, entirely ignorant of the law that a man is not obliged to discharge such a debt, actually borrowed the money, and lent it to the distressed and weeping mother. The father returned home, refused to pay the debt, and the person who had loaned the money was obliged to pay both principal and interest to the friend who lent it to her. Women should certainly know the laws by which they are governed, and from which they frequently suffer; yet they are kept in ignorance, nearly as profound, of their legal rights, and of the legislative enactments which are to regulate their actions, as slaves.

> "The husband, by the old law, might give his wife moderate correction, as he is to answer for her misbehavior. The law thought it reasonable to entrust him with this power of restraining her by domestic chastisement. The courts of law will still permit a husband to restrain a wife of her liberty, in case of any gross misbehavior."

What a mortifying proof this law affords, of the estimation in which woman is held! She is placed completely in the hands of a being subject like herself to the outbursts of passion, and therefore unworthy to be trusted with power. Perhaps I may be told respecting this law, that it is a dead letter, as I am sometimes told about the slave laws; but this is not true in either case. The slaveholder does kill his slave by moderate correction, as the law allows; and many a husband, among the poor, exercises the right given him by the law, of degrading woman by personal chastisement. And among the higher ranks, if actual imprisonment is not resorted to, women are not unfrequently restrained of the liberty of going to places of worship by irreligious husbands, and of doing many other things about which, as moral and responsible beings, *they* should be the *sole* judges. Such laws remind me of the reply of some little girls at a children's meeting held recently at Ipswich. The lecturer told them that God had created four orders of beings with which he had made us acquainted through the Bible. The first was angels, the second was man, the third beasts;

and now, children, what is the fourth? After a pause, several girls replied, "WOMEN."

> "A woman's personal property by marriage becomes absolutely her husband's, which, at his death, he may leave entirely away from her."

And farther, all the avails of her labor are absolutely in the power of her husband. All that she acquires by her industry is his; so that she cannot, with her own honest earnings, become the legal purchaser of any property. If she expends her money for articles of furniture, to contribute to the comfort of her family, they are liable to be seized for her husband's debts: and I know an instance of a woman, who by labor and economy had scraped together a little maintenance for herself and a do-little husband, who was left, at his death, by virtue of his last will and testament, to be supported by charity. I knew another woman, who by great industry had acquired a little money which she deposited in a bank for safe keeping. She had saved this pittance whilst able to work, in hopes that when age or sickness disqualified her for exertion, she might have something to render life comfortable, without being a burden to her friends. Her husband, a worthless, idle man, discovered this hid treasure, drew her little stock from the bank, and expended it all in extravagance and vicious indulgence. I know of another woman, who married without the least idea that she was surrendering her rights to all her personal property. Accordingly, she went to the bank as usual to draw her dividends, and the person who paid her the money, and to whom she was personally known as an owner of shares in that bank, remarking the change in her signature, withdrew the money, informing her that if she were married, she had no longer a right to draw her dividends without an order from her husband. It appeared that she intended having a little fund for private use, and had not even told her husband that she owned this stock, and she was not a little chagrined, when she found that it was not at her disposal. I think she was wrong to conceal the circumstance. The relation of husband and wife is too near and sacred to admit of secrecy about money matters, unless positive necessity demands it; and I can see no excuse for any woman entering into a marriage engagement with a design to keep her husband ignorant that she was possessed of property. If she was unwilling to give up her property to his disposal, she had infinitely better have remained single.

The laws above cited are not very unlike the slave laws of Louisiana.

"All that a slave possesses belongs to his master; he possesses nothing of his own, except what his master chooses he should possess."

"By the marriage, the husband is absolutely master of the profits of the wife's lands during the coverture, and if he has had a living child, and survives the wife, he retains the whole of those lands, if they are estates of inheritance, during his life; but the wife is entitled only to one third if she survives, out of the husband's estates of inheritance. But this she has, whether she has had a child or not." "With regard to the property of women, there is taxation without representation; for they pay taxes without having the liberty of voting for representatives."

And this taxation, without representation, be it remembered, was the cause of our Revolutionary war, a grievance so heavy, that it was thought necessary to purchase exemption from it at an immense expense of blood and treasure, yet the daughters of New England, as well as of all the other States of this free Republic, are suffering a similar injustice—but for one, I had rather we should suffer any injustice or oppression, than that my sex should have any voice in the political affairs of the nation.

The laws I have quoted, are, I believe, the laws of Massachusetts, and, with few exceptions, of all the States in this Union. "In Louisiana and Missouri, and possibly, in some other southern States, a woman not only has half her husband's property by right at his death, but may always be considered as possessed of half his gains during his life; having at all times power to bequeath that amount." That the laws which have generally been adopted in the United States, for the government of women, have been framed almost entirely for the exclusive benefit of men, and with a design to oppress women, by depriving them of all control over their property, is too manifest to be denied. Some liberal and enlightened men, I know, regret the existence of these laws; and I quote with pleasure an extract from Harriet Martineau's Society in America, as a proof of the assertion. "A liberal minded lawyer of Boston, told me that his advice to testators always is to leave the largest possible amount to the widow, subject to the condition of her leaving it to the children; but that it is with shame that he reflects that any woman should owe that to his professional advice, which the law should have secured to her as a right." I have known a few instances where men have left their whole property to their wives, when they have died, leaving only minor children; but I have known more instances of "the friend and helper of many years, being portioned off like a salaried domestic," instead of having a comfortable independence secured to her, while the children were amply provided for.

As these abuses do exist, and women suffer intensely from them, our brethren are called upon in this enlightened age, by every sentiment of honor, religion and justice, to repeal these unjust and unequal laws, and restore to woman those rights which they have wrested from her. Such laws approximate too nearly to the laws enacted by slaveholders for the government of their slaves, and must tend to debase and depress the mind of that being, whom God created as a help meet for man, or "helper like unto himself," and designed to be his equal and his companion. Until such laws are annulled, woman never can occupy that exalted station for which she was intended by her Maker.

And just in proportion as they are practically disregarded, which is the case to some extent, just so far is woman assuming that independence and nobility of character which she ought to exhibit.

The various laws which I have transcribed, leave women very little more liberty, or power, in some respects, than the slave. "A slave," says the civil code of Louisiana, "is one who is in the power of a master, to whom he belongs. He can possess nothing, nor acquire anything, but what must belong to his master." I do not wish by any means to intimate that the condition of free women can be compared to that of slaves in suffering, or in degradation; still, I believe the laws which deprive married women of their rights and privileges, have a tendency to lessen them in their own estimation as moral and responsible beings, and that their being made by civil law inferior to their husbands, has a debasing and mischievous effect upon them, teaching them practically the fatal lesson to look unto man for protection and indulgence.

Ecclesiastical bodies, I believe, without exception, follow the example of legislative assemblies, in excluding woman from any participation in forming the discipline by which she is governed. The men frame the laws, and, with few exceptions, claim to execute them on both sexes. In ecclesiastical, as well as civil courts, woman is tried and condemned, not by a jury of her peers, but by beings, who regard themselves as her superiors in the scale of creation. Although looked upon as an inferior, when considered as an intellectual being, woman is punished with the same severity as man, when she is guilty of moral offences. Her condition resembles, in some measure, that of the slave, who, while he is denied the advantages of his more enlightened master, is treated with even greater rigor of the law. Hoping that in the various reformations of the day, women may be relieved from some of their legal disabilities, I remain,

Thine in the bonds of womanhood,

Sarah M. Grimké

1872
Speech on Women's Rights

BY SUSAN B. ANTHONY

Susan Brownell Anthony was an abolitionist and women's
rights advocate. She was arrested for "illegal voting" in 1872,
and spent the next thirty-four years campaigning for women's
right to vote. She died fourteen years before the 1920 passage
of the 19th amendment, which gave women suffrage.

Friends and Fellow-Citizens:—I stand before you under indictment
for the alleged crime of having voted at the last presidential election,
without having a lawful right to vote. It shall be my work this
evening to prove to you that in thus doing, I not only committed no
crime, but instead simply exercised my citizen's right, guaranteed to
me and all United States citizens by the National Constitution
beyond the power of any State to deny.

Our democratic-republican government is based on the idea of the
natural right of every individual member thereof to a voice and a vote
in making and executing the laws. We assert the province of government to be to secure the people in the enjoyment of their inalienable
rights. We throw to the winds the old dogma that government can
give rights. No one denies that before governments were organized
each individual possessed the right to protect his own life, liberty and
property. When 100 to 1,000,000 people enter into a free government, they do not barter away their natural rights; they simply pledge
themselves to protect each other in the enjoyment of them through
prescribed judicial and legislative tribunals. They agree to abandon
the methods of brute force in the adjustment of their differences and

adopt those of civilization. . . . The Declaration of Independence, the United States Constitution, the constitutions of the several States and the organic laws of the Territories, all alike propose to *protect* the people in the exercise of their God-given rights. Not one of them pretends to bestow rights.

> All men are created equal, and endowed by their Creator with certain inalienable rights. Among these are life, liberty and the pursuit of happiness. To secure these, governments are instituted among men, deriving their just powers from the consent of the governed.

Here is no shadow of government authority over rights, or exclusion of any class from their full and equal enjoyment. Here is pronounced the right of all men, and "consequently," as the Quaker preacher said, "of all women," to a voice in the government. And here, in this first paragraph of the Declaration, is the assertion of the natural right of all to the ballot; for how can "the consent of the governed" be given, if the right to vote be denied? . . . The women, dissatisfied as they are with this form of government, that enforces taxation without representation—that compels them to obey laws to which they never have given their consent—that imprisons and hangs them without a trial by a jury of their peers—that robs them, in marriage, of the custody of their own persons, wages and children—are this half of the people who are left wholly at the mercy of the other half, in direct violation of the spirit and letter of the declarations of the framers of this government, every one of which was based on the immutable principle of equal rights to all. By these declarations, kings, popes, priests, aristocrats, all were alike dethroned and placed on a common level, politically, with the lowliest born subject or serf. By them, too, men, as such, were deprived of their divine right to rule and placed on a political level with women. By the practice of these declarations all class and caste distinctions would be abolished, and slave, serf, plebeian, wife, woman, all alike rise from their subject position to the broader platform of equality.

The preamble of the Federal Constitution says:

We, the people of the United States, in order to form a more perfect union, establish justice, insure domestic tranquillity, provide for the common defence, promote the general welfare and secure the blessings of liberty to ourselves and our posterity, do ordain and establish this Constitution for the United States of America.

It was we, the people, not we, the white male citizens, nor we, the male citizens; but we, the whole people, who formed this Union. We formed it not to give the blessings of liberty but to secure them; not to the half of ourselves and the half of our posterity, but to the whole people—women as well as men. It is downright mockery to talk to women of their enjoyment of the blessings of liberty while they are denied the only means of securing them provided by this democratic-republican government—the ballot.

The early journals of Congress show that, when the committee reported to that body the original articles of confederation, the very first one which became the subject of discussion was that respecting equality of suffrage. . . .

James Madison said:

Under every view of the subject, it seems indispensable that the mass of the citizens should not be without a voice in making the laws which they are to obey, and in choosing the magistrates who are to administer them. . . . Let it be remembered, finally, that it has ever been the pride and the boast of America that the rights for which she contended were the rights of human nature.

These assertions by the framers of the United States Constitution of the equal and natural right of all the people to a voice in the government, have been affirmed and reaffirmed by the leading statesmen of the nation throughout the entire history of our government. Thaddeus Stevens, of Pennsylvania, said in 1866: "I have made up my mind that the elective franchise is one of the inalienable rights meant to be secured by the Declaration of Independence." . . .

Charles Sumner, in his brave protests against the Fourteenth and Fifteenth Amendments, insisted that so soon as by the Thirteenth Amendment the slaves became free men, the original powers of the United States Constitution guaranteed to them equal rights—the right to vote and to be voted for. . . .

The preamble of the constitution of the State of New York declares the same purpose. It says: "We, the people of the State of New York, grateful to Almighty God for our freedom, in order to secure its blessings, do establish this constitution." Here is not the slightest intimation either of receiving freedom from the United States Constitution, or of the State's conferring the blessings of liberty upon the people; and the same is true of every other State constitution. Each and all declare rights God-given, and that to secure the people in the enjoyment of their inalienable rights is their one and only object in ordaining and establishing government. All of the State constitutions are equally emphatic in their recognition of the ballot as the means of securing the people in the enjoyment of these rights. . . .

I submit that in view of the explicit assertions of the equal right of the whole people, both in the preamble and previous article of the constitution, this omission of the adjective "female" should not be construed into a denial; but instead should be considered as of no effect. . . . No barriers whatever stand today between women and the exercise of their right to vote save those of precedent and prejudice, which refuse to expunge the word "male" from the construction.

. . . When, in 1871, I asked that senator to declare the power of the United States Constitution to protect women in their right to vote—as he had done for black men—he handed me a copy of all his speeches during that reconstruction period, and said:

> Put "sex" where I have "race" or "color," and you have here the best and strongest argument I can make for woman. There is not a doubt but women have the constitutional right to vote, and I will never vote for a Sixteenth Amendment to guarantee it to them. I voted for both the Fourteenth and Fifteenth under protest; would never have done it but for the pressing emergency of that hour; would have insisted that the power of the original Constitution to protect all citizens in the equal enjoyment of their rights should have been vindicated through the courts. But the newly-made freedmen had neither the intelligence, wealth nor time to await that slow process. Women do possess all these in an eminent degree, and I insist that they shall appeal to the courts, and through them establish the powers of our American magna charta to protect every citizen of the republic.

But, friends, when in accordance with Senator Sumner's counsel I went to the ballot-box, last November, and exercised my citizen's right to vote, the courts did not wait for me to appeal to them—they appealed to me, and indicted me on the charge of having voted illegally. Putting sex where he did color, Senator Sumner would have said:

> Qualifications can be in their nature permanent or insurmountable. Sex can not be a qualification any more than size, race,

color or previous condition of servitude. A permanent or insurmountable qualification is equivalent to a deprivation of the suffrage. In other words, it is the tyranny of taxation without representation, against which our Revolutionary mothers, as well as fathers, rebelled.

For any State to make sex a qualification, which must ever result in the disfranchisement of one entire half of the people, is to pass a bill of attainder, an ex post facto law, and is therefore a violation of the supreme law of the land. By it the blessings of liberty are forever withheld from women and their female posterity. For them, this government has no just powers derived from the consent of the governed. For them this government is not a democracy; it is not a republic. It is the most odious aristocracy ever established on the face of the globe. An oligarchy of wealth, where the rich govern the poor; an oligarchy of learning, where the educated govern the ignorant; or even an oligarchy of race, where the Saxon rules the African, might be endured; but this oligarchy of sex which makes father, brothers, husband, sons, the oligarchs over the mother and sisters, the wife and daughters of every household; which ordains all men sovereigns, all women subjects—carries discord and rebellion into every home of the nation. This most odious aristocracy exists, too, in the face of Section 4, Article IV, which says: "The United States shall guarantee to every State in the Union a republican form of government." . . .

It is urged that the use of the masculine pronouns *he, his* and *him* in all the constitutions and laws, is proof that only men were meant to be included in their provisions. If you insist on this version of the letter of the law, we shall insist that you be consistent and accept the other horn of the dilemma, which would compel you to exempt women from taxation for the support of the government and from penalties for the violation of laws. There is no *she* or *her* or *hers* in the tax laws, and this is equally true of all the criminal laws.

Take for example the civil rights law which I am charged with having violated; not only are all the pronouns in it masculine, but everybody knows that it was intended expressly to hinder the rebel men from voting. It reads, "If any person shall knowingly vote without *his* having a lawful right." . . . I insist if government officials may thus manipulate the pronouns to tax, fine, imprison and hang women, it is their duty to thus change them in order to protect us in our right to vote. . . .

Though the words persons, people, inhabitants, electors, citizens are all used indiscriminately in the national and State constitutions, there was always a conflict of opinion, prior to the war, as to whether they were synonymous terms, but whatever room there was for doubt, under the old regime, the adoption of the Fourteenth Amendment settled that question forever in its first sentence:

All persons born or naturalized in the United States, and subject to the jurisdiction thereof, are citizens of the United States, and of the State wherein they reside.

The second settles the equal status of all citizens:

No State shall make or enforce any law which shall abridge the privileges or immunities of citizens of the United States; nor shall any State deprive any person of life, liberty or property without due process of law, or deny to any person within its jurisdiction the equal protection of the laws.

The only question left to be settled now is: Are women persons? I scarcely believe any of our opponents will have the hardihood to say they are not. Being persons, then, women are citizens, and no State has a right to make any new law, or to enforce any old law, which shall abridge their privileges or immunities. Hence, every discrimination against women in the constitutions and laws of the several States is today null and void, precisely as is every one against negroes.

Is the right to vote one of the privileges or immunities of citizens? I think the disfranchised ex-rebels and ex-State prisoners all will agree that it is not only one of them, but the one without which all the others are nothing. Seek first the kingdom of the ballot and all things else shall be added, is the political injunction. . . .

I am proud to mention the names of the two United States judges who have given opinions honorable to our republican idea, and honorable to themselves—Judge Howe, of Wyoming Territory, and Judge Underwood, of Virginia. The former gave it as his opinion a year ago, when the legislature seemed likely to revoke the law enfranchising the women of that Territory that, in case they succeeded, the women would still possess the right to vote under the Fourteenth Amendment. The latter, in noticing the recent decision of Judge Cartter, of the Supreme Court of the District of Columbia, denying to women the right to vote under the Fourteenth and Fifteenth Amendments, says:

> If the people of the United States, by amendment of their Constitution, could expunge, without any explanatory or assisting legislation, an adjective of five letters from all State and local constitutions, and thereby raise millions of our most ignorant fellow-citizens to all of the rights and privileges of electors, why should not the same people, by the same amendment, expunge an adjective of four letters from the same State and local constitutions, and thereby raise other millions of more educated and better informed citizens to equal rights and privileges, without explanatory or assisting legislation?

If the Fourteenth Amendment does not secure to all citizens the right to vote, for what purpose was that grand old charter of the fathers lumbered with its unwieldy proportions? The Republican party, and Judges Howard and Bingham, who drafted the document, pretended it was to do something for black men; and if that something were not to secure them in their right to vote and hold office, what could it have been? For by the Thirteenth Amendment black men had become people, and hence were entitled to all the privileges and immunities of the government, precisely as were the women of the country and foreign men not naturalized. According to Associate-Justice Washington, they already had:

> Protection of the government, the enjoyment of life and liberty, with the right to acquire and possess property of every kind, and to pursue and obtain happiness and safety, subject to such restraints as the government may justly prescribe for the general welfare of the whole; the right of a citizen of one State to pass through or to reside in any other State for the purpose of trade, agriculture, professional pursuit, or otherwise; to claim the benefit of the writ of habeas corpus, to institute and maintain actions of any kind in the courts of the State; to take, hold, and dispose of property, either real or personal, and an exemption from higher taxes or impositions than are paid by the other citizens of the State.

Thus, you see, those newly-freed men were in possession of every possible right, privilege and immunity of the government, except that of suffrage, and hence needed no constitutional amendment for any other purpose. What right in this country has the Irishman the day after he receives his naturalization papers that he did not possess the day before, save the right to vote and hold office? The Chinamen now crowding our Pacific coast are in precisely the same position. What privilege or immunity has California or Oregon the right to deny them, save that of the ballot? Clearly, then, if the Fourteenth Amendment was not to secure to black men their right to vote it did nothing for them, since they possessed everything else before. But if it was intended to prohibit the States from denying or abridging their right to vote, then it did the same for all persons, white women included, born or naturalized in the United States; for the amendment does not say that all male persons of African descent, but that all persons are citizens.

The second section is simply a threat to punish the States by reducing their representation on the floor of Congress, should they disfranchise any of their male citizens, and can not be construed into a sanction to disfranchise female citizens, nor does it in any wise weaken or invalidate the universal guarantee of the first section.

However much the doctors of the law may disagree as to whether people and citizens, in the original Constitution, were one and the same, or whether the privileges and immunities in the Fourteenth Amendment include the right of suffrage, the question of the citizen's right to vote is forever settled by the Fifteenth Amendment. "The right of citizens of the United States to vote shall not be denied or abridged by the United States, or by any State, on account of race, color or previous condition of servitude." How can the State deny or abridge the right of the citizen, if the citizen does not possess it? There is no escape from the conclusion that to vote is the citizen's right, and the specifications of race, color or previous condition of servitude can in no way impair the force of that emphatic assertion that the citizen's right to vote shall not be denied or abridged. . . .

If once we establish the false principle that United States citizenship does not carry with it the right to vote in every State in this Union, there is no end to the petty tricks and cunning devices which will be attempted to exclude one and another class of citizens from the right of suffrage. It will not always be the men combining to disfranchise all women; native born men combining to abridge the rights of all naturalized citizens, as in Rhode Island. It will not always be the rich and educated who may combine to cut off the poor and ignorant; but we may live to see the hard-working, uncultivated day laborers, foreign and native born, learning the power of the ballot and their vast majority of numbers, combine and amend State constitutions so as to disfranchise the Vanderbilts, the Stewarts, the Conklings and the Fentons. It is a poor rule that won't work more ways than one. Establish this precedent, admit the State's right to deny suffrage, and there is no limit to the confusion, discord and disruption that may await us. There is and can be but one safe principle of government—equal rights to all. Discrimination against any class on account of color, race, nativity, sex, property, culture, can but embitter and disaffect that class, and thereby endanger the safety of the whole people. Clearly, then, the national government not only must define the rights of citizens, but must stretch out its powerful hand and protect them in every State in this Union.

If, however, you will insist that the Fifteenth Amendment's emphatic interdiction against robbing United States citizens of their suffrage "on account of race, color or previous condition of servitude," is a recognition of the right of either the United States or any State to deprive them of the ballot for any or all other reasons, I will prove to you that the class of citizens for whom I now plead are, by all the principles of our government and many of the laws of the States, included under the term "previous conditions of servitude."

Consider first married women and their legal status. What is servitude? "The condition of a slave." What is a slave? "A person who is robbed of the proceeds of his labor; a person who is subject to the will of another." By the laws of Georgia, South Carolina and all the States of the South, the negro had no right to the custody and control of his person. He belonged to his master. If he were disobedient, the master had the right to use correction. If the negro did not like the correction and ran away, the master had the right to use coercion to bring him back. By the laws of almost every State in this Union today, North as well as South, the married woman has no right to the custody and control of her person. The wife belongs to the husband; and if she refuses obedience he may use moderate correction, and if she does not like his moderate correction and leaves his "bed and board," the husband may use moderate coercion to bring her back. The little word "moderate," you see, is the saving clause for the wife, and would doubtless be overstepped should her offended husband administer his correction with the "cat-o'-nine-tails," or accomplish his coercion with blood-hounds.

Again the slave had no right to the earnings of his hands, they belonged to his master; no right to the custody of his children, they belonged to his master; no right to sue or be sued, or to testify in the courts. If he committed a crime, it was the master who must sue or be sued. In many of the States there has been special legislation, giving married women the right to property inherited or received by bequest, or earned by the pursuit of any avocation outside the home; also giving them the right to sue and be sued in matters pertaining to such separate property; but not a single State of this Union has ever secured the wife in the enjoyment of her right to equal ownership of the joint earnings of the marriage copartnership. And since, in the nature of things, the vast majority of married women never earn a dollar by work outside their families, or inherit a dollar from their fathers, it follows that from the day of their marriage to the day of the death of their husbands not one of them ever has a dollar, except it shall please her husband to let her have it. . . .

A good farmer's wife in Illinois, who had all the rights she wanted, had made for herself a full set of false teeth. The dentist pronounced them an admirable fit, and the wife declared it gave her fits to wear them. The dentist sued the husband for his bill; his counsel brought the wife as witness; the judge ruled her off the stand, saying, "A married woman can not be a witness in matters of joint interest between herself and her husband." Think of it, ye good wives, the false teeth in your mouths are a joint interest with your husbands, about which you are legally incompetent to speak! If a married woman is injured by accident, in nearly all of the States it is her husband who must sue, and it is to him that the damages will be awarded. . . . Isn't such a position humiliating enough to be called "servitude?" That husband sued and obtained damages for the loss of the services of his wife, precisely as he would have done had it been his ox, cow or horse; and exactly as the master, under the old regime, would have recovered for the services of his slave.

I submit the question, if the deprivation by law of the ownership of one's own person, wages, property, children, the denial of the right as an individual to sue and be sued and testify in the courts, is not a condition of servitude most bitter and absolute, even though under the sacred name of marriage? . . . The facts also prove that, by all the great fundamental principles of our free government, not only married women but the entire womanhood of the nation are in a "condition of servitude" as surely as were our Revolutionary fathers when they rebelled against King George. Women are taxed without representation, governed without their consent, tried, convicted and punished without a jury of their peers. Is all this tyranny any less humiliating and degrading to women under our democratic-republican government today than it was to men under their aristocratic, monarchial government one hundred years ago? . . .

Is anything further needed to prove woman's condition of

servitude sufficient to entitle her to the guarantees of the Fifteenth Amendment? Is there a man who will not agree with me that to talk of freedom without the ballot is mockery to the women of this republic, precisely as New England's orator, Wendell Phillips, at the close of the late war declared it to be to the newly emancipated black man? I admit that, prior to the rebellion, by common consent, the right to enslave, as well as to disfranchise both native and foreign born persons, was conceded to the States. But the one grand principle settled by the war and the reconstruction legislation, is the supremacy of the national government to protect the citizens of the United States in their right to freedom and the elective franchise, against any and every interference on the part of the several States; and again and again have the American people asserted the triumph of this principle by their overwhelming majorities for Lincoln and Grant.

The one issue of the last two presidential elections was whether the Fourteenth and Fifteenth Amendments should be considered the irrevocable will of the people; and the decision was that they should be, and that it is not only the right, but the duty of the national government to protect all United States citizens in the full enjoyment and free exercise of their privileges and immunities against the attempt of any State to deny or abridge. In this conclusion Republicans and Democrats alike agree. Senator Frelinghuysen said: "The heresy of State rights has been completely buried in these amendments, and as amended, the Constitution confers not only National but State citizenship upon all persons born or naturalized within our limits." . . .

Benjamin F. Butler, in a recent letter to me, said: "I do not believe anybody in Congress doubts that the Constitution authorizes the right of women to vote, precisely as it authorizes trial by jury and many other like rights guaranteed to citizens."

It is upon this just interpretation of the United States Constitution that our National Woman Suffrage Association, which celebrates the twenty-fifth anniversary of the woman's rights movement next May in New York City, has based all its arguments and action since the passage of these amendments. We no longer petition legislature or Congress to give us the right to vote, but appeal to women everywhere to exercise their too long neglected "citizen's right." We appeal to the inspectors of election to receive the votes of all United States citizens, as it is their duty to do. We appeal to United States commissioners and marshals to arrest, as is their duty, the inspectors who reject the votes of United States citizens, and leave alone those who perform their duties and accept these votes. We ask the juries to return verdicts of "not guilty" in the cases of law-abiding United States citizens who cast their votes, and inspectors of election who receive and count them.

We ask the judges to render unprejudiced opinions of the law, and wherever there is room for doubt to give the benefit to the side of liberty and equal rights for women, remembering that, as Sumner says, "The true rule of interpretation under our National Constitution, especially since its amendments, is that anything *for* human rights is constitutional, everything *against* human rights unconstitutional." It is on this line that we propose to fight our battle for the ballot—peaceably but nevertheless persistently—until we achieve complete triumph and all United States citizens, men and women alike, are recognized as equals in the government.

Demanding Full Equality

BY BETTY FRIEDAN

Feminist Betty Friedan's brief vignette recalls June 30, 1966, founding day of the National Organization of Women. Her story appeared in a 2003 *Time* feature about "days that changed the world."

"SEX DISCRIMINATION" WAS added to Title VII of the 1964 Civil Rights Act. But there was no group to lobby for enforcement. I had written *The Feminine Mystique* in 1963, and I became a magnet. Everyone was trying to pass the torch to me because I knew how to command media attention. Even surviving suffragists, who had chained themselves to the White House fence to win the vote, would call me up in the middle of the night and tell me to do something.

The government sought to pacify us and convened the Third National Conference of the Commissions on the Status of Women at the Washington Hilton in late June 1966. The omens were not good. That week President Johnson and Lady Bird invited a few of us to tea at the White House. The President said he wanted to appoint talented women, but the problem was "finding these women." It was a weekend of lip service.

We learned that we weren't allowed to pass resolutions at the conference. So on its final day, June 30, as dignitaries yammered at the podium, I joined other furious women at the two front lunch tables, passing along notes written on napkins. We were putting together the National Organization for Women under the noses of the people who wanted to put us off. I wrote on one napkin that NOW had "to take the actions needed to bring women into the mainstream of American society, now . . . in fully *equal* partnership with men." As people rushed to catch planes, the founding members collected $5 from one another as our charter budget. Anna Roosevelt Halstead, Eleanor's daughter, gave me $10.

1969
Do You Know the Facts About Marriage?

BY THE FEMINISTS

Activists wrote this leaflet for a demonstration at the New York City Marriage License Bureau.

DO YOU KNOW that rape is legal in marriage?

According to law, *sex* is the purpose of marriage. You have to have sexual intercourse in order to have a valid marriage.
Do you know that love and affection are not required in marriage?

If you can't have sex with your husband, he can get a divorce or annulment. If he doesn't love you, that's *not* grounds for divorce.

Do you know that you are your husband's prisoner?

You have to live with him wherever *he* pleases. If he decides to move someplace else, either you go with him or he can charge you with desertion, get a divorce and, according to law, you deserve nothing because *you're the guilty party.* And that's if *he* were the one who moved!

Do you know that, according to the United Nations, marriage is a "slavery-like practice"?

According to the marriage contract, your husband is entitled to more household services from you than he would be from a live-in maid. So, why aren't you getting paid? Under law, you're entitled only to "bed and board."

When you got married, did you know these facts? If you didn't know, what did you *think* you were consenting to? But these are the *laws*. If you *had* known the terms, would you have signed the contract?

Do You Resent This Fraud?

All the discriminatory practices against women are patterned and rationalized by this slavery-like practice. We can't destroy the inequities between men and women until we destroy marriage. *We must free ourselves. And marriage is the place to begin.*

1970
Principles

BY NEW YORK RADICAL WOMEN

Members of the women's movement that developed in the '60s and '70s often focused on issues such as abortion and equal rights in the workplace. They also questioned the most basic assumptions of capitalism and western culture.

WE TAKE THE woman's side in everything.

We ask not if something is "reformist," "radical," "revolutionary," or "moral." We ask: is it good for women or bad for women?

We ask not if something is "political." We ask: is it effective? Does it get us closest to what we really want in the fastest way?

We define the best interests of women as the best interests of the poorest, most insulted, most despised, most abused woman on earth. Her lot, her suffering and abuse is the threat that men use against all of us to keep us in line. She is what all women fear being called, fear being treated as and yet what we all really are in the eyes of men. She is Everywoman: ugly, dumb (dumb broad, dumb cunt), bitch, nag, hag, whore, fucking and breeding machine, mother of us all. Until Everywoman is free, no woman will be free. When her beauty and knowledge is revealed and seen, the new day will be at hand.

We are critical of all past ideology, literature and philosophy, products as they are of male supremacist culture. We are re-examining even our words, language itself.

We take as our source the hitherto unrecognized culture of women, a culture which from long experience of oppression developed an intense appreciation for life, a sensitivity to unspoken thoughts and the complexity of simple things, a powerful knowledge of human needs and feelings.

We regard our feelings as our most important source of political understanding.

We see the key to our liberation in our collective wisdom and our collective strength.

1987

We Do Abortions Here

BY SALLIE TISDALE

This article appeared in *Harper's*.

WE DO ABORTIONS here; that is all we do. There are weary, grim moments when I think I cannot bear another basin of bloody remains, utter another kind phrase of reassurance. So I leave the procedure room in the back and reach for a new chart. Soon I am talking to an eighteen-year-old woman pregnant for the fourth time. I push up her sleeve to check her blood pressure and find row upon row of needle marks, neat and parallel and discolored. She has been so hungry for her drug for so long that she has taken to using the loose skin of her upper arms; her elbows are already a permanent ruin of bruises. She is surprised to find herself nearly four months pregnant. I suspect she is often surprised, in a mild way, by the blows she is dealt. I prepare myself for another basin, another brief and chafing loss.

"How can you stand it?" Even the clients ask. They see the machine, the strange instruments, the blood, the final stroke that wipes away the promise of pregnancy. Sometimes I see that too: I watch a woman's swollen abdomen sink to softness in a few stuttering moments and my own belly flip-flops with sorrow. But all it takes for me to catch my breath is another interview, one more story that sounds so much like the last one. There is a numbing sameness lurking in this job: the same questions, the same answers, even the same trembling tone in the voices. The worst is the sameness of human failure, of inadequacy in the face of each day's dull demands.

In describing this work, I find it difficult to explain how much I enjoy it most of the time. We laugh a lot here, as friends and as professional peers. It's nice to be with women all day. I like the sudden, transient bonds I forge with some clients: moments when I am in my strength, remembering weakness, and a woman in weakness reaches out for my strength. What I offer is not power, but solidness, offered almost eagerly. Certain clients waken in me every tender urge I have—others make me wince and bite my tongue. Both challenge me to find a balance. It is a sweet brutality we practice here, a stark and loving dispassion.

I look at abortion as if I am standing on a cliff with a telescope, gazing at some great vista. I can sweep the horizon with both eyes, survey the scene in all its distance and size. Or I can put my eye to the lens and focus on the small details, suddenly so close. In abortion the absolute must always be tempered by the contextual, because both are real, both valid, both hard. How can we do this? How can we refuse? Each abortion is a measure of our failure to protect, to nourish our own. Each basin I empty is a promise—but a promise broken a long time ago.

I grew up on the great promise of birth control. Like many women my age, I took the pill as soon as I was sexually active. To risk pregnancy when it was so easy to avoid seemed stupid, and my contraceptive success, as it were, was part of the promise of social enlightenment. But birth control fails, far more frequently than laboratory trials predict. Many of our clients take the pill; its failure to protect them is a shocking realization. We have clients who have been sterilized, whose husbands have had vasectomies; each one is a statistical misfit, fine print come to life. The anger and shame of these women I hold in one hand, and the basin in the other. The distance between the two, the length I pace and try to measure, is the size of an abortion.

The procedure is disarmingly simple. Women are surprised, as though the mystery of conception, a dark and hidden genesis, requires an elaborate finale. In the first trimester of pregnancy, it's a mere few minutes of vacuuming, a neat tidying up. I give a woman a small yellow Valium, and when it has begun to relax her, I lead her into the back, into bareness, the stirrups. The doctor reaches in her, opening the narrow tunnel to the uterus with a succession of slim, smooth bars of steel. He inserts a plastic tube and hooks it to a hose on the machine. The woman is framed against white paper that crackles as she moves, the light bright in her eyes. Then the machine rumbles low and loud in the small windowless room; the doctor moves the tube back and forth with an efficient rhythm, and the long tail of it fills with blood that spurts and stumbles along into a jar. He is usually finished in a few minutes. They are long minutes for the woman; her uterus frequently reacts to its abrupt emptying with a powerful, unceasing cramp, which cuts off the blood vessels and enfolds the irritated, bleeding tissue.

I am learning to recognize the shadows that cross the faces of the women I hold. While the doctor works between her spread legs, the paper drape hiding his intent expression, I stand beside the table. I hold the woman's hands in mine, resting them just below her ribs. I watch her eyes, finger her necklace, stroke her hair. I ask about her job, her family; in a haze she answers me; we chatter, faces close, eyes meeting and sliding apart.

I watch the shadows that creep up unnoticed and suddenly darken her face as she screws up her features and pushes a tear out each side to slide down her cheeks. I have learned to anticipate the quiver of chin, the rapid intake of breath and the surprising sobs that rise soon after the machine starts to drum. I know this is when the cramp deepens, and the tears are partly the tears that follow pain—the sharp, childish crying when one bumps one's head on a cabinet door. But a well of woe seems to open beneath many women when they hear that thumping sound. The anticipation of the moment has finally come to fruit; the moment has arrived when the loss is no longer an imagined one. It has come true.

I am struck by the sameness and I am struck every day by the variety here—how this commonplace dilemma can so display the differences of women. A twenty-one-year-old woman, unemployed, uneducated, without family, in the fifth month of her fifth pregnancy. A forty-two-year-old mother of teenagers, shocked by her condition, refusing to tell her husband. A twenty-three-year-old mother of two having her seventh abortion, and many women in their thirties having their first. Some are stoic, some hysterical, a few giggle uncontrollably, many cry.

I talk to a sixteen-year-old uneducated girl who was raped. She has gonorrhea. She describes blinding headaches, attacks of breathlessness, nausea. "Sometimes, I feel like two different people," she tells me with a calm smile, "and I talk to myself."

I pull out my plastic models. She listens patiently for a time, and then holds her hands wide in front of her stomach.

"When's the baby going to go up into my stomach?" she asks.

I blink. "What do you mean?"

"Well," she says, still smiling, "when women get so big, isn't the baby in your stomach? Doesn't it hatch out of an egg there?"

My first question in an interview is always the same. As I walk down the hall with the woman, as we get settled in chairs and I glance through her files, I am trying to gauge her, to get a sense of the words, and the tone, I should use. With some I joke, with others I chat, sometimes I fall into a brisk, business-like patter. But I ask every woman, "Are you sure you want to have an abortion?" Most nod with grim knowing smiles. "Oh, yes," they sigh. Some seek forgiveness, offer excuses. Occasionally a woman will flinch and say, "Please don't use that word."

Later I describe the procedure to come, using care with my language. I don't say "pain" any more than I would say "baby." So many are afraid to ask how much it will hurt. "My sister told me—" I hear. "A friend of mine said—" and the dire expectations unravel. I prick the index finger of a woman for a drop of blood to test, and as the tiny lancet approaches the skin she averts her eyes, holding her trembling hand out to me and jumping at my touch.

It is when I am holding a plastic uterus in one hand, a suction tube in the other, moving them together in imitation of the scrubbing to come, that women ask the most secret question. I am speaking in a matter-of-fact voice about "the tissue" and "the contents" when the woman suddenly catches my eye and asks, "How big is the baby now?" These words suggest a quiet need for a definition of the boundaries being drawn. It isn't so odd, after all, that she feels relief when I describe the growing bud's bulbous shape, its miniature nature. Again I gauge, and sometimes lie a little, weaseling around its infantile features until its clinging power slackens.

But when I look in the basin, among the curdlike blood clots, I see an elfin thorax, attenuated, its pencilline ribs all in parallel rows with tiny knobs of spine rounding upwards. A translucent arm and hand swim beside.

A sleepy-eyed girl, just fourteen, watched me with a slight and goofy smile all through her abortion. "Does it have little feet and little fingers and all?" she'd asked earlier. When the suction was over she sat up woozily at the end of the table and murmured, "Can I see it?" I shook my head firmly.

"It's not allowed," I told her sternly, because I knew she didn't really want to see what was left. She accepted this statement of authority, and a shadow of confused relief crossed her plain, pale face. Privately, even grudgingly, my colleagues might admit the power of abortion to provoke emotion. But they seem to prefer the broad view and disdain the telescope. Abortion is a matter of choice, privacy, control. Its uncertainty lies in specific cases: retarded women and girls too young to give consent for surgery, women who are ill or hostile or psychotic. Such common dilemmas are met with both compassion and impatience: they slow things down. We are too busy to chew over ethics. One person might discuss certain concerns, behind closed doors, or describe a particularly disturbing dream. But generally there is to be no ambivalence.

Every day I take calls from women who are annoyed that we cannot see them, cannot do their abortion today, this morning, now. They argue the price, demand that we stay after hours to accommodate their job or class schedule. Abortion is so routine that one expects it to be like a manicure: quick, cheap, and painless.

Still, I've cultivated a certain disregard. It isn't negligence, but I don't always pay attention. I couldn't be here if I tried to judge each case on its merits; after all, we do over a hundred abortions a week. At some point each individual in this line of work draws a boundary and adheres to it. For one physician the boundary is a particular week of gestation; for another, it is a certain number of repeated abortions. But these boundaries can be fluid too: one physician overruled his own limit to abort a mature but severely malformed fetus. For me, the limit is allowing my clients to carry their own burden, shoulder the responsibility themselves. I shoulder the burden of trying not to judge them.

This city has several "crisis pregnancy centers" advertised in the Yellow Pages. They are small offices staffed by volunteers, and they offer free pregnancy testing, glossy photos of dead fetuses, and movies. I had a client recently whose mother is active in the anti-abortion movement. The young woman went to the local crisis center and was told that the doctor would make her touch her dismembered baby, that the pain would be the most horrible she could imagine, and that she might, after an abortion, never be able to have children. All lies. They called her at home and at work, over and over and over, but she had been wise enough to give a false name. She came to us a fugitive. We who do abortions are marked, by some, as impure. It's dirty work.

When a deliveryman comes to the sliding glass window by the reception desk and tilts a box toward me, I hesitate. I read the packing slip, assess the shape and weight of the box in light of its supposed contents. We request familiar faces. The doors are carefully locked; I have learned to half glance around at bags and boxes, looking for a telltale sign. I register with security when I arrive, and I am careful not to bang a door. We are all a little on edge here.

Concern about size and shape seem to be natural, and so is the relief that follows. We make the powerful assumption that the fetus is different from us, and even when we admit the similarities, it is too simplistic to be seduced by form alone. But the form is enormously potent—humanoid, powerless, palm-sized, and pure, it evokes an almost fierce tenderness when viewed simply as what it appears to be. But appearance, and even potential, aren't enough. The fetus, in becoming itself, can ruin others; its utter dependence has a sinister side. When I am struck in the moment by the contents in the basin, I am careful to remember the context, to note the tearful teenager and the woman sighing with something more than relief. One kind of question, though, I find considerably trickier.

"Can you tell what it is?" I am asked, and this means gender. This question is asked by couples, not women alone. Always couples would abort a girl and keep a boy. I have been asked about twins, and even if I could tell what race the father was.

An eighteen-year-old woman with three daughters brought her husband to the interview. He glared first at me, then at his wife, as he sank lower and lower in the chair, picking his teeth with a tooth-pick. He interrupted a conversation with his wife to ask if I could tell whether the baby would be a boy or a girl. I told him I could not.

"Good," he replied in a slow and strangely malevolent voice, " 'cause if was a boy I'd wring her neck."

In a literal sense, abortion exists because we are able to ask such questions, able to assign a value to the fetus which can shift with changing circumstances. If the human bond to a child were as prim-itive and unflinchingly narrow as that of other animals, there would be no abortion. There would be no abortion because there would be nothing more important than caring for the young and perpetuating the species, no reason for sex but to make babies. I sense this some-times, this wordless organic duty, when I do ultrasounds.

We do ultrasound, a sound-wave test that paints a faint, gray pic-ture of the fetus, whenever we're uncertain of gestation. Age is meas-ured by the width of the skull and confirmed by the length of the femur or thighbone; we speak of a pregnancy as being a cetain "femur length" in weeks. The usual concern is whether a pregnancy is within the legal limit for an abortion. Women this far along have bellies which swell out round and tight like trim muscles. When they lie flat, the mound rises softly above the hips, pressing the umbilicus upward.

It takes practice to read an ultrasound picture, which is grainy and etched as though in strokes of charcoal. But suddenly a rapid rhythmic motion appears—the beating heart. Nearby is a soft oval, scratched with lines—the skull. The leg is harder to find, and then suddenly the fetus moves, bobbing in the surf. The skull turns away, an arm slides across the screen, the torso rolls. I know the weight of a baby's head on my shoulder, the whisper of lips on ears, the delicate curve of a fragile spine in my hand. I know how heavy and correct a newborn cradled feels. The creature I watch in secret requires nothing from me but to be left alone, and that is precisely what won't be done.

These inadvertently made beings are caught in a twisting web of motive and desire. They are at least inconvenient, sometimes quite literally dangerous in the womb, but most often they fall somewhere in between—consequences never quite believed in come to roost. Their virtue rises and falls outside their own nature: they become only what we make them. A fetus created by accident is the most absolute kind of surprise. Whether the blame lies in a failed IUD, a slipped condom, or a false impression of safety, that fetus is a thing whose creation has been actively worked against. Its existence is an error. I think this is why so few women, even late in a pregnancy, will consider giving a baby up for adoption. To do so means making the fetus real—imagining it as something whole and outside oneself. The decision to terminate a pregnancy is sometimes so difficult and confounding that it creates an enormous demand for immediate action. The decision is a rejection; the pregnancy has become something to be rid of, a condition to be ended. It is a burden, a weight, a thing separate.

Women have abortions because they are too old, and too young, too poor, and too rich, too stupid, and too smart. I see women who berate themselves with violent emotions for their first and only abortion, and others who return three times, five times, hauling two or three children, who cannot remember to take a pill or where they put the diaphragm. We talk glibly about choice. But the choice for what? I see all the broken promises in lives lived like a series of impromptu obstacles. There are the sweet, light promises of love and intimacy, the glittering promise of education and progress, the warm promise of safe families, long years of innocence and community. And there is the promise of freedom: freedom from failure, from faithlessness. Freedom from biology. The early feminist defense of abortion asked many questions, but the one I remember is this: Is biology destiny? And the answer is yes, sometimes it is. Women who have the fewest choices of all exercise their right to abortion the most.

Oh, the ignorance. I take a woman to the back room and ask her to undress; a few minutes later I return and find her positioned discreetly behind a drape, still wearing underpants. "Do I have to take these off too?" she asks, a little shocked. Some swear they have not had sex, many do not know what a uterus is, how sperm and egg meet, how sex makes babies. Some late seekers do not believe themselves pregnant; they believe themselves impregnable. I was chastised when I began this job for referring to some clients as girls: it is a feminist heresy. They come so young, snapping gum, sockless and sneakered, and their shakily applied eyeliner smears when they cry. I call them girls with maternal benignity. I cannot imagine them as mothers.

The doctor seats himself between the woman's thighs and reaches into the dilated opening of a five-month pregnant uterus. Quickly he grabs and crushes the fetus in several places, and the room is filled with a low clatter and snap of forceps, the click of the tanaculum, and a pulling, sucking sound. The paper crinkles as the drugged and sleepy woman shifts, the nurse's low, honey-brown voice explains each step in delicate words.

I have fetus dreams, we all do here: dreams of abortions one after the other; of buckets of blood splashed on the walls; trees full of crawling fetuses. I dreamed that two men grabbed me and began to drag me away. "Let's do an abortion," they said with a sickening leer, and I began to scream; plunged into a vision of sucking, scraping pain, of being spread and torn by impartial instruments that do only what they are bidden; I woke from this dream barely able to breathe and thought of kitchen tables and coat hangers, knitting needles striped with blood, and women all alone clutching a pillow in their teeth to keep the screams from piercing the apartment-house walls. Abortion is the narrowest edge between kindness and cruelty. Done as well as it can be, it is still violence—merciful violence, like putting a suffering animal to death.

Maggie, one of the nurses, received a call at midnight not long ago. It was a woman in her twentieth week of pregnancy; the necessarily gradual process of cervical dilation begun the day before had stimulated labor, as it sometimes does. Maggie and one of the doctors met the woman at the office in the night. Maggie helped her onto the table, and as she lay down the fetus was delivered into Maggie's hands. When Maggie told me about it the next day, she cupped her hands into a small bowl—"It was just like a little kitten," she said softly, wonderingly. "Everything was still attached."

At the end of the day I clean out the suction jars, pouring blood into the sink, splashing the sides with flecks of tissue. From the sink rises a rich and humid smell, hot, earthy, and moldering; it is the smell of something recently alive beginning to decay. I take care of the plastic tub on the floor, filled with pieces too big to be trusted to the trash. The law defines the contents of the bucket I hold protectively against my chest as "tissue." Some would say my complicity in filling that bucket gives me no right to call it anything else. I slip the tissue gently into a bag and place it in the freezer, to be burned at another time. Abortion requires of me an entirely new set of assumptions. It requires a willingness to live with conflict, fearlessness, and grief. As I close the freezer door, I imagine a world where this won't be necessary, and then return to the world where it is.

labor

from *Lies My Teacher Told Me*

BY JAMES W. LOEWEN

James W. Loewen's 1995 book notes that labor history is
largely absent from American classrooms.

HIGH SCHOOL STUDENTS have eyes, ears, and television sets (all too
many have their own TV sets), so they know a lot about relative privilege in America. They measure their family's social position against
that of other families, and their community's position against other
communities. Middle-class students, especially, know little about
how the American class structure works, however, and nothing at all
about how it has changed over time. These students do not leave high
school merely ignorant of the workings of the class structure; they
come out as terrible sociologists. "Why are people poor?" I have
asked first-year college students. Or, if their own class position is
one of relative privilege, "Why is your family well off?" The answers
I've received, to characterize them charitably, are half-formed and
naïve. The students blame the poor for not being successful. They
have no understanding of the ways that opportunity is not equal in
America and no notion that social structure pushes people around,
influencing the ideas they hold and the lives they fashion.

High school history textbooks can take some of the credit for this
state of affairs. Some textbooks cover certain high points of labor history, such as the 1894 Pullman strike near Chicago that President Cleveland broke with federal troops, or the 1911 Triangle Shirtwaist fire that
killed 146 women in New York City, but the most recent event

mentioned in most books is the Taft-Hartley Act of fifty years ago. No book mentions the Hormel meat-packers' strike in the mid-1980s or the air traffic controllers' strike broken by President Reagan. Nor do textbooks describe any continuing issues facing labor, such as the growth of multinational corporations and their exporting of jobs overseas. With such omissions, textbook authors can construe labor history as something that happened long ago, like slavery, and that, like slavery, was corrected long ago. It logically follows that unions appear anachronistic. The idea that they might be necessary in order for workers to have a voice in the workplace goes unstated.

Textbooks' treatments of events in labor history are never anchored in any analysis of social class. This amounts to delivering the footnotes instead of the lecture! Six of the dozen high school American history textbooks I examined contain no index listing at all for "social class," "social stratification," "class structure," "income distribution," "inequality," or any conceivably related topic. Not one book lists "upper class," "working class," or "lower class." Two of the textbooks list "middle class," but only to assure students that America is a middle-class country. "Except for slaves, most of the colonists were members of the 'middling ranks,' " says *Land of Promise,* and nails home the point that we are a middle-class country by asking students to "Describe three 'middle-class' values that united free Americans of all classes." Several of the textbooks note the explosion of middle-class suburbs after World War II. Talking about the middle class is hardly equivalent to discussing social stratification, however; in fact, as Gregory Mantsios has pointed out, "such references appear to be acceptable precisely because they mute class differences."

Stressing how middle-class we all are is particularly problematic today, because the proportion of households earning between 75 percent and 125 percent of the median income has fallen steadily since 1967. The Reagan-Bush administrations accelerated this shrinkage of the middle class, and most families who left its ranks fell rather than rose. This is the kind of historical trend one would think history books would take as appropriate subject matter, but only four of the twelve books in my sample provide any analysis of social stratification in the United States. Even these fragmentary analyses are set mostly in colonial America. *Land of Promise* lives up to its reassuring title by heading its discussion of social class "Social Mobility." "One great difference between colonial and European society was that the colonists had more social mobility," echoes *The American Tradition.* "In contrast with contemporary Europe, eighteenth-century America was a shining land of equality and opportunity—with the notorious exception of slavery," chimes in *The American Pageant.* Although *The Challenge of Freedom* identifies three social classes—upper, middle, and lower—among whites in colonial society, compared to Europe "there was greater *social mobility.*"

Never mind that the most violent class conflicts in American history—Bacon's Rebellion and Shays's Rebellion—took place in and just after colonial times. Textbooks still say that colonial society was relatively classless and marked by upward mobility. And things have gotten rosier since. "By 1815," *The Challenge of Freedom* assures us, two classes had withered away and "America was a country of middle class people and of middle class goals." This book returns repeatedly, at intervals of every fifty years or so, to the theme of how open opportunity is in America. "In the years after 1945, *social mobility*—movement from one social class to another—became more widespread in America," *Challenge* concludes. "This meant that people had a better chance to move upward in society." The stress on upward mobility is striking. There is almost nothing in any of these textbooks about class inequalities or barriers of any kind to social mobility. "What conditions made it possible for poor white immigrants to become richer in the colonies?" *Land of Promise* asks. "What conditions made/make it difficult?" goes unasked. Textbook authors thus present an America in which, as preachers were fond of saying in the nineteenth century, men start from "humble origins" and attain "the most elevated positions."

Social class is probably the single most important variable in society. From womb to tomb, it correlates with almost all other social characteristics of people that we can measure. Affluent expectant mothers are more likely to get prenatal care, receive current medical advice, and enjoy general health, fitness, and nutrition. Many poor and working-class mothers-to-be first contact the medical profession in the last month, sometimes the last hours, of their pregnancies. Rich babies come out healthier and weighing more than poor babies. The infants go home to very different situations. Poor babies are more likely to have high levels of poisonous lead in their environments and their bodies. Rich babies get more time and verbal interaction with their parents and higher quality day care when not with their parents. When they enter kindergarten, and through the twelve years that follow, rich children benefit from suburban schools that spend two to three times as much money per student as schools in inner cities or impoverished rural areas. Poor children are taught in classes that are often 50 percent larger than the classes of affluent children. Differences such as these help account for the higher school-dropout rate among poor children.

Even when poor children are fortunate enough to attend the same school as rich children, they encounter teachers who expect only children of affluent families to know the right answers. Social science research shows that teachers are often surprised and even distressed when poor children excel. Teachers and counselors believe they can predict who is "college material." Since many working-class children give off the wrong signals, even in first grade, they end up in the "general education" track in high school. "If you are the child of low-income parents, the chances are good that you will receive limited and often careless attention from adults in your high school," in the words of Theodore Sizer's best-selling study of American high schools, *Horace's Compromise.* "If you are the child of upper-middle-income parents, the chances are good that you will receive substantial and careful attention." Researcher Reba Page has provided vivid accounts of how high school American history courses use rote learning to turn off lower-class students. Thus schools have put into practice Woodrow Wilson's recommendation: "We want one class of persons to have a liberal education, and we want another class of persons, a very much larger class of necessity in every society, to forgo the privilege of a liberal education and fit themselves to perform specific difficult manual tasks."

As if this unequal home and school life were not enough, rich teenagers then enroll in the Princeton Review or other coaching sessions for the Scholastic Aptitude Test. Even without coaching, affluent children are advantaged because their background is similar to that of the test-makers, so they are comfortable with the vocabulary and subtle subcultural assumptions of the test. To no one's surprise, social class correlates strongly with SAT scores.

All these are among the reasons why social class predicts the rate of college attendance and the type of college chosen more effectively than does any other factor, including intellectual ability, however measured. After college, most affluent children get white-collar jobs, most working-class children get blue-collar jobs, and the class differences continue. As adults, rich people are more likely to have hired an attorney and to be a member of formal organizations that increase their civic power. Poor people are more likely to watch TV. Because affluent families can save some money while poor families must spend what they make, wealth differences are ten times larger than income differences. Therefore most poor and working-class families cannot accumulate the down payment required to buy a house, which in turn shuts them out from our most important tax shelter, the writeoff of home mortgage interest. Working-class parents cannot afford to live in elite subdivisions or hire high-quality day care, so the process of educational inequality replicates itself in the next generation. Finally, affluent Americans also have longer life expectancies than lower- and working-class people, the largest single cause of which is better access to health care. Echoing the results of Helen Keller's study of blindness, research has determined that poor health is not distributed randomly about the social structure but is concentrated in the lower class. Social Security then becomes a huge transfer system, using monies contributed by all Americans to pay benefits disproportionately to longer-lived affluent Americans.

Ultimately, social class determines how people think about social class. When asked if poverty in America is the fault of the poor or the fault of the system, 57 percent of business leaders blamed the poor; just 9 percent blamed the system. Labor leaders showed sharply reversed choices: only 15 percent said the poor were at fault while 56 percent blamed the system. (Some replied "don't know" or chose a middle position.) The largest single difference between our two main political parties lies in how their members think about social class: 55 percent of Republicans blamed the poor for their poverty, while only 13 percent blamed the system for it; 68 percent of Democrats, on the other hand, blamed the system, while only 5 percent blamed the poor.

Few of these statements are news, I know, which is why I have not documented most of them, but the majority of high school students do not know or understand these ideas. Moreover, the processes have changed over time, for the class structure in America today is not the same as it was in 1890, let alone in colonial America. Yet in *Land of Promise*, for example, social class goes unmentioned after 1670.

Many teachers compound the problem by avoiding talking about social class. Recent interviews with teachers "revealed that they had a much broader knowledge of the economy, both academically and experientially, than they admitted in class." Teachers "expressed fear that students might find out about the injustices and inadequacies of their economic and political institutions." By never blaming the system, American history courses thus present "Republican history."

Historically, social class is intertwined with all kinds of events and processes in our past. Our governing system was established by rich men, following theories that emphasized government as a bulwark of the propertied class. Although rich himself, James Madison worried about social inequality and wrote *The Federalist* #10 to explain how the proposed government would not succumb to the influence of the affluent. Madison did not fully succeed, according to Edward Pessen, who examined the social-class backgrounds of all American presidents through Reagan. Pessen found that more than 40 percent hailed from the upper class, mostly from the upper fringes of that elite group, and another 15 percent originated in families located between the upper and upper-middle classes. More than 25 percent came from a solid upper-middle-class background, leaving just six presidents, or 15 percent, to come from the middle and lower-middle classes and just one, Andrew Johnson, representing any part of the lower class. For good reason, Pessen titled his book *The Log Cabin Myth.* While it was sad when the great ship *Titanic* went down, as the old song refrain goes, it was saddest for the lower classes: among women, only 4 of 143 first-class passengers were lost, while 15 of 93 second-class passengers drowned, along with 81 of 179 third-class women and girls. The crew ordered third-class passengers to remain below deck, holding some of them there at gunpoint. More recently, social class played a major role in determining who fought in the Vietnam War: sons of the affluent won educational and medical deferments through most of the conflict. Textbooks and teachers ignore all this.

Teachers may avoid social class out of a laudable desire not to embarrass their charges. If so, their concern is misguided. When my students from nonaffluent backgrounds learn about the class system, they find the experience liberating. Once they see the social processes that have helped keep their families poor, they can let go of their negative self-image about being poor. If to understand is to pardon, for working-class children to understand how stratification works is to pardon *themselves* and their families. Knowledge of the social-class system also reduces the tendency of Americans from other social classes to blame the victim for being poor. Pedagogically, stratification provides a gripping learning experience. Students are fascinated to discover how the upper class wields disproportionate power relating to everything from energy bills in Congress to zoning decisions in small towns.

Consider a white ninth-grade student taking American history in a predominantly middle-class town in Vermont. Her father tapes Sheet-rock, earning an income that in slow construction seasons leaves the family quite poor. Her mother helps out by driving a school bus part-time, in addition to taking care of her two younger siblings. The girl lives with her family in a small house, a winterized former summer cabin, while most of her classmates live in large suburban homes. How is this girl to understand her poverty? Since history textbooks present the American past as 390 years of progress and portray our society as a land of opportunity in which folks get what they deserve and deserve what they get, the failures of working-class Americans to transcend their class origin inevitably get laid at their own doorsteps.

Within the white working-class community the girl will probably find few resources—teachers, church parishioners, family members—who can tell her of heroes or struggles among people of her background, for, except in pockets of continuing class conflict, the working class usually forgets its own history. More than any other group, white working-class students believe that they deserve their low status. A subculture of shame results. This negative self-image is foremost among what Richard Sennett and Jonathan Cobb have called "the hidden injuries of class." Several years ago, two students of mine provided a demonstration: they drove around Burlington, Vermont, in a big, nearly new, shiny black American car (probably a Lexus would be more appropriate today) and then in a battered ten-year-old subcompact. In each vehicle, when they reached a stoplight and it turned green, they waited until they were honked at before driving on. Motorists averaged less than seven seconds to honk at them in the subcompact, but in the luxury car the students enjoyed 13.2 seconds before anyone honked. Besides providing a good reason to buy a luxury car, this experiment shows how Americans unconsciously grant respect to the educated and successful. Since motorists of all social stations honked at the subcompact more readily, working-class drivers were in a sense disrespecting themselves while deferring to their betters. The biting quip "If you're so smart, why aren't you rich?" conveys the injury done to the self-image of the poor when the idea that America is a meritocracy goes unchallenged in school.

Part of the problem is that American history textbooks describe American education itself as meritocratic. A huge body of research confirms that education is dominated by the class structure and operates to replicate that structure in the next generation. Meanwhile, history textbooks blithely tell of such federal largesse to education as the Elementary and Secondary Education Act, passed under Pres. Lyndon Johnson. Not one textbook offers any data on or analysis of inequality within educational institutions. None mentions how school districts in low-income areas labor under financial constraints so shocking that Jonathan Kozol calls them "savage inequalities." No textbook ever suggests that students might research the history of their own school and the population it serves. The only two textbooks that relate education to the class system at all see it as a remedy! Schooling "was a key to upward mobility in postwar America," in the words of *The Challenge of Freedom*.

The tendency of teachers and textbooks to avoid social class as if it were a dirty little secret only reinforces the reluctance of working-class families to talk about it. Paul Cowan has told of interviewing the children of Italian immigrant workers involved in the famous 1912 Lawrence, Massachusetts, mill strike. He spoke with the daughter of one of the Lawrence workers who testified at a Washington congressional hearing investigating the strike. The worker, Camella Teoli, then thirteen years old, had been scalped by a cotton-twisting machine just before the strike and had been hospitalized for several months. Her testimony "became front-page news all over America." But Teoli's daughter, interviewed in 1976 after her mother's death, could not help Cowan. Her mother had told her nothing of the incident, nothing of her trip to Washington, nothing about her impact on America's conscience—even though almost every day, the daughter "had combed her mother's hair into a bun that disguised the bald spot." A professional of working-class origin told me a similar story about being ashamed of her uncle "for being a steelworker." A certain defensiveness is built into working-class culture; even its successful acts of working-class resistance, like the Lawrence strike, necessarily presuppose lower status and income, hence connote a certain inferiority. If the larger community is so good, as textbooks tell us it is, then celebrating or even passing on the memory of conflict with it seems somehow disloyal.

Textbooks do present immigrant history. Around the turn of the century immigrants dominated the American urban working class, even in cities as distant from seacoasts as Des Moines and Louisville. When more than 70 percent of the white population was native stock, less than 10 percent of the urban working class was. But when textbooks tell the immigrant story, they emphasize Joseph Pulitzer, Andrew Carnegie, and their ilk—immigrants who made supergood. Several textbooks apply the phrases *rags to riches* or *land of opportunity* to the immigrant experience. Such legendary successes were achieved, to be sure, but they were the exceptions, not the rule.

Ninety-five percent of the executives and financiers in America around the turn of the century came from upper-class or upper-middle-class backgrounds. Fewer than 3 percent started as poor immigrants or farm children. Throughout the nineteenth century, just 2 percent of American industrialists came from working-class origins. By concentrating on the inspiring exceptions, textbooks present immigrant history as another heartening confirmation of America as the land of unparalleled opportunity.

Again and again, textbooks emphasize how America has differed from Europe in having less class stratification and more economic and social mobility. This is another aspect of the archetype of American exceptionalism: our society has been uniquely fair. It would never occur to historians in, say, France or Australia, to claim that their society was exceptionally equalitarian. Does this treatment of the United States prepare students for reality? It certainly does not accurately describe our country today. Social scientists have on many occasions compared the degree of economic equality in the United States with that in other industrial nations. Depending on the measure used, the United States has ranked sixth of six, seventh of seven, ninth of twelve, or fourteenth of fourteen. In the United States the richest fifth of the population earns eleven times as much income as the poorest fifth, one of the highest ratios in the industrialized world; in Great Britain the ratio is seven to one, in Japan just four to one. In Japan the average chief executive officer in an automobile-manufacturing firm makes 20 times as much as the average worker in an automobile assembly plant; in the United States he (and it is not she) makes 192 times as much. The Jeffersonian conceit of a nation of independent farmers and merchants is also long gone: only one working American in thirteen is self-employed, compared to one in eight in Western Europe. Thus not only do we have far fewer independent entrepreneurs compared to two hundred years ago, we have fewer compared to Europe today.

Since textbooks claim that colonial America was radically less stratified than Europe, they should tell their readers when inequality set in. It surely was not a recent development. By 1910 the top 1 percent of the United States population received more than a third of all personal income, while the bottom fifth got less than one-eighth. This level of inequality was on a par with that in Germany or Great Britain. If textbooks acknowledged inequality, then they could describe the changes in our class structure over time, which would introduce their students to fascinating historical debate.

For example, some historians argue that wealth in colonial society was more equally distributed than it is today and that economic inequality increased during the presidency of Andrew Jackson—a period known, ironically, as the age of the common man. Others believe that the flowering of the large corporation in the late nineteenth century made the class structure more rigid. Walter Dean Burnham has argued that the Republican presidential victory in 1896 (McKinley over Bryan) brought about a sweeping political realignment that changed "a fairly democratic regime into a rather broadly based oligarchy," so by the 1920s business controlled public policy. Clearly the gap between rich and poor, like the distance between blacks and whites, was greater at the end of the Progressive Era in 1920 than at its beginning around 1890. The story is not all one of increasing stratification, for between the depression and the end of World War II income and wealth in America gradually became more equal. Distributions of income then remained reasonably constant until President Reagan took office in 1981, when inequality began to grow. Still other scholars think that little change has occurred since the Revolution. Lee Soltow, for example, finds "surprising inequality of wealth and income" in America in 1798. At least for Boston, Stephan Thernstrom concludes that inequalities in life chances owing to social class show an eerie continuity. All this is part of American history. But it is not part of American history as taught in high school.

To social scientists, the level of inequality is a portentous thing to know about a society. When we rank countries by this variable, we find Scandinavian nations at the top, the most equal, and agricultural societies like Colombia and India near the bottom. The policies of the Reagan and Bush administrations, which openly favored the rich, abetted a secular trend already in motion, causing inequality to increase measurably between 1981 and 1992. For the United States to move perceptibly toward Colombia in social inequality is a development of no small import. Surely high school students would be interested to learn that in 1950 physicians made two and a half times what unionized industrial workers made but now make six times as much. Surely they need to understand that top managers of clothing firms, who used to earn fifty times what their American employees made, now make 1,500 times what their Malaysian workers earn. Surely it is wrong for our history textbooks and teachers to withhold the historical information that might prompt and inform discussion of these trends.

Why might they commit such a blunder? First and foremost, publisher censorship of textbook authors. "You always run the risk, if you talk about social class, of being labeled Marxist," the editor for social studies and history at one of the biggest publishing houses told me. This editor communicates the taboo, formally or subtly, to every writer she works with, and she implied that most other editors do too.

Publisher pressure derives in part from textbook adoption boards and committees in states and school districts. These are subject in turn to pressure from organized groups and individuals who appear before them. Perhaps the most robust such lobby is Educational Research Analysts, led by Mel Gabler of Texas. Gabler's stable of right-wing critics regards even alleging that a textbook contains some class analysis as a devastating criticism. As one writer has put it, "Formulating issues in terms of class is unacceptable, perhaps even un-American." Fear of not winning adoption in Texas is a prime source of publisher angst, and might help explain why *Life and Liberty* limits its social-class analysis to colonial times in *England!* By contrast, "the colonies were places of great opportunity," even back then. Some Texans cannot easily be placated, however. Deborah L. Brezina, a Gabler ally, wrote that *Life and Liberty* describes America "as an unjust society," unfair to lower economic groups, and therefore should not be approved. Such pressure is hardly new. Harold Rugg's *Introduction to Problems of American Culture* and his popular history textbook, written during the depression, included some class analysis. In the early 1940s, according to Frances FitzGerald, the National Association of Manufacturers attacked Rugg's books, partly for this feature, and "brought to an end" social and economic analysis in American history textbooks.

More often the influence of the upper class is less direct. The most potent rationale for class privilege in American history has been Social Darwinism, an archetype that still has great power in American culture. The notion that people rise and fall in a survival of the fittest may not conform to the data on intergenerational mobility in the United States, but that has hardly caused the archetype to fade away from American education, particularly from American history classes. Facts that do not fit with the archetype, such as the entire literature of social stratification, simply get left out.

Textbook authors may not even need pressure from publishers, the right wing, the upper class, or cultural archetypes to avoid social stratification. As part of the process of heroification, textbook authors treat America itself as a hero, indeed as *the* hero of their books, so they remove its warts. Even to report the facts of income and wealth distribution might seem critical of America the hero, for it is difficult to come up with a theory of social justice that can explain why 1 percent of the population controls almost 40 percent of the wealth. Could the other 99 percent of us be *that* lazy or otherwise undeserving? To go on to include some of the mechanisms—

unequal schooling and the like—by which the upper class stays upper would clearly involve criticism of our beloved nation.

For any or all of these reasons, textbooks minimize social stratification. They then do something less comprehensible: they fail to explain the benefits of free enterprise. Writing about an earlier generation of textbooks, Frances FitzGerald pointed out that the books ignored "the virtues as well as the vices of their own economic system." Teachers might mention free enterprise with respect, but seldom do the words become more than a slogan. This omission is strange, for capitalism has its advantages, after all. Basketball star Michael Jordan, Chrysler executive Lee Iacocca, and ice-cream makers Ben and Jerry all got rich by supplying goods and services that people desired. To be sure, much social stratification cannot be justified so neatly, because it results from the abuse of wealth and power by those who have these advantages to shut out those who do not. As a social and economic order, the capitalist system offers much to criticize but also much to praise. America *is* a land of opportunity for many people. And for all the distortions capitalism imposes upon it, democracy also benefits from the separation of power between public and private spheres. Our history textbooks never touch on these benefits.

Publishers or those who influence them have evidently concluded that what American society needs to stay strong is citizens who assent to its social structure and economic system without thought. As a consequence, today's textbooks defend our economic system mindlessly, with insupportable pieties about its unique lack of stratification; thus they produce alumni of American history courses unable to criticize or defend our system of social stratification knowledgeably.

But isn't it nice simply to believe that America is equal? Maybe the "land of opportunity" archetype is an empowering myth—maybe believing in it might even help make it come true. For if students *think* the sky is the limit, they may reach for the sky, while if they don't, they won't.

The analogy of gender points to the problem with this line of thought. How could high school girls understand their place in American history if their textbooks told them that, from colonial America to the present, women have had equal opportunity for upward mobility and political participation? How could they then explain why no woman has been president? Girls would have to infer, perhaps unconsciously, that it has been their own gender's fault, a conclusion that is hardly empowering.

Textbooks do tell how women were denied the right to vote in many states until 1920 and faced other barriers to upward mobility. Textbooks also tell of barriers confronting racial minorities. The final question *Land of Promise* asks students following its "Social Mobility" section is "What social barriers prevented blacks, Indians, and women from competing on an equal basis with white male colonists?" After its passage extolling upward mobility, *The Challenge of Freedom* notes, "Not all people, however, enjoyed equal rights or an equal chance to improve their way of life," and goes on to address the issues of sexism and racism. But neither here nor anywhere else do *Promise* or *Challenge* (or most other textbooks) hint that opportunity might not be equal today for white Americans of the lower and working classes. Perhaps as a result, even business leaders and Republicans, the respondents statistically most likely to engage in what sociologists call "blaming the victim," blame the social system rather than African Americans for black poverty and blame the system rather than women for the latter's unequal achievement in the workplace. In sum, affluent Americans, like their textbooks, are willing to credit racial discrimination as the cause of poverty among blacks and Indians and sex discrimination as the cause of women's inequality but don't see class discrimination as the cause of poverty in general.

More than math or science, more even than American literature, courses in American history hold the promise of telling high school students how they and their parents, their communities, and their society came to be as they are. One way things are unequal is by social class. Although poor and working-class children usually cannot identify the cause of their alienation, history often turns them off because it justifies rather than explains the present. When these students react by dropping out, intellectually if not physically, their poor school performance helps convince them as well as their peers in the faster tracks that the system is meritocratic and that they themselves lack merit. In the end, the absence of social-class analysis in American history courses amounts to one more way that education in America is rigged against the working class.

1920
The 1920 Strike

BY JEREMY BRECHER, JERRY LOMBARDI, AND JAN STACKHOUSE

The American brass industry for more than 150 years was centered in "Brass Valley," a region along the Naugatuck River in Connecticut. A 1920 strike mobilized more than 15,000 workers—most of them immigrants from countries that included Italy, France and Germany.

THE 1919 WALKOUT showed the power of the Brass Valley workers to shut down the entire local industry and win concessions from their employers. In the midst of the strike, workers began organizing. The largest organization was the Waterbury Workers Association (later changed to the New England Workers Association). Competing with it was Local 16712 of the AFL, set up to organize unskilled brass workers. Each had many thousands of members.

Both of these "unions" were organized, not by plant or even by industry, but by ethnic group. Each had sections for Italians, Lithuanians, Poles, Russians, Portuguese, French, or other groups. Ethnic community leaders—foreign language newspaper editors, for example—often played significant roles within these sections, even though they did not work in the plants. These were not, in short, unions in today's sense, but organizations of the immigrant social groups.

At the same time, the machinists' union began substantial organizing among the skilled workers in the Valley. Their activities at times supported, at times undermined, those of the unskilled.

The 1920 strike began in Ansonia, where it lasted for several weeks. Just as it began to abate there, it spread up the Valley to Waterbury, where it continued for nearly twelve weeks, hitting nearly every industrial plant in the city. As many as 16,000 workers may have been out in the Valley at one time or another during the course of the strike.

James Tiso remembers the origins of the organization and strike.

James Tiso: We were working in misery. I was working for a dollar a day, ten and twelve hours. All over. If you give me a dollar and this guy gives me a dollar and a quarter, I leave you; I go get a dollar and a quarter.

We started the union over there for a lousy quarter to join. We had a pretty good strong union. But there were rats, agents, that would rat to the boss.

It happened like this: "We'll go to the union. We'll pay dues, we pay a quarter."

Everything was fine. We make a pretty good strong union. They joined at Scovill; they joined at American Brass; they joined at Chase. We want to call a strike.

Then they started making a mess, mixing them up. One union for the carpenters, a union for the bricklayers, a union for the laborers; everybody looking for a buck, like a bird. We're the sucker. You belong to the union for carpentry work; he belongs to the [union for] laborers. I said, make one, one. That's the one they got to be in, one [union for all the workers].

There was a guy from Massachusetts. He came down to organize the people in Waterbury. He started talking. None of the Italian people could understand English; we were all green. When they talked in English, he would explain to us what they meant. He was Italian. We had some people from Town Plot. They were anarchists. Italian people.

That's what happened in the first union. It came in with all the nations: all Italian, French, German people.

This guy [from Massachusetts] talked against the factory, against the people that were traitors to the working people. He spoke against the law, against the police, against the firemen, against the factory.

Some of the police wanted to pinch him. They pinched him. They took him over to the police station. Everybody went. The chief of police told him, "Where are you coming from?" "From Massachusetts." "You go back to Massachusetts, or I'll put you in jail for six months." Just because he was a talker—he didn't do anything, the poor guy.

He opened the eyes of the people in the state of Connecticut. How they're going to do, how they're going to work. And that's how the union was started.

They wanted so much for the people. The company didn't want to give it to you. What you do? You call a strike. You shut off the goddamn motors. You shut off the machines.

The demands of the strike grew directly out of the poor working conditions and the economic needs of the immigrant community.

On April 21 mass meetings were held throughout Waterbury, where votes for a general walkout were taken. On April 24 the New England Workers Association issued the following demands:

"1. Seventy five cents per hour the minimum—Female employees to be given same consideration of rate doing same work.

"2. Eight hours work per day—44 hours per week labor namely Monday-Tuesday-Wednesday-Thursday-Friday from 8 a.m. to 12 and from 1 p.m. to 5—from 8 a.m. to 12 on Saturday.

"3. The re-employment of all members discharged for Union activities without any discrimination belonging to the N.E.W. Ass.

"4. The abolishment of all piece work.

"5. Casters helpers will receive for Brass 20 cents per pot—four rounds limit—for Copper 25 and for Silver 30 cents per pot—three rounds limit. It is asked also an additional helper and should same be absent for any reason his pay to be divided among others doing his work.

"6. The Recognition of a Shop Committee."[*]

A meeting between the "Unfailing Committee" (strike leaders) of the New England Workers Association and a committee appointed by the mayor brought out some of the basic issues:

"—The majority of members had rejected the idea of dealing with the manufacturers through separate shop committees, and insisted that they deal with the organization as a whole. Their reason was that different wage scales would result in different factories, and further labor troubles and possibly another strike would follow. They declared that to treat with the manufacturers separately would be to destroy their unity and lessen their chances of winning the strike.

"—The workers walked out of the factories because they realized

---

[*] Copy of demands in Scovill collection, Baker Library.

that they must get more money if prices kept soaring upwards. Agitators might have precipitated the strike, but the increasing cost of living was actually responsible for the labor trouble. The perpendicular climbs in the prices of commodities of sugar, clothes, and other things were cited as examples.

"—Efforts to state their cases to the heads of factories had been in vain. The department foremen paid no attention to them. The 'bosses' in one factory were described as 'kaisers.' Grievances presented to foremen were ignored, and it was impossible to reach men higher up.

"—Favoritism in factories was also alleged. Italians, Lithuanians, Russians, and Poles were given all of the poor jobs on piece work.

"—Many of the married women of the Brooklyn section had been forced to go to work to help their husband support their children.

"—Members of the strike committee criticized the system they said was maintained by the factories whereby a man's record is passed on from one factory to another. They said if a man is receiving the minimum wage at one factory and becoming dissatisfied decides to go to another, to look for more money, he will find that all of the other factories of the city have been 'tipped off' not to exceed the minimum in that worker's case. The result was that the man was forced to remain in his old position at his old rate of pay."[*]

Because many companies officially kept their plants open, workers developed an unusual tactic to meet their economic needs and still continue the strike. Richard Giacin, a participant in the strike, recalled that workers originally maintained they would rather starve than give in to the manufacturers. Anyone who even mentioned giving in was ostracized, beaten up, or both. However, as money

---

[*] Waterbury *American,* April 30, 1920.

became more and more scarce, people would go to work one or two days a week to earn just enough to get by. This is confirmed by the Scovill strike statistics, which show a decline in absences at the beginning of each week with a return to high levels thereafter.

The role of skilled workers in the strike was ambiguous. Usually of ethnic groups that had immigrated to the Valley earlier than the unskilled, they held privileged positions within the plants. Yet their positions were being eroded by new technologies. Thus, they had numerous grievances of their own.

Through the early weeks of the strike, machinists and other skilled workers continued to work. In May, however, the International Association of Machinists—representing the skilled workers—issued demands of its own for a 44-hour week, a 35-percent wage increase, and recognition of shop committees. When, on May 19, American Brass refused to recognize the machinists' committee, skilled workers began to join the strike. On June 13 national IAM organizer Joe Tone arrived to organize machinists, but he announced that union recognition would not be a condition of settlement.

Joe Tone, subsequently Connecticut State Labor Commissioner, recalled that the police would not allow the organizers to address strikers' meetings. However, there was no rule against organizers' talking to each other. Consequently, each meeting was attended by two organizers, seated at opposite ends of the hall, who would discuss whatever pertinent information needed to be relayed—loudly enough for every striker in the hall to hear. [*]

The strike was met by organized repression from local authorities.

---

[*] M.S. Foucher, "The Labor Movement in Connecticut—An Introductory History," unpublished manuscript, pp. 37–38.

More than 100 strikers were arrested; some were held for deportation. Meetings were forbidden; authorities even broke into churches to disrupt meetings. There were numerous charges that employers and police had infiltrated strike leadership. These allegations had at least some basis in fact.

John Driscoll: Joe Tone [of the machinists] told me that his local was infiltrated by company spies. He said he found out later that all but one member of the local lodge executive board were company operatives.

In the 1950s I ran into a barber who told me he had acted as an informant for the Department of Justice. He gave them the names of people who were active in the strike and succeeded in getting them deported. A. Mitchell Palmer had organized the so-called red raids. Apparently a lot of the strike leaders were bundled into railroad cars and shipped out.

Police repression climaxed with the Bridge Street Incident, in which two policemen were wounded and a young striker, Liberto Tiso, was shot dead. Police accused Tiso of firing on the policemen. James Tiso, Liberto's older brother, tells his version of the story.

James Tiso: Over ten thousand on Baldwin Street, ten thousand on East Main. We march—we're walking our own business; we didn't do nothing wrong. Near Scovill we find a set of policemen. "Stay back. Who are you?" "We're not bothering you. We're just walking our own business. We're just showing the shop how many people are out of the goddamn hole."

One sonofabitch of a copper, he goes to the front of the line where all the younger fellows are, eighteen or nineteen years old. He says, "Get the hell out of there, you —— bastards! What do you think you are?"

There was a rain. My brother had an umbrella. He pushed the horse. Near the bridge. The boy said, "What's the matter?" "Stand back, you goddamn guinea bastard!" Pow! Well, [my brother] didn't want to see him swing the goddamn stick. So he stuck the umbrella in his belly. When he swing the umbrella, that guy [the policeman] took a pistol and boom! boom! He drop on the ground.

Now before he drop on the ground—he had a gun. He pulled the gun. He shoot to left then—toom! toom! When he got up, blood everywhere. And the cops, they get him. The cop on top of the horse took off, and they took him right in the door at St. Mary's Hospital. Everybody pick him up, help him. Put him in the hospital. Call a doctor.

My brother fell on the street, on the sidewalk. Somebody threw a brick and hit another police, boom! He fall across my brother. My brother still had a pistol in his hand. That guy was afraid they were going to shoot him. He took a pistol, boom! boom! boom!

The police came with a machine gun on top of a truck—it was a big revolution.

The police, after policing the crowd, then they went for the truck to pick up all the fellows that were hurt. There were eighteen fellows hurt, but not like my brother.

They put my brother on the truck, just like a pig.

Seventeen young fellows were all in one room. But he was bad. They tied him up like a dog. Blood. He couldn't speak. I said, "Tell me what happened to you. Who did that? Do you know?" He said, "Brother, no. You've got the kids."

Before I go, I start to cry.

Finally they say [to my father], "Your son is dead."

My father—I'll tell you the truth—if he knew who killed his boy, he'd get them right on the street, anyplace. We don't say we're anarchists, Fascists, or Communists. We've got tolerance. But that ain't right, what they did.

Liberto Tiso's funeral provided a focal point for strikers' emotions, and his death became a symbol of their solidarity across ethnic lines.

• • •

James Tiso: They took him to a funeral home. We had all combination of people.

All over the state they had to go to send a motor troop from New Haven, Bridgeport, all around. They brought them over to the city: machine guns and everything.

We had one German fellow, big guy, he wouldn't cave in to nobody. He wasn't scared to talk. He picked up on the city, on the police, on the shop, on how they treated the people, how they really are in this America.

The line never stopped, day and night, day and night.

They made a collection, put the money in.

Down there [at the cemetery], all people. The German fellow was with the union. All Polish people, all Italian people, French, German, all mixed. Before putting my brother on the grave. All the police came down on the road.

[The German] made a speech. Against the police, against the factory, against the judge, against the law we've got in the United States of America. Then he rose and said, "The man was on the ground, and they shot him. You've got to have a lot of guts. This is respect in America!" He talk all right.

What was the matter? Was [my brother] an anarchist? Was he a Communist? Was he a Bolshevik? What was this man? He was a Catholic like the rest of the people in America.

And that was the trouble of my brother.

In the wake of the Bridge Street Incident, Governor Holcomb put the state guard at the disposal of the mayor of Waterbury, sent in a machine gun batallion, and stationed sentinels with fixed bayonets around City Hall. The superintendent of police ordered that no permits be granted for strikers' meetings and that policemen carry riot guns with orders to shoot. The newspapers predicted that the strike would immediately collapse. But the strikers, outraged by what they considered a denial of their rights, continued the strike for another six weeks.

After only a little more than a month on strike, the skilled workers returned to work. The Ansonia workers had gone back to work as well. Waterbury strikers held out till mid-July. Ultimately, they were defeated by a combination of repression and the economic power of the companies—the brass masters could afford to wait, while the strikers went hungry.

Despite its outcome, the strike constituted a memorable effort by tens of thousands of people, mostly immigrant workers of all nationalities, to overcome their divisions and use their power over production to make a better life for themselves, their families, and their communities.

1930s
from *Hard Times*
by Studs Terkel

Studs Terkel's 1970 oral history of the Great Depression included conversations with coal miners and their family members.

Buddy Blankenship

A West Virginian émigré, living in Chicago. Illness has kept him jobless. Children, ranging wide in age from late adolescence to babyhood, stepchildren, son-in-law, grandchild and a weary wife are seated or wandering about the apartment: trying to keep cool on this hot, muggy summer afternoon. Hand-me-down furniture is in evidence in all the rooms.

I've been in a depression ever since I've been in the world. Still, it's better and worse. '31, '32, that's about the worst we ever been through.

I told my dad I wasn't going to school any more. He said: Why, you just come on and go work with me. I went in the mines, and I went to work. From '31 to about the last of '32. The Depression got so bad, we went to farming, raising our own stuff. He worked in the mines fifty-one years. He was sixty-three when he got killed. A boy shot him.

We lived eight miles from the mine, and we had to ride it horseback. I was riding behind my dad. Many times I'd have to git off and hammer his feet out of the stirrups. They'd be froze in the stirrups. It was cold, you know. When you come out of the mines, your feet would be wet of sweat and wet where you're walking on the bottom. And get up on those steel stirrups, while you're riding by eight miles, your feet'd be frozen and you couldn't git 'em out of the stirrups. I'd have to hammer 'em out. His feet were numb, and they wouldn't hurt till they started to get warm, and then they would get to hurtin'.

We got up at five in the mornin', start at six. We got out at ten that night. We'd work about sixteen hours a day, seventeen hours. The boss said we had to clean up. We didn't clean it up, the next morning there'd be another man in the mine to clean it up. The motor man would say: How many cars you got? Five more. Well, hurry up, we want to get out of here. They was gettin' a dollar seventy-five a day. We'd get sixty to sixty-five ton a day—that is, both us, me and Dad, Then they changed me off and let me get a dollar and a half a day. I was trappin'.

Trappin'? The trap door was shut so the air would circulate through the mine. Then the motor come along, I'd open it up. I had to stay there till everybody quit. Then we'd walk about two miles and a half till we got outside. We walked about a mile before we got to where we could get our horses. We got down to the horses, why we rode about eight miles before we got to home. Summertimes it wasn't too bad. But in wintertime, boy, it was rough. You'd get snowbound and it would get so you couldn't get in and out. Ice'd be so bad . . . an' dangerous. Of course, we had to go to work. We didn't eat if we didn't go.

They had what they called safety devices, but it wasn't real safety. They had an axe and a saw and you cut your own timbers. You brought 'em in, strapped on your back. You went out on the mountain with your one-man saw. You sawed down a bush or whatever size prop you wanted and you tuck 'em in on your back. On Sunday, I packed timbers on my back, about two miles to the place . . . to set 'em on Monday. Company furnished the timber but you had to cut 'em. You had to lay your own track. . . .

I've seen several accidents. I've had to take four out of the mines dead. I didn't think about nothin' like that, though. I packed one for seven miles, and he got up and walked better'n I could. I was gonna give out, and he wasn't hurtin' any bit. There was some rock on him, and I took a jack and lifted it up and pulled 'im out. Just his breath knocked out of 'im. . . .

About '32, it got so they wouldn't let us work but two days a week. We saved $20 in the office. They laid us off two weeks till we traded that $20 in the store. We had to trade it out in the store, or we didn't get to work no more. It was a company store. What we made, we had to go next evening and trade it off. If we didn't, they'd lay us off. They didn't let you draw no money at all. It was scrip. They had a man top of the hill who took your tonnage down, how many tons you loaded, and it was sent up to the scrip office. If you made $20 over your expenses—for house, rent, lights and all—why, then they laid you off till you spent that $20.

This town you lived in . . .

It was a cave, a coal cave. Thirty-two families lived in the caves. It was nice buildings, built up inside, but they was just rough lumber. The company was the landlord, too. They owned it all. They still got company houses yet.

I worked about two years on the mines, then we went back to the farm from '32 to '37. It seemed like you lived a lot better on the farm than today. The works was bad, but you didn't have to pay some big price for the stuff. You raised your own hogs, you could have your own cattle. And you had your own meat, your own bacon, lard. You didn't have to buy nothin' but flour and meal. You raised your own potatoes. You never had money because you didn't make it to have it. It was a pretty bad time. It seemed just like a dream to me, the Depression did. I was young and didn't pay no attention to it. I didn't get the clothes or the underwear or stuff like that, but the eatin' part was good. I'd rather be back on the farm than anything I ever done.

Then we went to camp—minin'—in '37. The same mines. Roosevelt brought the mines arolling again. Things got to moving, and money got to circulating through. I worked the mine from '37 up to '57. Then it was a lot different. They had the union there and we worked just seven hours and fifteen minutes. We didn't work as hard as when the Depression was on. And they wouldn't let us stay no overtime, 'cause they didn't want to pay the overtime. I guess. We made some good money, me and my dad both. He worked up to '41 and they cut him out. Age. He never did get a pension. He never worked long enough in the union to get a pension.

I took part in four strikes. They fined us one time for takin' a strike. A wildcat, that's what they called it. I helped organize about six mines. Now the company didn't like this, and they was kickin' on us all at the same time. They'd do anything, they'd kill and everything else. One place in West Virginia, they was shootin' us all to pieces. They had guns of all kinds there.

They had three hundred state troopers there. They was on the labor's side, and they took a lot of smoke bombs out of the men's pockets, the scabs. They said: "If you fellows wants to sign up or not wants to sign up . . . but go to carryin' no guns. You fellas ain't paid to carry 'em and ain't paid to use 'em, we're paid to use 'em. If you want to sign 'em up, you go ahead and sign 'em up." And they signed up.

It surprised everyone that these three hundred state police come— on our side. The captain said: If they don't want to organize, shut 'em down. He walked into the bathhouse and, boy, they had guns hanging out all around, the scabs. See, the company furnished 'em guns. They had machine guns and everything. They took the state police in there to take all them guns out. I know the name of the Governor if I could think of it—he was on labor's side.[*] That was '42.

As he remembers, past and present fuse. . . . "The mines were runnin' out, except this little wagon of a mine, and it didn't have no tracks. You had to get on your knees, coal was so low. Coal was just twenty-eight inches. Panther Creek, West Virginia. We drove tunnels clear through the mountain to the other side. We'd drive up as far as we could go without air, and we'd come back and get a sniff and drive it up again as far as we could again without air. We could get breakthroughs to the other place and get air, you see.

"They cut one tunnel there was twelve miles long one way and twenty-eight miles long the other way, 'cause it was a ridge one way. They took twenty-eight inches of rock from the top, make it high enough for the men to

---

[*] M.M. Neely, Governor of West Virginia, 1941–1945

work. I traveled about seven miles a day back and forth on my knees. They'd be knots on 'em big as your double fist. . . ."

I liked the mines till it got so I couldn't work no more. My wind was too short, and there was too much dead air and I just choked up and couldn't do no good. I went to work for a dollar an hour . . . on the roads. Till that run out. And I come to Chicago.

MARY OWSLEY

Before setting off with his family for Oklahoma in 1929, to follow the oil boom, her husband was a dynamite man in Kentucky mines.

One day he noticed on the side of the boiler a place as big as a saucer. They call it a breather—it's a weak place on the boiler. He told the boss that had to be fixed, because he didn't want to get killed. Monday morning, I saw him comin' back home. They hadn't fixed it, hadn't done a thing about it. He told 'em in less than three weeks there'll be an explosion. Sure enough, there was. Killed three men and two mine mules from that very thing. He left.

We lived in a company house. We had to buy every bucket of water we used, 'cause the company undermined things so bad, they ruined all the water wells. I bought my food from the company store, and we bought our furniture from the company store, and we paid three prices on it. I've seen my husband have to borry from his next pay check—what they call scrip—to buy just medicine and things like that. And we didn't live extravagant either. We paid over 260 some odd dollars for furniture from the coal company. We paid it all back but $20. And when he went and got another job, he bought a truck down there for the furniture. And they took the whole thing away from us. They wouldn't let us pay the $20.

Because he was a troublemaker . . . ?

• • •

No, because he quit that job there where the breather was on that boiler. That's the kind of troublemaker he was, you're mighty right he was. He wanted to live.

We lived in this coal mine camp, this next one, and there was a pump out in the middle between four houses. The four families of us shared that one pump. In the wintertime, that thing would get covered up with ice a foot thick. Us women had to keep a tub of water on our coal stove hot. The men would have to get up at three in the morning to get out there and melt the ice off the pump before they went to work. Just for the simple want of a shed built over a water pump. It might deflate the company's bank account.

AARON BARKHAM

"I'm too young to retire and too old to work in the coal mines. When a man gets to be up around thirty-five, forty years old, been in a mine ten or twelve years, they want somebody younger. When they get the chance, they'll replace him."

He is from West Virginia. His father, a miner all his life, died in a coal camp. "Silicosis wasn't even heard of. He died of hardened arteries. * *Dad belonged to the Oddfellows, and they paid Mother about $11 a month. We had a cow and a hog. When things got tight, we let loose of that. We had a hardscrabble farm, worn-out ground, not worth much. From the time I was four years old, that's all I knowed, hard times."*

People worked fifteen hours a day, loaded a four-ton car, they got a

---

* "Several hundred autopsies have confirmed that many miners die of heart failure when coal dust clamps the small arteries in their lungs in a stiff unyielding cast which eventually puts a critical load on their hearts." Robert G. Sherrill, *The Nation* April 28, 1969, p. 533.

dollar out of it. If the company could, it'd take that. (Laughs.) I think they made about $2 a day, most of 'em. We had boarders from the coal camp, others weren't that lucky. My oldest brother, he was fifteen, he went to work as a breaker boy at the tipple.

Years before, he and my other brother, who was twelve, got the idea of sellin' moonshine. We'd pay a dollar a gallon and sell it for twenty-five cents a pint. So that worked all right. We sold sometimes three gallons a day. During Prohibition, and after, people that got the relief checks was the ones that bought the whiskey. We'd get it in half-gallon jars and put it in pint bottles.

That's where a playful little boy comes in. A little boy—I was about six, seven—could get aholt of somethin' and carry it right along the road where a man could get arrested. 1931 was when that started and come to about 1936. That was 'bout the only family income. The only obstacle I had, I had with my own second cousin. He was a deputy sheriff. He was big and fat, and I could get around him. He chased me miles through the thickets.

Nine revenuers were split up into three bunches. Work in the woods, lookin' for stills. They'd put down a marker. It was my job to switch the markers. And they'd get all confused. Everybody bootlegged. It kind of got to be a legitimate business. You had to be foxier than the foxes, that's all.

That second cousin, he was on the political side of the fence. So when WPA come in, we didn't get any relief from the local politicians. My mother was a Republican. I think it was her pride that wouldn't change our politics. Not much use complainin' about somethin' like that. We had enough to eat from the bootleg. About four out of five was unemployed in the county till 'bout 1938.

I never did get a whole year of school—maybe five or six months. I started workin' when I was thirteen. In a sawmill at ten cents an hour. I worked for the guy that had all the timber monopoly for the company. I worked for the bulldozers. I finally got twenty-five cents an hour, but he raised the board to seventy-five cents a day. Get up at four o'clock in the mornin', we clumb on a big truck and was hauled about fifteen miles. We started about a quarter to five and worked till we couldn't see. Then we'd quit. It was nearer sixteen hours than it was eight hours. I know we'd get into bed and turn over one time, and they'd be yellin' for breakfast.

It got bad in '29. The Crash caught us with one $20 gold piece. All mines shut down—stores, everything. One day they was workin', the next day the mines shut down. Three or four months later, they opened up. Run two, three days a week, mostly one. They didn't have the privilege of calling their souls their own. Most people by that time was in debt so far to the company itself, they couldn't live.

Some of them been in debt from '29 till today, and never got out. Some of them didn't even try. It seem like whenever they went back to work, they owed so much. The company got their foot on 'em even now.

When the Crash come, they got about ten cents an hour—that is, if they begged the supervisor for a job. They had to load a seven-ton car for fifty cents. If they found three pieces of slate as big as your hand, they took that car, and you didn't get paid. That's what they called the dock. A man couldn't predict what's gonna fall on that car, goin' through maybe a couple of miles of tunnel, and everything fallin' anyhow.

One time they hauled a mule out. They fired the guy that got that mule killed. They told him a mule's worth more'n a man. They had to pay $50 for a mule, but a man could be got for nothin'. He never had worked another day since. Blackballed for costin' 'em that money.

I remember one time, the Red Cross shipped in about four ton of flour in twenty-four pound bags. Unloaded it in the company warehouse. It was a Red Cross gift. But the company said they have to work a day to get a sack of flour. That started it. Pretty much like walkin' the inferno.

An old woman, about sixty years, she come down from Canyon Creek. One time she was makin' a speech near a railroad track. She was standin' on a box. The strikebreakers shot her off with a shot gun. So she come down to Logan County where we was and made speeches and helped get them organized. But they had a time.

The county sheriff had a hundred strikebreakers. They were called deputies. The company paid him ten cents a ton on all the coal carried down the river, to keep the union out. He was beaten in the election by T. Hatfield of the feudin' Hatfields. He was for the union. They had pretty much a full-scale war out there for about three years.

They brought the army in. The county was under martial law, stayed till about '31. What strikes me is the soldiers along the company road, dispersin' people. When people'd gather together, they couldn't talk. Two guys could, but three couldn't.

About that time, a bunch of strikebreakers come in with shotguns and axe handles. Tried to break up union meetings. The UMW deteriorated and went back to almost no existence. It didn't particularly get full strength till about 1949. And it don't much today in West Virginia. So most people ganged up and formed the Ku Klux Klan.

The Ku Klux was the real controllin' factor in the community. They was the law. It was in power to about 1932. My dad and my older brother belonged to it. My dad was one of the leaders till he died. The company called in the army to get the Ku Klux out, but it didn't work. The union and the Ku Klux was about the same thing.

The superintendent of the mine got the big idea of makin' it rougher than it was. They hauled him off in a meat wagon, and about ten more of the company officials. Had the mine shut down. They didn't kill 'em, but they didn't come back. They whipped one of the foremen and got him out of the county. They gave him twelve hours to get out, get his family out.

The UMW had a field representative, he was a lawyer. They tarred and feathered 'im for tryin' to edge in with the company. He come around, got mad, tryin' to tell us we were wrong, when we called a wildcat. He was takin' the side of the company. I used the stick to help tar 'im. And it wasn't the first time.

The Ku Klux was formed on behalf of people that wanted a decent living, both black and white. Half the coal camp was colored. It wasn't anti-colored. The black people had the same responsibilities as the white. Their lawn was just as green as the white man's. They got the same rate of pay. There was two colored who belonged to it. I remember those two niggers comin' around my father and askin' questions about it. They joined. The pastor of our community church was a colored man. He was Ku Klux. It was the only protection the workin' man had.

Sure, the company tried to play the one agin' the other. But it didn't work. The colored and the whites lived side by side. It was somethin' like a checkerboard. There'd be a white family and a colored family. No sir, there was no racial problem. Yeah, they had a certain feelin' about the colored. They sure did. They had a certain feelin' about the white, too. Anyone come into the community had unsatisfactory dealin's, if it was colored or white, he didn't stay.

I remember one family moved in from acrost us. They had a bunch of women. I remember where I saw out the window, it didn't look right. The Ku Klux warned 'em once. Gave 'em twenty-four hours. They didn't take the warning. The next night they whipped Hughie (that was the man), his wife and his niece, his uncle and his aunt, and whipped six more that was acrowdin' around. They whipped 'em with switches and run 'em out, all of 'em. They was white; they wasn't niggers.

One time a Negro slapped a white boy. They didn't give him no warning. They whipped 'im and run 'im out of town. If a white man'd slapped a colored kid, they'd a done the same thing. They didn't go in for beatin' up niggers because they was niggers. What they done was kept the community decent to live in. What they did object to was obscenity and drinkin'.

What about bootlegging?

Oh, they objected to raisin' a fuss in town. What you do private, that's your business. You're talkin' about mountain people now. This ain't the Deep South.

People'd get their temper rubbed off quick. In organizin' the union, we didn't go through the Labor Relations Board. We went through what we called "mule train." We'd figure how many people were workin' at that certain mine, and we'd just tell 'em to organize it or we'd close 'em. We'd give 'em three days. Sometimes they'd stand at the mouth of the mine with a club. There was seventeen thousand in the whole district. I have knowd every one of them to come out on account of one man bein' called out. And join the UMW.

At a UMW meeting, they'd iron it out themselves. I had to pull out a .38 once to get out of a union meetin'. Our chairman of the local was thick with the superintendent of the mine, and I made mention of it in the meeting. Some guys didn't like it: they followed him close. We was in a school building. I was up next to the blackboard, and the door was on the other end of the room. So they blocked the door. My wife's half-brother was sittin' about half way back. So he pulled out his gun and throwd it to me. I told 'em I'm goin' out and anybody stops me, I'm gonna shoot. They followed me outside, there was about fifty. They blocked the gate. So I told 'em I'm gonna shoot the first six gets in my way.

The next day I went back to work. I took my gun with me. They cooled off. It took 'em a week, they cooled off.

In my life, I've found people won't take anything. If things get real bad again, I'm afraid there'd be some millionaires made paupers because they'd take their money. They'd take it the rough way. The people are gonna take care of their families, if they'd have to shoot somebody else. And you can't blame 'em for that. You think I wouldn't take what you got if you had a million dollars and I had to protect my family? I sure would. I'd take your money one way or the other. Some people don't have courage enough to fight for what they have comin'. Until 1934, more than half the people of Logan County were scabbin'. Gives you an idea how they don't know. . . .

Explosions? Had one back in '35, killed a few men. They had one in Bartley, killed 136 men. In Macbeth the same year—when was that?—a fire and explosion killed eighteen and twenty men. Then in 1947, they had an explosion that killed a couple of men.

They sent me for a job in Virginia. Shaft was fifteen hundred feet deep. I went down and looked it over and went up and didn't go. Gas and dust. That was 1965. Supposed to have been the most safest mine in the world. They had an explosion about four months after that. Killed two men, injured nine more. . . .

Postscript: *Suddenly, a light laugh: "I remember the first radio come to Mingo County, next to Logan. Wayne Starbuck, a cousin to me, brought that in in 1934. That was a boon. It was a little job, got more squeals and squeaks than anything else. Everybody came from miles around to look at it. We didn't have any electricity. So he hooked up two car batteries. We got 'Grand Old Opry' on it."*

Edward Santander

A director of adult education at a small Midwestern college. "I never had the slightest intention of being anything other than a schoolteacher. My whole life is bound up in this. The Depression played a role: if I could just add my two cents worth to making life better. . . ."

My first real memories come about '31. It was simply a gut issue then: eating or not eating, living or not living. My father was a coal miner, outside a small town in Illinois. My dad, my grandfather and my uncle worked in this same mine. He had taken a cut in wages, but we were still doing pretty well. We were sitting in a '27 Hudson, when I saw a line of men waiting near the I.C. tracks. I asked him what was the trouble. They were waiting to get something to eat.

When the mine temporarily closed down in the early Thirties, my dad had to hunt work elsewhere. He went around the state, he'd paint barns, anything.

I went to an old, country-style schoolhouse, a red-stripe. One building that had eight rows in it, one for each grade. Seven rows were quiet, while the eighth row recited. The woman teacher got the munificent sum of $30 a month. She played the organ, an old pump organ with pedals, she taught every subject, and all eight grades. This was 1929, '30, '31. . . . At the back corner was a great pot-bellied stove that kept the place warm. It had about an acre of ground, a playground with no equipment. Out there were the toilets, three-holers, and in the winter—You remember Chic Sale?* You had moons, crescents or stars on the doors. You'd be surprised at the number of people in rural areas that didn't have much in this way, as late as the Thirties.

One of the greatest contributions of the WPA was the standardized outdoor toilet, with modern plumbing. (Laughs.) They built thousands of them around here. You can still see some of 'em standing. PAW built new schools and the City Hall in this town. I remember NYA. I learned a good deal of carpentry in this.

Roosevelt was idolized in that area. The county had been solidly Republican from the Civil War on. And then was Democratic till the end of Truman's time. F.D.R. was held in awe by most people, but occasionally you'd run across someone who said: "Well, he has

---

* A "rube" vaudevillian, best known for "The Specialist," a routine based on outhouse humor.

syphillis, and it's gone to his brain." The newspaper in the area hated Roosevelt, just hated him. (Laughs.)

Almost everybody was in the same boat, pretty poorly off. I remember kids who didn't have socks. We all wore long-handles—you could get 'em red, you could get 'em white. These boys would cut the bottoms off their long-handles and stuff 'em into the top of their shoes and make it look like they had socks.

We had epidemics of typhoid and diptheria. Houses would be placarded with signs. This one girl who came to school had had typhoid and had lost all her hair. There was absolutely no way they could purchase a wig for her. This was the shame of it. The girl had to go around bald-headed for as long as I knew her. It wasn't the physical thing because we all got used to that. But what did it do to her inside? Along about '34 and '35, the state began giving diptheria and typhoid shots and all this sort of thing.

His grandfather was the patriarch of the family; a huge man, born in a log cabin; took home correspondence courses and became a hoisting engineer in the mines. He was a Socialist, a strong supporter of Debs and was elected a three-term mayor of Central City, near Centralia. "In those days, women had just received the right to vote. Many of them were hesitant. He urged them to vote, no matter what ticket, as long as they went to the polls."

There were any number of Socialists in this area. Today people don't think and discuss as much as they did in those days. I remember men with thick calluses on their hands from handling shovels. They would be discussing Daniel De Leon and Debs and Christian Socialism and Syndicalism and Anarchism. A lot of them came out of the IWW into the miners' movement. Many were first generation, Polish, Italian, Croatian. . . . They changed the spelling of their names as they've gone along. The ones who couldn't read, someone would read it to them. There were thousands of presses that would run off little booklets, like the group in Girard, Kansas.[*] My grandfather, father and uncle were self-educated men. There were less distractions then.

Was drinking a problem when the Depression hit?

I remember driving through one town that had less than a thousand people in it. There were ten taverns. But they always did put it away rather heavily. They were a hard-drinking society under any standards. Many of them made their home brew. One old fellow I remember would drink his own during the week. On Saturday, he would become royalty and go to town and drink what they called factory-made. (Laughs.)

My grandmother was a very saving woman. The women in our family took care of the money. When the Depression really hit us in 1936, when the mine closed down completely, there was no income. We tried opening a filling station and went absolutely broke on that. The only livelihood these men had was mining coal. Where would you go? Down in Harlan County, Kentucky? They were out of work, too. West Frankfort? Carterville? They had the same problems.

Natural gas was being used, and cities began having ordinances against dirty coal in those days. This mine was simply not making a profit. The family that owned it, pretty decent people, decided to sell. The miners, bullheadedly—who could read the handwriting on the wall, anyway?—decided they would buy the mine themselves. This was '36, '37. So they sold shares of stock. They collected $33,000. The owner's widow accepted it rather than a $38,000 bid from a St. Louis scrap dealer, who was going to close it up.

---

[*] E. Haldemann-Julius blue books. They were sold for a nickel or a dime: philosophical, political, scientific and literary classics.

For eighteen months, these men worked for nothing to get the mine back in shape to show a profit. It started with four hundred men. The mine operated until the Fifties. By that time, only eighteen men were left. . . .

Some people go into strip mining. Fifteen or twenty of them get together and get the mining rights from someone. Then they put a ladder and a shaft in and strip down the area. There are very few pit mines left in this state.

This area was not ready to convert to any other type of work. The people who had the money were absentee owners. There was plenty going out but nothing coming in. When the mines decided it wasn't profitable to operate, they closed down. That took away whatever income this area had.

In the Thirties, UMW came along. The union was the only salvation the people had. It grew violent at times, quite violent. If mines did open with scabs, it wasn't long before someone was done away with.

Do you recall any mine disasters?

I can take you to a cemetery where there is only one mausoleum. Everybody else is buried underground. In this mausoleum is a miner who died in an accident at Junction City. He oft expressed himself that he had spent so many years below ground that when he died, he wanted to spend the rest of it above. This was always on their minds: an accident.

He remembers the Centralia disaster of '47. "When number Five blew up." 111 men were killed. He remembers '51, West Frankfort: 119 were killed. "Illinois had always been notoriously lax in its rules regarding the safety of the mines. Even the old-fashioned method of using birds to check the gas—not too many of them did this."

His uncle was killed in the Centralia disaster. He recalls: "All the mines had wash houses. After a miner got done washing up, he'd go home and sit in a galvanized tub and just soak. Because he'd have this coal dust under his fingernails and ground into his skin. In the morning, they hang their clothes up on a hook in the wash house. They'd pull a chain and the clothes would go up to the ceiling. . . .

"In this '47 thing, we'd all be sitting in the wash house. It was damp and cold. Someone would unwind the chain, and he'd let these clothes down. And the most profound silence. No weeping or anything like that. You've seen these pictures of women in their babushkas, waiting patiently, hoping. . . . In this '47 thing, all were killed. When the rescue team got to one group, they were still warm.

"In Centralia, they turned about everything into a mortuary. In the funeral home where my uncle was . . . my cousin said, 'I've got to see him.' The man lifted up the sheet. It wasn't even human. 'Is this your father?' He said, 'No.' He lifted up another one—and my cousin said to me, 'I've had enough.' My father went and identified him by his wedding ring. There was only one open coffin in the whole place: the mailman, who had died a natural death."

People in the Thirties did feel a bit different. When the pig-killing was going on, the farmers would kill the pigs well enough, but they'd tell the people where they buried them, and they'd go dig 'em up and take 'em home. The farmers couldn't sell the pigs anyway, so they weren't out anything.

It isn't true that people who have very little won't share. When everybody is in the same position, they haven't anything to hide from one another. So they share. But when prosperity comes around, you hear: Look at that son of a bitch. When he didn't have anything, he was all right. Look at him now.

The Depression was such a shock to some people that when World War II was over—you'd hear men in the army say it: "When I get back,

I'm going to get a good job, a house and a car, some money in the bank, and I'm never going to worry again. These people have passed this on to their kids." In many cases, youngsters rebel against this.

I never heard anyone who expressed feeling that the United States Government, as it existed, was done for. It was quite the opposite. The desire to restore the country to the affluence it had. This was uppermost in people's minds. Even the Socialists who talked about taking the corporate system out were just talking, that's all.

If we had a severe depression today—I'm basically an optimist—I don't think this country would survive. Many people today are rootless. When you have this rootlessness, we're talking about the Germany of the Twenties. You'd see overt dictatorship take over. You would see your camps. . . .

Postscript: *"We used to talk a great deal about keeping solvent and the morality of not going into debt. I was almost thirty years old before I went into debt."*

ROGER

He is fourteen. He was brought to Chicago from West Virginia eight years ago. His mother is dead. His father, whom he sees once in a while, is somewhere in the Appalachian community. Though he stays with his sister-in-law, his life is on the streets of the city. He's pretty much on his own.

If I say the word—"Depression"—what does that mean?

I wouldn't know, 'cause I never heard the word before.

What do you think it means?

I figure maybe you're all tensed up or somethin'. That's the only thing I could think of "depression" meanin'.

Ever hear of the time when millions of people weren't working, in the 1930s—long before you were born . . . ?

I heard about it. They didn't have no food and money. Couldn't keep their children fed and in clothes. People say, like a long time ago it was, coal miners worked real hard for a couple of dollars, and you couldn't hardly get a job. Especially in my home town and places like that.

Well, we still had it hard when we come up here. I was six. My father and my mother, they told me about how hard it was to get a job up here. That's why I tried to get him to go back to West Virginia, after I was up here a while. See, I never knowd hard times when we was down there. So I said to Dad, "Let's go back to West Virginia." He says, "There's no jobs for us down there, we can't make a living. We have to stay here." He said: "Some days, sometimes maybe if it get easy to get jobs down there, maybe we go down there."

It's so damn hard. Seems like everybody's takin' advantage of you. See, I never heard that word "depression" before. They would all just say "hard times" to me. It is still. People around this neighborhood still has hard times. Like you see, the buildin's are all tore up and not a decent place to live. My house isn't fit to live in. These buildin's ain't no good. If we tear 'em down, they ain't gonna build new ones for us. So we have to live in 'em.

Dearborn Massacre

A crowd of 3,000 to 5,000 unemployed workers, organized by
the Communist Party, marched from downtown Detroit to
the Ford Plant in Dearborn on March 7, 1932. Their demands
ranged from jobs for laid-off workers to equal hiring rights for
black workers. The police met them with firehoses and guns.
This article appeared in *The New York Times.*

NEARLY 3,000 OF Detroit's unemployed, with Communists in their
midst, took part in a riot today at the gates of the Ford Motor Company's
plant in Dearborn. Their demonstration culminated in a
furious fight in which four men were killed and at least fifty others
were injured.

The demonstration by the unemployed, who had planned to ask
Ford company officials, through a committee, to give them work,
started quietly, but before it was over Dearborn pavements were
stained with blood, streets were littered with broken glass and the
wreckage of bullet-ridden automobiles and nearly every window in
the Ford plant's employment building had been broken. . . .

The march, plans for which were completed on Sunday evening,
according to one of the wounded demonstrators, was orderly at the
start. In accordance with the program, the work-seekers gathered at
Fort Street and Oakland Boulevard at about 2 o'clock this afternoon
and set out for the Ford plant in Dearborn, more than two miles
away, where they intended to send a committee of officials to the factory
with the demand that the company immediately employ a large
number of those out of work.

Carrying banners and signs demanding jobs, the demonstrators marched in orderly fashion along Fort Street to Miller Road, where they halted for a few minutes to hold a conference. The conference was soon over and once more they resumed the march, swinging along Miller Road to the Dearborn city limits.

There they encountered a squad of Dearborn police, who warned them to turn back to Detroit.

Ignoring the warning, the marchers surged over the city lines, and instantly the fighting broke out. The police hurled a barrage of tear bombs into the crowd, causing the vanguard of the parade to fall back along the Rouge River and the railroad tracks.

Wind Carries Off Gas Fumes

But in a few minutes the police had exhausted their supply of bombs and, to add to their troubles, the prevailing high winds quickly cleared the air of tear-gas fumes.

Quick to take advantage of the situation, the marchers began a second charge, hurling rocks and jagged chunks of frozen mud at the police.

Dodging the missiles, the police drew their guns, pointing them threateningly at the angry mob. Once more the marchers scattered, this time along Miller Road to Dearborn Road, where they encountered more gas bombs which had been rushed to the scene during the lull of their first retreat.

Meanwhile, Dearborn firemen had stationed themselves on an overhead walk that crosses Miller Road at Gate 3, in front of the main plant, around which the worst of the fighting took place.

On the viaduct, out of reach of the missiles flung by the rioters, the firemen turned a hose on them, holding them back temporarily with the icy stream of water.

But the rioters were held at bay only for a few minutes. Soon they swarmed up the embankment and were surging to the gate of the Ford Motor Company's employment office.

Shot Starts General Melee

There they were met by squads of police with drawn guns and by the Ford Company's fire department.

The demonstrators had just made their request for a hearing in the employment office, when someone started to shoot. The report of the pistol shot started a general melee. Hand-to-hand fighting began, the police defensive being aided by streams of water from the firemen's hoses.

Men fell with gunshot wounds in their legs and were carried out of further harm's way by their comrades, who tried to commandeer automobiles to take the wounded away. When automobile drivers refused to help, their cars were stoned.

The fighting continued meanwhile, but it was finally checked with the arrival, in answer to calls for aid, of reinforcements of State and Detroit police. . . .

One man declared that the marchers were fired upon by the Ford police before they could present their appeal.

1998
from *Nickel and Dimed*

BY BARBARA EHRENREICH

Barbara Ehrenreich's research for her 2002 best-seller included several months of trying to make a living at low-wage jobs. She found out why so many Americans who

work full-time are poor. Ehrenreich began her odyssey in
the Spring of 1998, moving to Key West and taking a job
as a waitress.

MOSTLY OUT OF laziness, I decide to start my low-wage life in the
town nearest to where I actually live, Key West, Florida, which with
a population of about 25,000 is elbowing its way up to the status of
a genuine city. The downside of familiarity, I soon realize, is that it's
not easy to go from being a consumer, thoughtlessly throwing money
around in exchange for groceries and movies and gas, to being a
worker in the very same place. I am terrified, especially at the beginning, of being recognized by some friendly business owner or erstwhile
neighbor and having to stammer out some explanation of my project.
Happily, though, my fears turn out to be entirely unwarranted:
during a month of poverty and toil, no one recognizes my face or my
name, which goes unnoticed and for the most part unuttered. In this
parallel universe where my father never got out of the mines and I
never got through college, I am "baby," "honey," "blondie," and,
most commonly, "girl."

My first task is to find a place to live. I figure that if I can earn $7
an hour—which, from the want ads, seems doable—I can afford to
spend $500 on rent or maybe, with severe economies, $600 and still
have $400 or $500 left over for food and gas. In the Key West area,
this pretty much confines me to flophouses and trailer homes—like
the one, a pleasing fifteen-minute drive from town, that has no air-
conditioning, no screens, no fans, no television, and, by way of diver-
sion, only the challenge of evading the landlord's Doberman
pinscher. The big problem with this place, though, is the rent, which
at $675 a month is well beyond my reach. All right, Key West is
expensive. But so is New York City, or the Bay Area, or Jackson,

Wyoming, or Telluride, or Boston, or any other place where tourists and the wealthy compete for living space with the people who clean their toilets and fry their hash browns. Still, it is a shock to realize that "trailer trash" has become, for me, a demographic category to aspire to.

So I decide to make the common trade-off between affordability and convenience and go for a $500-a-month "efficiency" thirty miles up a two-lane highway from the employment opportunities of Key West, meaning forty-five minutes if there's no road construction and I don't get caught behind some sun-dazed Canadian tourists. I hate the drive, along a roadside studded with white crosses commemorating the more effective head-on collisions, but it's a sweet little place—a cabin, more or less, set in the swampy backyard of the converted mobile home where my landlord, an affable TV repairman, lives with his bartender girlfriend. Anthropologically speaking, the trailer park would be preferable, but here I have a gleaming white floor and a firm mattress, and the few resident bugs are easily vanquished.

The next piece of business is to comb through the want ads and find a job. I rule out various occupations for one reason or another: hotel front-desk clerk, for example, which to my surprise is regarded as unskilled and pays only $6 or $7 an hour, gets eliminated because it involves standing in one spot for eight hours a day. Waitressing is also something I'd like to avoid, because I remember it leaving me bone-tired when I was eighteen, and I'm decades of varicosities and back pain beyond that now. Telemarketing, one of the first refuges of the suddenly indigent, can be dismissed on grounds of personality. This leaves certain supermarket jobs, such as deli clerk, or house-keeping in the hotels and guest houses, which pays about $7 and, I imagine, is not too different from what I've been doing part-time, in my own home, all my life.

So I put on what I take to be a respectable-looking outfit of ironed Bermuda shorts and scooped-neck T-shirt and set out for a tour of the local hotels and supermarkets. Best Western, Econo Lodge, and HoJo's all let me fill out application forms, and these are, to my relief, mostly interested in whether I am a legal resident of the United States and have committed any felonies. My next stop is Winn-Dixie, the supermarket, which turns out to have a particularly onerous application process, featuring a twenty-minute "interview" by computer since, apparently, no human on the premises is deemed capable of representing the corporate point of view. I am conducted to a large room decorated with posters illustrating how to look "professional" (it helps to be white and, if female, permed) and warning of the slick promises that union organizers might try to tempt me with. The interview is multiple-choice: Do I have anything, such as child care problems, that might make it hard for me to get to work on time? Do I think safety on the job is the responsibility of management? Then, popping up cunningly out of the blue: How many dollars' worth of stolen goods have I purchased in the last year? Would I turn in a fellow employee if I caught him stealing? Finally, "Are you an honest person?"

Apparently I ace the interview, because I am told that all I have to do is show up in some doctor's office tomorrow for a urine test. This seems to be a fairly general rule: if you want to stack Cheerios boxes or vacuum hotel rooms in chemically fascist America, you have to be willing to squat down and pee in front of a health worker (who has no doubt had to do the same thing herself.)[*] The wages Winn-Dixie

---

[*] Eighty-one percent of large employers now require preemployment drug testing, up from 21 percent in 1987. Among all employers, the rate of testing is highest in the South. The drug most likely to be detected—marijuana, which can be detected weeks after use—is also the most innocuous, while heroin and cocaine are generally undetectable three days after use. Alcohol, which clears the body within hours after ingestion, is not tested for.

is offering—$6 and a couple of dimes to start with—are not enough, I decide, to compensate for this indignity.

I lunch at Wendy's, where $4.99 gets you unlimited refills at the Mexican part of the Super-bar, a comforting surfeit of refried beans and cheese sauce. A teenage employee, seeing me studying the want ads, kindly offers me an application form, which I fill out, though here, too, the pay is just $6 and change an hour. Then it's off for a round of the locally owned inns and guest houses in Key West's Old Town, which is where all the serious sightseeing and guzzling goes on, a couple of miles removed from the functional end of the island, where the discount hotels make their homes. At The Palms, let's call it, a bouncy manager actually takes me around to see the rooms and meet the current housekeepers, who, I note with satisfaction, look pretty much like me—faded ex-hippie types in shorts with long hair pulled back in braids. Mostly, though, no one speaks to me or even looks at me except to proffer an application form. At my last stop, a palatial B & B, I wait twenty minutes to meet "Max," only to be told that there are no jobs now but there should be one soon, since "nobody lasts more than a couple weeks."

Three days go by like this and, to my chagrin, no one from the approximately twenty places at which I've applied calls me for an interview. I had been vain enough to worry about coming across as too educated for the jobs I sought, but no one even seems interested in finding out how overqualified I am. Only later will I realize that the want ads are not a reliable measure of the actual jobs available at any particular time. They are, as I should have guessed from Max's comment, the employers' insurance policy against the relentless turnover of the low-wage workforce. Most of the big hotels run ads almost continually, if only to build a supply of applicants to replace the current workers as they drift away or are fired, so finding a job is just a matter of being in the right place at the right time and flexible enough to take whatever is being offered that day. This finally happens to me at one of the big discount chain hotels where I go, as usual, for housekeeping and am sent instead to try out as a waitress at the attached "family restaurant," a dismal spot looking out on a parking garage, which is featuring "Pollish sausage and BBQ sauce" on this 95-degree day. Phillip, the dapper young West Indian who introduces himself as the manager, interviews me with about as much enthusiasm as if he were a clerk processing me for Medicare, the principal questions being what shifts I can work and when I can start. I mutter about being woefully out of practice as a waitress, but he's already on to the uniform: I'm to show up tomorrow wearing black slacks and black shoes; he'll provide the rust-colored polo shirt with "Hearthside," as we'll call the place, embroidered on it, though I might want to wear my own shirt to get to work, ha ha. At the word *tomorrow,* something between fear and indignation rises in my chest. I want to say, "Thank you for your time, sir, but this is just an experiment, you know, not my actual life."

So begins my career at the Hearthside, where for two weeks I work from 2:00 till 10:00 p.m. for $2.43 an hour plus tips.[*] Employees are barred from using the front door, so I enter the first day through the kitchen, where a red-faced man with shoulder-length blond hair is throwing frozen steaks against the wall and yelling, "Fuck this shit!" "That's just Billy," explains Gail, the wiry middle-aged waitress who is assigned to train me. "He's on the rag again"—a condition occasioned, in this instance, by the fact that the cook on the morning

---

[*] According to the Fair Labor Standards Act, employers are not required to pay "tipped employees," such as restaurant servers, more than $2.13 an hour in direct wages. However, if the sum of tips plus $2.13 an hour falls below the minimum wage, or $5.15 an hour, the employer is required to make up the difference. This fact was not mentioned by managers or otherwise publicized at either of the restaurants where I worked.

shift had forgotten to thaw out the steaks. For the next eight hours, I run after the agile Gail, absorbing bits of instruction along with fragments of personal tragedy. All food must be trayed, and the reason she's so tired today is that she woke up in a cold sweat thinking of her boyfriend, who was killed a few months ago in a scuffle in an upstate prison. No refills on lemonade. And the reason he was in prison is that a few DUIs caught up with him, that's all, could have happened to anyone. Carry the creamers to the table in a "monkey bowl," never in your hand. And after he was gone she spent several months living in her truck, peeing in a plastic pee bottle and reading by candlelight at night, but you can't live in a truck in the summer, since you need to have the windows down, which means anything can get in, from mosquitoes on up.

At least Gail puts to rest any fears I had of appearing overqualified. From the first day on, I find that of all the things that I have left behind, such as home and identity, what I miss the most is competence. Not that I have ever felt 100 percent competent in the writing business, where one day's success augurs nothing at all for the next. But in my writing life, I at least have some notion of *procedure:* do the research, make the outline, rough out a draft, etc. As a server, though, I am beset by requests as if by bees: more iced tea here, catsup over there, a to-go box for table 14, and where are the high chairs, anyway? Of the twenty-seven tables, up to six are usually mine at any time, though on slow afternoons or if Gail is off, I sometimes have the whole place to myself. There is the touch-screen computer-ordering system to master, which I suppose is meant to minimize server-cook contacts but in practice requires constant verbal fine-tuning: "That's gravy on the mashed, OK? None on the meatloaf," and so forth. Plus, something I had forgotten in the years since I was eighteen: about a third of a server's job is "side work" invisible to customers—sweeping, scrubbing, slicing, refilling, and restocking.

If it isn't all done, every little bit of it, you're going to face the 6:00 p.m. dinner rush defenseless and probably go down in flames. I screw up dozens of times at the beginning, sustained in my shame entirely by Gail's support—"It's OK, baby, everyone does that sometime"— because, to my total surprise and despite the scientific detachment I am doing my best to maintain, I *care.*

The whole thing would be a lot easier if I could just skate through it like Lily Tomlin in one of her waitress skits, but I was raised by the absurd Booker T. Washingtonian precept that says: If you're going to do something, do it well. In fact, "well" isn't good enough by half. Do it better than anyone has ever done it before. Or so said my father, who must have known what he was talking about because he managed to pull himself, and us with him, up from the mile-deep copper mines of Butte to the leafy suburbs of the Northeast, ascending from boiler-makers to martinis before booze beat out ambition. As in most endeavors I have encountered in my life, "doing it better than anyone" is not a reasonable goal. Still, when I wake up at 4 a.m. in my own cold sweat, I am not thinking about the writing deadlines I'm neglecting; I'm thinking of the table where I screwed up the order and one of the kids didn't get his kiddie meal until the rest of the family had moved on to their Key lime pies. That's the other powerful motivation—the customers, or "patients," as I can't help thinking of them on account of the mysterious vulnerability that seems to have left them temporarily unable to feed themselves. After a few days at Hearthside, I feel the service ethic kick in like a shot of oxytocin, the nurturance hormone. The plurality of my customers are hardworking locals—truck drivers, construction workers, even housekeepers from the attached hotel—and I want them to have the closest to a "fine dining" experience that the grubby circumstances will allow. No "you guys" for me; everyone over twelve is "sir" or "ma'am." I ply them with iced tea and coffee refills; I return, midmeal, to inquire how everything is; I doll up their salads with chopped raw mushrooms, summer squash slices, or whatever bits of produce I can find that have survived their sojourn in the cold storage room mold-free.

There is Benny, for example, a short, tight-muscled sewer repairman who cannot even think of eating until he has absorbed a half hour of air-conditioning and ice water. We chat about hyperthermia and electrolytes until he is ready to order some finicky combination like soup of the day, garden salad, and a side of grits. There are the German tourists who are so touched by my pidgin *"Wilkommen"* and *"Ist alles gut?"* that they actually tip. (Europeans, no doubt spoiled by their trade union-ridden, high-wage welfare states, generally do not know that they are supposed to tip. Some restaurants, the Hearthside included, allow servers to "grat" their foreign customers, or add a tip to the bill. Since this amount is added before the customers have a chance to tip or not tip, the practice amounts to an automatic penalty for imperfect English.) There are the two dirt-smudged lesbians, just off from their shift, who are impressed enough by my suave handling of the fly in the piña colada that they take the time to praise me to Stu, the assistant manager. There's Sam, the kindly retired cop who has to plug up his tracheotomy hole with one finger in order to force the cigarette smoke into his lungs.

Sometimes I play with the fantasy that I am a princess who, in penance for some tiny transgression, has undertaken to feed each of her subjects by hand. But the nonprincesses working with me are just as indulgent, even when this means flouting management rules—as to, for example, the number of croutons that can go on a salad (six). "Put on all you want," Gail whispers, "as long as Stu isn't looking." She dips into her own tip money to buy biscuits and gravy for an out-of-work mechanic who's used up all his money on dental surgery, inspiring me to pick up the tab for his pie and milk. Maybe the same high levels of agape can be found throughout the "hospitality industry." I remember the poster decorating one of the apartments I looked at, which said, "If you seek happiness for yourself you will never find it. Only when you seek happiness for others will it come to you," or words to that effect—an odd sentiment, it seemed to me at the time, to find in the dank one-room basement apartment of a bellhop at the Best Western. At Hearthside, we utilize whatever bits of autonomy we have to ply our customers with the illicit calories that signal our love. It is our job as servers to assemble the salads and desserts, pour the dressings, and squirt the whipped cream. We also control the number of butter pats our customers get and the amount of sour cream on their baked potatoes. So if you wonder why Americans are so obese, consider the fact that waitresses both express their humanity and earn their tips through the covert distribution of fats.

Ten days into it, this is beginning to look like a livable lifestyle. I like Gail, who is "looking at fifty," agewise, but moves so fast she can alight in one place and then another without apparently being anywhere between. I clown around with Lionel, the teenage Haitian busboy, though we don't have much vocabulary in common, and loiter near the main sink to listen to the older Haitian dishwashers' musical Creole, which sounds, in their rich bass voices, like French on testosterone. I bond with Timmy, the fourteen-year-old white kid who buses at night, by telling him I don't like people putting their baby seats right on the tables: it makes the baby look too much like a side dish. He snickers delightedly and in return, on a slow night, starts telling me the plots of all the *Jaws* movies (which are perennial favorites in the shark-ridden Keys): "She looks around, and the water-skier isn't there anymore, then SNAP! The whole boat goes . . ."

I especially like Joan, the svelte fortyish hostess, who turns out to be a militant feminist, pulling me aside one day to explain that "men run everything—we don't have a chance unless we stick together." Accordingly, she backs me up when I get overpowered on the floor, and in return I give her a chunk of my tips or stand guard while she sneaks off for an unauthorized cigarette break. We all admire her for standing up to Billy and telling him, after some of his usual nastiness about the female server class, to "shut the fuck up." I even warm up to Billy when, on a slow night and to make up for a particularly unwarranted attack on my abilities, or so I imagine, he tells me about his glory days as a young man at "coronary school" in Brooklyn, where he dated a knockout Puerto Rican chick—or do you say "culinary"?

I finish up every night at 10:00 or 10:30, depending on how much side work I've been able to get done during the shift, and cruise home to the tapes I snatched at random when I left my real home—Marianne Faithfull, Tracy Chapman, Enigma, King Sunny Ade, Violent Femmes—just drained enough for the music to set my cranium resonating, but hardly dead. Midnight snack is Wheat Thins and Monterey Jack, accompanied by cheap white wine on ice and whatever AMC has to offer. To bed by 1:30 or 2:00, up at 9:00 or 10:00, read for an hour while my uniform whirls around in the land-lord's washing machine, and then it's another eight hours spent fol-lowing Mao's central instruction, as laid out in the Little Red Book, which was: Serve the people.

I could drift along like this, in some dreamy proletarian idyll, except for two things. One is management. If I have kept this subject to the margins so far it is because I still flinch to think that I spent all those weeks under the surveillance of men (and later women) whose job it was to monitor my behavior for signs of sloth, theft, drug abuse, or worse. Not that managers and especially "assistant man-agers" in low-wage settings like this are exactly the class enemy.

Mostly, in the restaurant business, they are former cooks still capable of pinch-hitting in the kitchen, just as in hotels they are likely to be former clerks, and paid a salary of only about $400 a week. But everyone knows they have crossed over to the other side, which is, crudely put, corporate as opposed to human. Cooks want to prepare tasty meals, servers want to serve them graciously, but managers are there for only one reason—to make sure that money is made for some theoretical entity, the corporation, which exists far away in Chicago or New York, if a corporation can be said to have a physical existence at all. Reflecting on her career, Gail tells me ruefully that she swore, years ago, never to work for a corporation again. "They don't cut you no slack. You give and you give and they take."

Managers can sit—for hours at a time if they want—but it's their job to see that no one else ever does, even when there's nothing to do, and this is why, for servers, slow times can be as exhausting as rushes. You start dragging out each little chore because if the manager on duty catches you in an idle moment he will give you something far nastier to do. So I wipe, I clean, I consolidate catsup bottles and recheck the cheesecake supply, even tour the tables to make sure the customer evaluation forms are all standing perkily in their places—wondering all the time how many calories I burn in these strictly theatrical exercises. In desperation, I even take the desserts out of their glass display case and freshen them up with whipped cream and bright new maraschino cherries; anything to look busy. When, on a particularly dead afternoon, Stu finds me glancing at a *USA Today* a customer has left behind, he assigns me to vacuum the entire floor with the broken vacuum cleaner, which has a handle only two feet long, and the only way to do that without incurring orthopedic damage is to proceed from spot to spot on your knees.

On my first Friday at Hearthside there is a "mandatory meeting for all restaurant employees," which I attend, eager for insight into our overall marketing strategy and the niche (your basic Ohio cuisine with a tropical twist?) we aim to inhabit. But there is no "we" at this meeting. Phillip, our top manager except for an occasional "consultant" sent out by corporate headquarters, opens it with a sneer: "The break room—it's disgusting. Butts in the ashtrays, newspapers lying around, crumbs." This windowless little room, which also houses the time clock for the entire hotel, is where we stash our bags and civilian clothes and take our half-hour meal breaks. But a break room is not a right, he tells us, it can be taken away. We should also know that the lockers in the break room and whatever is in them can be searched at any time. Then comes gossip; there has been gossip; gossip (which seems to mean employees talking among themselves) must stop. Off-duty employees are henceforth barred from eating at the restaurant, because "other servers gather around them and gossip." When Phillip has exhausted his agenda of rebukes, Joan complains about the condition of the ladies' room and I throw in my two bits about the vacuum cleaner. But I don't see any backup coming from my fellow servers, each of whom has slipped into her own personal funk; Gail, my role model, stares sorrowfully at a point six inches from her nose. The meeting ends when Andy, one of the cooks, gets up, muttering about breaking up his day off for this almighty bullshit.

Just four days later we are suddenly summoned into the kitchen at 3:30 p.m., even though there are live tables on the floor. We all— about ten of us—stand around Phillip, who announces grimly that there has been a report of some "drug activity" on the night shift and that, as a result, we are now to be a "drug-free" workplace, meaning that all new hires will be tested and possibly also current employees on a random basis. I am glad that this part of the kitchen is so dark because I find myself blushing as hard as if I had been caught toking up in the ladies' room myself: I haven't been treated this way—lined up in the corridor, threatened with locker searches, peppered with carelessly aimed accusations—since at least junior high school. Back on the floor, Joan cracks, "Next they'll be telling us we can't have *sex* on the job." When I ask Stu what happened to inspire the crackdown, he just mutters about "management decisions" and takes the opportunity to upbraid Gail and me for being too generous with the rolls. From now on there's to be only one per customer and it goes out with the dinner, not with the salad. He's also been riding the cooks, prompting Andy to come out of the kitchen and observe—with the serenity of a man whose customary implement is a butcher knife—that "Stu has a death wish today."

Later in the evening, the gossip crystallizes around the theory that Stu is himself the drug culprit, that he uses the restaurant phone to order up marijuana and sends one of the late servers out to fetch it for him. The server was caught and she may have ratted out Stu, at least enough to cast some suspicion on him, thus accounting for his pissy behavior. Who knows? Personally, I'm ready to believe anything bad about Stu, who serves no evident function and presumes too much on our common ethnicity, sidling up to me one night to engage in a little nativism directed at the Haitian immigrants: "I feel like I'm the foreigner here. They're taking over the country." Still later that evening, the drug in question escalates to crack. Lionel, the busboy, entertains us for the rest of the shift by standing just behind Stu's back and sucking deliriously on an imaginary joint or maybe a pipe.

The other problem, in addition to the less-than-nurturing management style, is that this job shows no sign of being financially viable. You might imagine, from a comfortable distance, that people who live, year in and year out, on $6 to $10 an hour have discovered some survival stratagems unknown to the middle class. But no. It's not hard to get my coworkers talking about their living situations, because housing, in almost every case, is the principal source of disruption in their lives, the first thing they fill you in on when they arrive for their shifts. After a week, I have compiled the following survey:

Gail is sharing a room in a well-known downtown flophouse for $250 a week. Her roommate, a male friend, has begun hitting on her, driving her nuts, but the rent would be impossible alone.

Claude, the Haitian cook, is desperate to get out of the two-room apartment he shares with his girlfriend and two other, unrelated people. As far as I can determine, the other Haitian men live in similarly crowded situations.

Annette, a twenty-year-old server who is six months pregnant and abandoned by her boyfriend, lives with her mother, a postal clerk.

Marianne, who is a breakfast server, and her boyfriend are paying $170 a week for a one-person trailer.

Billy, who at $10 an hour is the wealthiest of us, lives in the trailer he owns, paying only the $400-a-month lot fee.

The other white cook, Andy, lives on his dry-docked boat, which, as far as I can tell from his loving descriptions, can't be more than twenty feet long. He offers to take me out on it once it's repaired, but the offer comes with inquiries as to my marital status, so I do not follow up on it.

Tina, another server, and her husband are paying $60 a night for a room in the Days Inn. This is because they have no car and the Days Inn is in walking distance of the Hearthside. When Marianne is tossed out of her trailer for subletting (which is against trailer park rules), she leaves her boyfriend and moves in with Tina and her husband.

Joan, who had fooled me with her numerous and tasteful outfits (hostesses wear their own clothes), lives in a van parked behind a shopping center at night and showers in Tina's motel room. The clothes are from thrift shops.[*]

It strikes me, in my middle-class solipsism, that there is gross improvidence in some of these arrangements. When Gail and I are wrapping silverware in napkins—the only task for which we are permitted to sit—she tells me she is thinking of escaping from her roommate by moving into the Days Inn herself. I am astounded: how she can even think of paying $40 to $60 a day? But if I was afraid of sounding like a social worker, I have come out just sounding like a fool. She squints at me in disbelief: "And where am I supposed to get a month's rent and a month's deposit for an apartment?" I'd been feeling pretty smug about my $500 efficiency, but of course it was made possible only by the $1,300 I had allotted myself for start-up costs when I began my low-wage life: $1,000 for the first month's rent and deposit, $100 for initial groceries and cash in my pocket, $200 stuffed away for emergencies. In poverty, as in certain propositions in physics, starting conditions are everything.

There are no secret economies that nourish the poor; on the contrary, there are a host of special costs. If you can't put up the two months' rent you need to secure an apartment, you end up paying through the nose for a room by the week. If you have only a room, with a hot plate at best, you can't save by cooking up huge lentil stews that can be frozen for the week ahead. You eat fast food or the hot dogs and Styrofoam cups of soup that can be microwaved in a

---

[*] I could find no statistics on the number of employed people living in cars or vans, but according to a 1997 report of the National Coalition for the Homeless, "Myths and Facts about Homelessness," nearly one-fifth of all homeless people (in twenty-nine cities across the nation) are employed in full- or part-time jobs.

convenience store. If you have no money for health insurance—and the Hearthside's niggardly plan kicks in only after three months—you go without routine care or prescription drugs and end up paying the price. Gail, for example, was doing fine, healthwise anyway, until she ran out of money for estrogen pills. She is supposed to be on the company health plan by now, but they claim to have lost her application form and to be beginning the paperwork all over again. So she spends $9 a pop for pills to control the migraines she wouldn't have, she insists, if her estrogen supplements were covered. Similarly, Marianne's boyfriend lost his job as a roofer because he missed so much time after getting a cut on his foot for which he couldn't afford the prescribed antibiotic.

My own situation, when I sit down to assess it after two weeks of work, would not be much better if this were my actual life. The seductive thing about waitressing is that you don't have to wait for payday to feel a few bills in your pocket, and my tips usually cover meals and gas, plus something left over to stuff into the kitchen drawer I use as a bank. But as the tourist business slows in the summer heat, I sometimes leave work with only $20 in tips (the gross is higher, but servers share about 15 percent of their tips with the busboys and bartenders). With wages included, this amounts to about the minimum wage of $5.15 an hour. The sum in the drawer is piling up but at the present rate of accumulation will be more than $100 short of my rent when the end of the month comes around. Nor can I see any expenses to cut. True, I haven't gone the lentil stew route yet, but that's because I don't have a large cooking pot. potholders, or a ladle to stir with (which would cost a total of about $30 at Kmart, somewhat less at a thrift store), not to mention onions, carrots, and the indispensable bay leaf. I do make my lunch almost every day—usually some slow-burning, high-protein combo like frozen chicken patties with melted cheese on top and canned pinto beans on the side. Dinner is at the Hearthside, which offers its employees a choice of BLT, fish sandwich, or hamburger for only $2. The burger lasts longest, especially if it's heaped with gut-puckering jalapenos, but by midnight my stomach is growling again.

So unless I want to start using my car as a residence, I have to find a second or an alternative job.

2001

Can My Mommy Have Her Paycheck?

BY KATHARINE MIESZKOWSKI

Katharine Mieszkowski interviewed filmmakers Deborah Kaufman and Alan Snitow about their 2001 documentary "Secrets of Silicon Valley." The film describes the poor treatment of workers in Silicon Valley's technology industry. This interview originally appeared on salon.com.

How did you decide to do a film about Silicon Valley?

ALAN SNITOW: Living here in the Bay Area, we've been subjected for years to unrelenting hype about technology and the Internet being the Second Coming—all people will benefit, and any individual can become a billionaire with hard work and a good idea.

DEBORAH KAUFMAN: The media here has been a part of this hype machine. And it's really unfortunate that the criticism is only beginning with the NASDAQ fall. But maybe that's an opportunity to look with more clearheadedness at what's happened.

Silicon Valley really hasn't been treated in all of its nuance and complexity. There are a lot of stereotypes about geeks, but there is zero representation of everybody else who lives there. There is a rich multicultural community, immigrants, all kinds of people living in San Jose and Santa Clara, but you never hear about them.

What's the significance of the industry myth that there is no physical production in Silicon Valley, that it's all about bits and bytes, ones and zeroes?

D.K.: It's part of the entire worldview of flexibility of the new economy. It's about not allowing the reality of manufacturing and assembly and exploited workers to come out to the public. I think that they [the companies] want to cover it up. I didn't really think about who made my computer or printer before we started this film. And now I can't look at a cellphone or any gadget without thinking that human hands made this.

A.S.: There is an active silencing in the industry. People who are working on these assembly lines are not a part of American democracy. They have no freedom of speech. For them to say that their conditions are intolerable is to invite immediate termination and economic blackballing.

The best metaphor that we've heard about it is that it's like feudalism. The castle is a brand-name company like Hewlett-Packard. Inside the castle, you get stock options. You get paid well. You get health benefits. And then outside the walls of the castle are the temporary workers and the manufacturing employees. Those people are exposed to the elements, to the marauding hordes, the vandals. That is the nature of our economic organization now. That is what is happening in this country and around the world.

And the moat around the castle is the Manpower temporary agency. So a company like Hewlett-Packard can say: We're not employing these people; it's the subcontractor, or it's the temporary agency.

The temp economy just keeps growing because it's cheaper. You don't have to pay health benefits. No one has job security. Jobs can be eliminated on a minute's notice. If you create an economy that has that kind of "flexibility," then you save a lot of money and that money goes into annual reports, which increases your stock price.

Did you try to talk to Hewlett-Packard? Have you had any reaction from the company?

D.K.: We requested an interview with Carly Fiorina—she couldn't do it for whatever reason. In the end, we feel that Hewlett-Packard is a full character in the film with all of its contradictions showing.

A.S.: Hewlett-Packard has refused to come on the air on TV to be interviewed with us about the film. [Officials there] said they hadn't seen the film, so they don't know whether we "have our facts right."

D.K.: But the people from the Packard Foundation, which is separate from HP, have seen it and liked it, and have requested a copy.

How did you get inside the factories?

A.S.: When we asked for the interview with Carly Fiorina, we also asked to get into the factory where Raj worked. [A central character in the film, labor activist Raj Jayadev, is a temp worker organizing on the front lines.] They said: "We don't have any factories in San Jose."

D.K.: The factory where Raj worked was in San Jose.

A.S.: This is the secret of Silicon Valley. Cisco doesn't make routers. Hewlett-Packard doesn't make computers or printers.

We called the HP subcontractor, a company called Manufacturing Services Limited, and said: "Can we get into the factory?"

And [company representatives] said this factory is on Hewlett-Packard land, it's a Hewlett-Packard warehouse, it makes Hewlett-Packard printers, it has Hewlett-Packard security—but Hewlett-Packard won't allow us to put out a press release saying that we're running the factory for them.

So they said, "There's no way."

How did you get the footage you used?

A.S.: Ultimately, we used stock footage, Hewlett-Packard video news releases. Every news outlet in the country has the exact same footage. There are no international security secrets in these factories. There is nothing that industrial espionage is going to uncover. There is no possible liability of a camera crew going in there.

What they're doing is [ensuring] that the media and the public have no access to these people, and these people have no access to the media and the public.

Is HP the only company doing this?

D.K.: We wanted to have people in the film who are sympathetic, socially conscious, who have values. Carly Fiorina is known to have social values, as is Hewlett-Packard, with "the HP way."

The whole idea was to show how the system is bad. HP is meant to be symbolic of the whole system—we're not trying to do, "Now,

now, HP." The film is really meant as a larger exploration of the values of the new economy.

What was the most surprising thing you learned in the process of making the film?

A.S.: We found this industry to be completely committed to the idea that the market can solve all human problems much better than the government can.

D.K.: The anti-government animus is profound. What's very disturbing is the fact that you've got these levels of society living so close, side by side, and they're not speaking to each other. And you have tens of thousands of working people left out of the conversation about the future of the place they live. The development of the valley is going at breakneck speed, without an opportunity for people to participate in the discussion. It's being left to the high rollers.

We're creating two societies, and the middle is getting washed out. It's the haves and the have-nots, and it's really disturbing.

A.S.: Also, there's the intensity of the resistance in the industry to any kind of union organizing—it's bitter.

D.K.: Because temps are the backbone of the economy; the temp economy is the backbone of high tech. It has to be. That's what people mean by "speed" and "flexibility"—they mean temps. They can lay them off the next day if they need to. That is what they mean; it's a euphemism.

Do you think that there's any hope for organizing these temp workers in Silicon Valley?

D.K.: I think it's going to be a long struggle, but it's going to have to happen, because the industry is not capable of self-regulating. The idea that they can have their own codes of conduct and self-regulate is another one of the myths.

A.S.: Each big, huge company points to the next huge company, saying: "We have to keep up with them." "The HP way" is dead because they're now becoming a flexible company just like all the other companies. "We have to move fast. We have to start laying off people." And that wasn't the HP way. The HP way was to not subcontract. It was to provide health benefits to people on the assembly lines, not just to the highest-paid software designers.

There were people whom Raj met in the factory who 10 years ago were earning twice as much money, with health benefits, working for HP as they're earning today.

D.K.: Originally, HP was one of the great companies to work for. But this is HP in the 21st century; it's not the same.

What are some of the ways that workers have fought back?
A.S.: One of the stories that Raj told us that we loved the most is that apparently when the workers weren't getting paid properly, they would have their children call Manpower and say: "My mommy is not being paid."

D.K.: "My mommy can't buy the groceries."

A.S.: This is the mouth that is not being fed. Apparently the Manpower management was very pissed off. "How can you have these people calling us? We work hard too."

D.K.: First, [Manpower officials] said it was an error—a computer error or something—and then they got angry.

How did you choose your subjects?

A.S.: We didn't want to show the downtrodden worker who is just a victim, because I think there is a trend in documentaries to make people cry and to show the most victims that you can, to just constantly look for the worst off, the most screwed over, the massacred. We were looking for characters who are actors, not victims, to see what kind of choices they make—moral choices and other choices—against the backdrop of history.

D.K.: When we were talking about our film, at a certain point people were saying: "Oh yeah, show Larry Ellison's house and then some really horrible little hut." But we didn't want to do that. We really wanted to show people in the middle who are trying to cope with social issues. The intent was to show people who are organizers and activists, young people who care. There is also a kind of stereotype that young people don't care.

[Escobar and Jayadev, the two Silicon Valley organizers featured in the film] are not against technology; in fact they love technology, both of them. They had an optimism that had very distinct strategies for resisting the wrongs that are taking place in the valley.

D.S.: What was really important was to show that you could be an activist or in community service and succeed.

civil rights

The Negro Artist and the Racial Mountain

BY LANGSTON HUGHES

Langston Hughes' writing helped define the 1920s literary
revival known as the Harlem Renaissance. This piece originally appeared in *The Nation*.

ONE OF THE most promising of the young Negro poets said to me
once, "I want to be a poet—not a Negro poet," meaning, I believe,
"I want to write like a white poet"; meaning subconsciously, "I would
like to be a white poet"; meaning behind that, "I would like to be
white." And I was sorry the young man said that, for no great poet
has ever been afraid of being himself. And I doubted then that, with
his desire to run away spiritually from his race, this boy would ever
be a great poet. But this is the mountain standing in the way of any
true Negro art in America—this urge within the race toward white-
ness, the desire to pour racial individuality into the mold of American standardization, and to be as little Negro and as much American
as possible.

But let us look at the immediate background of this young poet.
His family is of what I suppose one would call the Negro middle
class: people who are by no means rich yet never uncomfortable nor
hungry—smug, contented, respectable folk, members of the Baptist
church. The father goes to work every morning. He is a chief
steward at a large white club. The mother sometimes does fancy
sewing or supervises parties for the rich families of the town. The
children go to a mixed school. In the home they read white papers

and magazines. And the mother often says "Don't be like niggers" when the children are bad. A frequent phrase from the father is, "Look how well a white man does things." And so the word white comes, to be unconsciously a symbol of all the virtues. It holds for the children beauty, morality, and money. The whisper of "I want to be white" runs silently through their minds. This young poet's home is, I believe, a fairly typical home of the colored middle class. One sees immediately how difficult it would be for an artist born in such a home to interest himself in interpreting the beauty of his own people. He is never taught to see that beauty. He is taught rather not to see it, or if he does, to be ashamed of it when it is not according to Caucasian patterns.

For racial culture the home of a self-styled "high-class" Negro has nothing better to offer. Instead there will perhaps be more aping of things white than in a less cultured or less wealthy home. The father is perhaps a doctor, lawyer, landowner, or politician. The mother may be a social worker, or a teacher, or she may do nothing and have a maid. Father is often dark but he has usually married the lightest woman he could find. The family attend a fashionable church where few really colored faces are to be found. And they themselves draw a color line. In the North they go to white theaters and white movies. And in the South they have at least two cars and a house "like white folks." Nordic manners, Nordic faces, Nordic hair, Nordic art (if any), and an Episcopal heaven. A very high mountain indeed for the would-be racial artist to climb in order to discover himself and his people.

But then there are the low-down folks, the so-called common element, and they are the majority—may the Lord be praised. The people who have their nip of gin on Saturday nights and are not too important to themselves or the community, or too well fed, or too learned to watch the lazy world go round. They live on Seventh Street in Washington or State Street in Chicago and they do not particularly care whether they are like white folks or anybody else. Their joy runs, bang! into ecstasy. Their religion soars to a shout. Work maybe a little today, rest a little tomorrow. Play awhile. Sing awhile. O, let's dance! These common people are not afraid of spirituals, as for a long time their more intellectual brethren were, and jazz is their child. They furnish a wealth of colorful, distinctive material for any artist because they still hold their own individuality in the face of American standardizations. And perhaps these common people will give to the world its truly great Negro artist, the one who is not afraid to be himself. Whereas the better-class Negro would tell the artist what to do, the people at least let him alone when he does appear. And they are not ashamed of him—if they know he exists at all. And they accept what beauty is their own without question.

Certainly there is, for the American Negro artist who can escape the restrictions the more advanced among his own group would put upon him, a great field of unused material ready for his art. Without going outside his race, and even among the better classes with their "white" culture and conscious American manners, but still Negro enough to be different, there is sufficient matter to furnish a black artist with a lifetime of creative work. And when he chooses to touch on the relations between Negroes and whites in this country with their innumerable overtones and undertones, surely, and especially for literature and the drama, there is an inexhaustible supply of themes at hand. To these the Negro artist can give his racial individuality, his heritage of rhythm and warmth, and his incongruous humor that often, as in the Blues, becomes ironic laughter mixed with tears. But let us look again at the mountain.

A prominent Negro clubwoman in Philadelphia paid eleven dollars to hear Raquel Meller sing Andalusian popular songs. But she told me a few weeks before she would not think of going to hear "that woman," Clara Smith, a great black artist, sing Negro folksongs. And many an upper-class Negro church, even now, would not dream of employing a spiritual in its services. The drab melodies in white folks' hymnbooks are much to be preferred. "We want to worship the Lord correctly and quietly. We don't believe in 'shouting.' Let's be dull like the Nordics," they say, in effect.

The road for the serious black artist, then, who would produce a racial art is most certainly rocky and the mountain is high. Until recently he received almost no encouragement for his work from either white or colored people. The fine novel of Chestnutt go out of print with neither race noticing their passing. The quaint charm and humor of Dunbar's dialect verse brought to him, in his day, largely the same kind of encouragement one would give a sideshow freak (A colored man writing poetry! How odd!) or a clown (How amusing!).

The present vogue in things Negro, although it may do as much harm as good for the budding colored artist, has at least done this: it has brought him forcibly to the attention of his own people among whom for so long, unless the other race had noticed him beforehand, he was a prophet with little honor. I understand that Charles Gilpin acted for years in Negro theaters without any special acclaim from his own, but when Broadway gave him eight curtain calls, Negroes, too, began to beat a tin pan in his honor. I know a young colored writer, a manual worker by day, who had been writing well for the colored magazines for some years, but it was not until he recently broke into the white publications and his first book was accepted by a prominent New York publisher that the "best" Negroes in his city took the trouble to discover that he lived there. Then almost immediately they decided to give a grand dinner for him. But the society ladies were careful to whisper to his mother that perhaps she'd better not come. They were not sure she would have an evening gown.

The Negro artist works against an undertow of sharp criticism and misunderstanding from his own group and unintentional bribes from the whites. "O, be respectable, write about nice people, show how good we are," say the Negroes. "Be stereotyped, don't go too far, don't shatter our illusions about you, don't amuse us too seriously. We will pay you," say the whites. Both would have told Jean Toomer not to write *Cane*. The colored people did not praise it. The white people did not buy it. Most of the colored people who did read *Cane* hate it. They are afraid of it. Although the critics gave it good reviews the public remained indifferent. Yet (excepting the work of DuBois) *Cane* contains the finest prose written by a Negro in America. And like the singing of Robeson, it is truly racial.

But in spite of the Nordicized Negro intelligentsia and the desires of some white editors we have an honest American Negro literature already with us. Now I await the rise of the Negro theater. Our folk music, having achieved world-wide fame, offers itself to the genius of the great individual American Negro composer who is to come. And within the next decade I expect to see the work of a growing school of colored artists who paint and model the beauty of dark faces and create with new technique the expressions of their own soul-world. And the Negro dancers who will dance like flame and the singers who will continue to carry our songs to all who listen—they will be with us in even greater numbers tomorrow.

Most of my own poems are racial in theme and treatment, derived from the life I know. In many of them I try to grasp and hold some of the meanings and rhythms of jazz. I am sincere as I know how to be in these poems and yet after every reading I answer questions like these from my own people: Do you think Negroes should always write about Negroes? I wish you wouldn't read some of your poems to white folks. How do you find anything interesting in a place like a cabaret? Why do you write about black people? You aren't black. What makes you do so many jazz poems?

But jazz to me is one of the inherent expressions of Negro life in America: the eternal tom-tom beating in the Negro soul—the tom-tom of revolt against weariness in a white world, a world of subway trains, and work, work, work; the tom-tom of joy and laughter, and pain swallowed in a smile. Yet the Philadelphia clubwoman is ashamed to say that her race created it and she does not like me to write about it. The old subconscious "white is best" runs through her mind. Years of study under white teachers, a life-time of white books, pictures, and papers, and white manners, morals, and Puritan standards made her dislike the spirituals. And now she turns up her nose at jazz and all its manifestations—likewise almost everything else distinctly racial. She doesn't care for the Winold Reiss portraits of Negroes because they are "too Negro." She does not want a true picture of herself from anybody. She wants the artist to flatter her, to make the white world believe that all Negroes are as smug and as near white in soul as she wants to be. But, to my mind, it is the duty of the younger Negro artist, if he accepts any duties at all from outsiders, to change through the force of his art that old whispering "I want to be white," hidden in the aspirations of his people, to "Why should I want to be white? I am a Negro—and beautiful!"

So I am ashamed for the black poet who says, "I want to be a poet, not a Negro poet," as though his own racial world were not as interesting as any other world. I am ashamed, too, for the colored artist who runs from the painting of Negro faces to the painting of sunsets after the manner of the academicians because he fears the strange un-white-ness of his own features. An artist must be free to choose what he does, certainly, but he must also never be afraid to do what he might choose.

Let the blare of Negro jazz bands and the bellowing voice of Bessie Smith singing Blues penetrate the closed ears of the colored near-intellectuals until they listen and perhaps understand. Let Paul Robeson singing "Water Boy," and Rudolph Fisher writing about the streets of Harlem, and Jean Toomer holding the heart of Georgia in his hands, and Aaron Douglas drawing strange black fantasies cause the smug Negro middle class to turn from their white, respectable, ordinary books and papers to catch a glimmer of their own beauty.

We younger Negro artists who create now intend to express our individual dark-skinned selves without fear or shame. If white people are pleased we are glad. If they are not, it doesn't matter. We know we are beautifuL And ugly too. The tom-tom cries and the tom-tom laughs. If colored people are pleased we are glad. If they are not, their displeasure doesn't matter either. We build our temples for tomorrow, strong as we know how, and we stand on top of the mountain, free within ourselves.

1942
Non-Violence vs. Jim Crow
By Bayard Rustin

Bayard Rustin during the early '40s organized local nonviolent direct-action groups that later formed the Congress of Racial Equality (CORE). He went on to play a crucial role in many achievements of the civil rights movement, including the 1963 March on Washington. This article originally appeared in *Fellowship.*

Recently I was planning to go from Louisville to Nashville by bus. I bought my ticket, boarded the bus and, instead of going to the back, sat down in the second seat back. The driver saw me, got up, and came back to me.

"Hey you, you're supposed to sit in the back seat."

"Why?"

"Because that's the law. Niggers ride in back."

I said, "My friend, I believe that is an unjust law. If I were to sit in back I would be condoning injustice."

Angry, but not knowing what to do, he got out and went into the station, but soon came out again, got into his seat, and started off.

This routine was gone through at each stop, but each time nothing came of it. Finally the driver, in desperation, must have phoned ahead, for about thirteen miles north of Nashville I heard sirens approaching. The bus came to an abrupt stop, and a police car and two motorcycles drew up beside us with a flourish. Four policemen got into the bus, consulted shortly with the driver, and came to my seat.

"Get up, you ——nigger!"

"Why?" I asked.

"Get up, you black —— !"

"I believe that I have a right to sit here," I said quietly. "If I sit in the back of the bus I am depriving that child—" I pointed to a little white child of five or six—"of the knowledge that there is injustice here, which I believe it is his right to know. It is my sincere conviction that the power of love in the world is the greatest power existing. If you have a greater power, my friend, you may move me."

How much they understood of what I was trying to tell them I do not know. By this time they were impatient and angry. As I would not move they began to beat me about the head and shoulders, and I shortly found myself knocked to the floor. Then they dragged me out of the bus and continued to kick and beat me.

Knowing that if I tried to get up or protect myself in the first heat of their anger they would construe it as an attempt to resist and beat me down again, I forced myself to be still and wait for their kicks, one after another. Then I stood up, spreading out my arms parallel to the ground, and said, "There is no need to beat me. I am not resisting you."

At this three white men, obviously Southerners by their speech, got out of the bus and remonstrated with the police. Indeed, as one of the policemen raised his club to strike me, one of them, a little fellow, caught hold of it and said, "Don't you do that!" A second policeman raised his club to strike the little man, and I stepped between them, facing the man, and said, "Thank you, but there is no need to do that. I do not wish to fight. I am protected well."

An elderly gentleman, well-dressed and also a Southerner, asked the police where they were taking me.

They said "Nashville."

"Don't worry, son," he said to me. "I'll be there to see that you get justice."

I was put into the back seat of the police car, between two policemen. Two others sat in front. During the thirteen-mile ride to town they called me every conceivable bad name and said anything they could think of to incite me to violence. I found that I was shaking with nervous strain, and to give myself something to do, I took out a piece of paper and a pencil, and began to write from memory a chapter from one of Paul's letters.

When I had written a few sentences the man on my right said, "What're you writing?" and snatched the paper from my hand. He read it, then crumpled it into a ball and pushed it in my face. The man on the other side gave me a kick.

A moment later I happened to catch the eye of the young policeman in the front seat. He looked away quickly, and I took a renewed courage from the realization that he could not meet my eyes because he was aware of the injustice being done. I began to write again, and after a moment I leaned forward and touched him on the shoulder. "My friend," I said, "how do you spell 'difference'?"

He spelled it for me—incorrectly—and I wrote it correctly and went on.

When we reached Nashville a number of policemen were lined up on both sides of the hallway down which I had to pass on my way to the captain's office. They tossed me from one to another like a volley-ball. By the time I reached the office the lining of my best coat was torn, and I was considerably rumpled. I straightened myself as best I could and went in. They had my bag, and went through it and my papers, finding much of interest, especially in the *Christian Century* and *Fellowship*.

Finally the captain said, "Come here, nigger."

I walked directly to him. "What can I do for you?" I asked.

"Nigger," he said menacingly, "you're supposed to be scared when you come in here!"

"I am fortified by truth, justice and Christ," I said. "There is no need for me to fear."

He was flabbergasted and, for a time, completely at a loss for words. Finally he said to another officer, "I believe the nigger's crazy!"

They sent me into another room and went into consultation. The wait was long, but after an hour and a half they came for me and I was taken for another ride, across town. At the courthouse, I was taken down the hall to the office of the Assistant District Attorney, Mr. Ben West. As I got to the door I heard a voice, "Say, you colored fellow, hey!" I looked around and saw the elderly gentleman who had been on the bus.

"I'm here to see that you get justice," he said.

The Assistant District Attorney questioned me about my life, the *Christian Century*, the F.O.R., pacifism, and the war, for half an hour. Then he asked the police to tell their side of what had happened. They did, stretching the truth a good deal in spots and including several lies for seasoning. Mr. West then asked me to tell my side.

"Gladly," I said, "and I want *you*," turning to the young policeman who had sat in the front seat, "to follow what I say, and stop me if I deviate from the truth in the least."

Holding his eyes with mine, I told the story exactly as it had happened, stopping often to say "Is that right?" or "Isn't that what happened?" to the young policeman. During the whole time he never once interrupted me, and when I was through I said, "Did I tell the truth just as it happened?" and he said, "Well——"

Then Mr. West dismissed me, and I was sent to wait alone in a dark room. After an hour, Mr. West came in and said, very kindly, "you may go, *Mister* Rustin."

I left the courthouse, believing all the more strongly in the nonviolent approach, for I am certain that I was addressed as "Mister," as no Negro is ever addressed in the South; that I was assisted by those three men; and that the elderly gentleman interested himself in my predicament because I had, without fear, faced the four policemen, and said, "There is no need to beat me. I offer you no resistance."

1945
Adventures in Dining
By Langston Hughes

This piece originally appeared in the *Chicago Defender.*

EATING IN DINING cars south of the Mason-Dixon line these days is, for Negroes, often quite an adventure. Until recently, for some strange reason, southern white people evidently did not think that colored travellers ever got hungry while travelling, or if they did get hungry they were not expected to eat. Until the war came along, and the Mitchell Case was won, most Southern trains made no arrangements at all for Negroes to eat in the diners.

But now some Southern trains do arrange for Negroes to eat at times by having one or two tables curtained off in the dining car, and serving colored travellers behind the curtain. But not all trains do this. Some expect Negro passengers to eat early, others expect them to eat late, and others still expect them not to eat at all, but just go hungry until they get where they are going.

I have just come out of the South, having been during this lecture season from the Carolinas to Texas. On some trains heading southward from Washington through Virginia, I have been served without difficulty at any table in the diner, with white passengers eating with me. Further South, I have encountered the curtain, behind which I had to sit in order to eat, often being served with the colored Pullman porters and brakemen. On other trains there has been no curtain and no intention for Negroes to eat.

Coming out of Chattanooga on such a train, I went into the diner on the first call for dinner because sometimes these days if you wait for the second call everything will be gone. As I entered the diner, I said to the white steward, "One, please." He looked at me in amazement and walked off toward the other end of the car. The diner was filling rapidly, but there were still a couple of empty tables in the center of the car, so I went ahead and sat down.

Three whites soon joined me, then all the seats in the dining car were taken. The steward came and gave the three whites menus, but ignored me. Every time he passed, though, he would look at me and frown. Finally he leaned over and whispered in my ear.

"Say, fellow, are you Puerto Rican?"

"No," I said, "I'm American."

"Not American Negro, are you?" he demanded.

"I'm just hungry," I said loudly.

He gave me a menu! The colored waiters grinned. They served me with great courtesy, a quality which I have always found our dining car waiters to possess.

A few days later, in the great state of Alabama, I was riding in a Pullman that was half sleeping-car and half diner. There were only six tables in the dining portion of the car so, when the Filipino steward announced luncheon, I got up and went forward. I took a seat at one of the middle tables. Two white Navy men and a WAVE occupied the table with me. The Filipino steward looked very perturbed.

He walked up and down the aisle and gave a menu to everybody but me. Then he gave order checks to everybody but me. Then he disappeared in the kitchen. Finally he came out and addressed me nervously in broken English.

"Chef want to see you in kitchen," he mumbled.

I said, "What?"

He repeated, "Chef want see you in kitchen."

"I have nothing to do with the kitchen!" I said. "Tell the chef to come here."

He disappeared again. Finally he came back and gave me a menu. Since he was both waiter and steward, he served me himself. Nothing more was said.

On some dining cars in Texas, I found that they have colored stewards, although they do not term them stewards, but "waiters-in-charge." It happened that I knew one "waiter-in-charge," an intelligent and progressive young Negro, who invited me to be his personal guest at dinner. He told me that he seated colored passengers right along with the others. Certainly there is great variation in railroad dining for the race these days in the South. Just exactly what to expect still remains a mystery for Negroes—but it has the aura of adventure.

I would advise Negro travellers in the South to use the diners more. In fact, I wish we would use the diners in droves—so that whites may get used to seeing us in diners. It has been legally established that Negro passengers have a lawful right to eat while travelling. If we are refused service or ejected on grounds of color, we can sue. Several cases have been won and damages assessed recently. So, folks, when you go South by train, be sure to eat in the diner. Even if you are not hungry, eat anyhow—to help establish that right. Besides, it will be fun to see how you will be received.

1955

Interview with Jo Ann Robinson from *Eyes on the Prize*

BY JUAN WILLIAMS

On December 1, 1955, Rosa Parks, forty-three, was arrested after she refused to yield to a white man her seat on a Montgomery, Alabama bus. Jo Ann Robinson and her fellow activists at the Women's Political Council were ready. The protest that followed helped launch the civil rights movement, and made Martin Luther King, Jr. a national figure.

THE WOMAN'S POLITICAL Council was an organization begun in 1946 after dozens of black people had been arrested on the buses. We witnessed the arrests and humiliations and the court trials and the fines paid by people who just sat down on empty seats. We knew something had to be done.

We organized the Women's Council and within a month's time we had over a hundred members. We organized a second chapter and a third, and soon we had more than 300 members. We had members in every elementary, junior high, and senior high school. We had them organized from federal and state and local jobs; wherever there were more than ten blacks employed, we had a member there. We were organized to the point that we knew that in a matter of hours we could corral the whole city.

The evening that Rosa Parks was arrested, Fred Gray called me and told me that her case would be [heard] on Monday. As president of the main body of the Women's Political Council, I got on the phone and called all the officers of the three chapters. I told them that Rosa Parks had been arrested and she would be tried. They said, "You have the plans, put them into operation."

I didn't go to bed that night. I cut those stencils and took them to [the] college. The fellow who let me in during the night is dead now . . . he was in the business department. I ran off 35,000 copies.

I talked with every member [of the Women's Council] in elementary, junior high and senior high schools and told them to have somebody on the campus. I told them I would be there to deliver them [the handbills]. I taught my classes from 8:00 to 10:00. When my 10:00 class was over, I took two senior students with me. I would drive to the place of dissemination and a kid would be there to grab [the handbills].

After we had circulated those 35,000 circulars, we went by the church. That was about 3:30 in the afternoon. We took them to the minister . . . The [ministers] agreed to meet that night to decide what should be done about the boycott after the first day. You see, the Women's Council planned it only for Monday, and it was left up to the men to take over after we had forced them to really decide whether or not it had been successful enough to continue, and how long it was to be continued.

They had agreed at the Friday night meeting that they would call this meeting at Holt Street Church and they would let the audience determine whether or not they would continue the bus boycott or end it in one day.

Monday night, the ministers held their meeting. The church itself holds four or five thousand people. But there were thousands of people outside the church that night. They had to put up loudspeakers so they would know what was happening. When they got through reporting that very few people had ridden the bus, that the boycott was really a success—I don't know if there was one vote that said 'No, don't continue that boycott'—they voted unanimously to continue the boycott. And instead of it lasting one day as the Women's Council had planned it, it lasted for thirteen months.

The spirit, the desire, the injustices that had been endured by thousands of people through the years . . . I think people were fed up, they had reached the point that they knew there was no return. That they had to do it or die. And that's what kept it going. It was the sheer spirit for freedom, for the feeling of being a man or a woman.

Now when you ask why the courts had to come in, they had to come in. You get 52,000 people in the streets and nobody's showing any fear, something had to give. So the Supreme Court had to rule that segregation was not the way of life . . . We [met] after the news came through. All of these people who had fought got together to communicate and to rejoice and to share that built-up emotion and all the other feelings they had lived with during the past thirteen months. And we just rejoiced together.

1955
from *Coming of Age in Mississippi*
By Anne Moody

Anne Moody was born in 1940 to sharecroppers in Centerville, Mississippi. Her 1969 memoir includes this passage about how her community responded to the death of Emmett Till, black Chicago boy murdered in August 1955, while visiting family in Mississippi. His white killers suspected Till of disrespectful behavior toward a white woman.

I WAS NOW working for one of the meanest white women in town, and a week before school started Emmett Till was killed.

Up until his death, I had heard of Negroes found floating in a river or dead somewhere with their bodies riddled with bullets. But I didn't know the mystery behind these killings then. I remember once when I was only seven I heard Mama and one of my aunts talking about some Negro who had been beaten to death. "Just like them low-down skunks killed him they will do the same to us," Mama had said. When I asked her who killed the man and why, she said, "An Evil Spirit killed him. You gotta be a good girl or it will kill you too." So since I was seven, I had lived in fear of that "Evil Spirit." It took me eight years to learn what that spirit was.

I was coming from school the evening I heard about Emmet Till's death. There was a whole group of us, girls and boys, walking down the road headed home. A group of about six high school boys were walking a few paces ahead of me and several other girls. We were laughing and talking about something that had happened in school that day. However, the six boys in front of us weren't talking very loud. Usually they kept up so much noise. But today they were just walking and talking among themselves. All of a sudden they began to shout at each other.

"Man, what in the hell do you mean?"

"What I mean is these goddamned white folks is gonna start some shit here you just watch!"

"That boy wasn't but fourteen years old and they killed him. Now what kin a fourteen-year-old boy do with a white woman? What if he did whistle at her, he might have thought the whore was pretty."

"Look at all these white men here that's fucking over our women. Everybody knows it too and what's done about that? Look how many white babies we got walking around in our neighborhoods. Their mama's ain't white either. That boy was from Chicago, shit, everybody fuck everybody up there. He probably didn't even think of the bitch as white."

What they were saying shocked me. I knew all of those boys and I had never heard them talk like that. We walked on behind them for a while listening. Questions about who was killed, where, and why started running through my mind. I walked up to one of the boys.

"Eddie, what boy was killed?"

"Moody, where've you been?" he asked me. "Everybody talking about that fourteen-year-old boy who was killed in Greenwood by some white men. You don't know nothing that's going on besides what's in them books of yours, huh?"

Standing there before the rest of the girls, I felt so stupid. It was then that I realized I really didn't know what was going on all around me. It wasn't that I was dumb. It was just that ever since I was nine, I'd had to work after school and do my lessons on lunch hour. I never had time to learn anything, to hang around with people my own age. And you never were told anything by adults.

That evening when I stopped off at the house on my way to Mrs. Burke's, Mama was singing. Any other day she would have been yelling at Adline and Junior them to take off their school clothes. I wondered if she knew about Emmet Till. The way she was singing she had something on her mind and it wasn't pleasant either.

I got a shoe, you got a shoe,
All of God's chillun got shoes;
When I get to hebben, I'm gonna put on my shoes,
And gonna tromp all over God's hebben.
When I get to hebben, I'm gonna put on my shoes,
And gonna walk all over God's hebben.

Mama was dishing up beans like she didn't know anyone was home. Adline, Junior, and James had just thrown their books down and sat themselves at the table. I didn't usually eat before I went to work. But I wanted to ask Mama about Emmett Till. So I ate and thought of some way of asking her.

"These beans are some good, Mama," I said, trying to sense her mood.

"Why is you eating anyway? You gonna be late for work. You know how Miss Burke is," she said to me.

"I don't have much to do this evening. I kin get it done before I leave work," I said.

The conversation stopped after that. Then Mama started humming that song again.

When I get to hebben, I'm gonna put on my shoes,
And gonna tromp all over God's hebben.

She put a plate on the floor for Jennie Ann and Jerry.

"Jennie Ann! you and Jerrry sit down here and eat and don't put beans all over this floor."

Ralph, the baby, started crying, and she went in the bedroom to give him his bottle. I got up and followed her.

"Mama, did you hear about that fourteen-year-old Negro boy who was killed a little over a week ago by some white men?" I asked her.

"Where did you hear that?" she said angrily.

"Boy, everybody really thinks I am dumb or deaf or something. I heard Eddie them talking about it this evening coming from school."

"Eddie them better watch how they go around here talking. These white folks git a hold of it they gonna be in trouble," she said.

"What are they gonna be in trouble about, Mama? People got a right to talk, ain't they?"

"You go on to work before you is late. And don't you let on like you know nothing about that boy being killed before Miss Burke them. Just do your work like you don't know nothing," she said. "That boy's a lot better off in heaven than he is here," she continued and then started singing again.

On my way to Mrs. Burke's that evening, Mama's words kept running through my mind. "Just do your work like you don't know nothing." "Why is Mama acting so scared?" I thought. "And what if Mrs. Burke knew we knew? Why must I pretend I don't know? Why are these people killing Negroes? What did Emmett Till do besides whistle at that woman?"

By the time I got to work, I had worked my nerves up some. I was shaking as I walked up on the porch. "Do your work like you don't know nothing." But once I got inside, I couldn't have acted normal if Mrs. Burke were paying me to be myself.

I was so nervous, I spent most of the evening avoiding them going about the house dusting and sweeping. Everything went along fairly well until dinner was served.

"Don, Wayne, and Mama, y'all come on to dinner. Essie, you can wash up the pots and dishes in the sink now. Then after dinner you won't have as many," Mrs. Burke called to me.

If I had the power to mysteriously disappear at that moment, I would have. They used the breakfast table in the kitchen for most of their meals. The dining room was only used for Sunday dinner or when they had company. I wished they had company tonight so they could eat in the dining room while I was at the kitchen sink.

"I forgot the bread," Mrs. Burke said when they were all seated. "Essie, will you cut it and put it on the table for me?"

I took the cornbread, cut it in squares, and put it on a small round dish. Just as I was about to set it on the table, Wayne yelled at the cat, I dropped the plate and the bread went all over the floor.

"Never mind, Essie," Mrs. Burke said angrily as she got up and got some white bread from the breadbox.

I didn't say anything. I picked up the cornbread from around the table and went back to the dishes. As soon as I got to the sink, I dropped a saucer on the floor and broke it. Didn't anyone say a word until I had picked up the pieces.

"Essie, I bought some new cleanser today. It's setting on the bathroom shelf. See if it will remove the stains in the tub," Mrs. Burke said.

I went to the bathroom to clean the tub. By the time I got through with it, it was snow white. I spent a whole hour scrubbing it. I had removed the stains in no time but I kept scrubbing until they finished dinner.

When they had finished and gone into the living room as usual to watch TV, Mrs. Burke called me to eat. I took a clean plate out of the cabinet and sat down. Just as I was putting the first forkful of food in my mouth, Mrs. Burke entered the kitchen.

"Essie, did you hear about that fourteen-year-old boy who was killed in Greenwood?" she asked me, sitting down in one of the chairs opposite me.

"No, I didn't hear that," I answered, almost choking on the food.

"Do you know why he was killed?" she asked and I didn't answer.

"He was killed because he got out of his place with a white

woman. A boy from Mississippi would have known better than that. This boy was from Chicago. Negroes up North have no respect for people. They think they can get away with anything. He just came to Mississippi and put a whole lot of notions in the boys' heads here and stirred up a lot of trouble," she said passionately.

"How old are you, Essie?" she asked me after a pause.

"Fourteen. I will soon be fifteen though," I said.

"See, that boy was just fourteen too. It's a shame he had to die so soon." She was so red in the face, she looked as if she was on fire.

When she left the kitchen I sat there with my mouth open and my food untouched. I couldn't have eaten now if I were starving. "Just do your work like you don't know nothing" ran through my mind again and I began washing the dishes.

I went home shaking like a leaf on a tree. For the first time out of all her trying, Mrs. Burke had made me feel like rotten garbage. Many times she had tried to instill fear within me and subdue me and had given up. But when she talked about Emmett Till there was something in her voice that sent chills and fear all over me.

Before Emmett Till's murder, I had known the fear of hunger, hell, and the Devil. But now there was a new fear known to me—the fear of being killed just because I was black. This was the worst of my fears. I knew once I got food, the fear of starving to death would leave. I also was told that if I were a good girl, I wouldn't have to fear the Devil or hell. But I didn't know what one had to do or not do as a Negro not to be killed. Probably just being a Negro period was enough, I thought.

A few days later, I went to work and Mrs. Burke had about eight women over for tea. They were all sitting around in the living room when I got there. She told me she was having a "guild meeting," and asked me to help her serve the cookies and tea.

After helping her, I started cleaning the house. I always swept the hallway and porch first. As I was sweeping the hall, I could hear them talking. When I heard the word "nigger," I stopped sweeping and listened. Mrs. Burke must have sensed this, because she suddenly came to the door.

"Essie, finish the hall and clean the bathroom," she said hesitantly. "Then you can go for today. I am not making dinner tonight." Then she went back in the living room with the rest of the ladies.

Before she interrupted my listening, I had picked up the words "NAACP" and "that organization." Because they were talking about niggers, I knew NAACP had something to do with Negroes. All that night I kept wondering what could that NAACP mean?

Later when I was sitting in the kitchen at home doing my lessons, I decided to ask Mama. It was about twelve-thirty. Everyone was in bed but me. When Mama came in to put some milk in Ralph's bottle, I said, "Mama, what do NAACP mean?"

"Where did you git that from?" she asked me, spilling milk all over the floor.

"Mrs. Burke had a meeting tonight—"

"What kind of meeting?" she asked, cutting me off.

"I don't know. She had some women over—she said it was a guild meeting," I said.

"A guild meeting," she repeated.

"Yes, they were talking about Negroes and I heard some woman say 'that NAACP' and another 'that organization,' meaning the same thing."

"What else did they say?" she asked me.

"That's all I heard. Mrs. Burke must have thought I was listening, so she told me to clean the bathroom and leave."

"Don't you ever mention that word around Mrs. Burke or no other white person, you heah! Finish your lesson and cut that light out and go to bed," Mama said angrily and left the kitchen.

"With a Mama like that you'll never learn anything," I thought as I got into bed. All night long I thought about Emmet Till and the NAACP. I even got up to look up NAACP in my little concise dictionary. But I didn't find it.

The next day at school, I decided to ask my homeroom teacher Mrs. Rice the meaning of NAACP. When the bell sounded for lunch, I remained in my seat as the other students left the room.

"Are you going to spend your lunch hour studying again today, Moody?" Mrs. Rice asked me.

"Can I ask you a question, Mrs. Rice?" I asked her.

"You *may* ask me a question, yes, but I don't know if you *can* or not," she said.

"What does the word NAACP mean?" I asked.

"Why do you want to know?"

"The lady I worked for had a meeting and I overheard the word mentioned."

"What else did you hear?"

"Nothing. I didn't know what NAACP meant, that's all." I felt like I was on the witness stand or something.

"Well, next time your boss has another meeting you listen more carefully. NAACP is a Negro organization that was established a long time ago to help Negroes gain a few basic rights," she said.

"What's it gotta do with the Emmett Till murder?" I asked.

"They are trying to get a conviction in Emmett Till's case. You see the NAACP is trying to do a lot for the Negroes and get the right to vote for Negroes in the South. I shouldn't be telling you all this. And don't you dare breathe a word of what I said. It could cost me my job if word got out I was teaching my students such. I gotta go to lunch and you should go outside too because it's nice and sunny out today," she said leaving the room. "We'll talk more when I have time."

About a week later, Mrs. Rice had me over for Sunday dinner, and

I spent about five hours with her. Within that time, I digested a good meal and accumulated a whole new pool of knowledge about Negroes being butchered and slaughtered by whites in the South. After Mrs. Rice had told me all this, I felt like the lowest animal on earth. At least when other animals (hogs, cows, etc.) were killed by man, they were used as food. But when man was butchered or killed by man, in the case of Negroes by whites, they were left lying on a road or found floating in a river or something.

Mrs. Rice got to be something like a mother to me. She told me anything I wanted to know. And made me promise that I would keep all this information she was passing on to me to myself. She said she couldn't, rather didn't, want to talk about these things to the other teachers, that they would tell Mr. Willis and she would be fired. At the end of that year she was fired. I never found out why. I haven't seen her since then.

1963
The View from the Front of the Bus

By Marlene Nadle

The August, 1963 March on Washington is forever associated with Martin Luther King's celebrated "I Have a Dream" speech. Marlene Nadle as a young reporter covered the event for the *Village Voice*.

"THERE'S NO PLACE for Uncle Tom on this bus, man." The voice of the Negro echoed down the neon-bathed Harlem street as he mounted the steps of Bus 10 ready to start for Washington.

It was 2 a.m. on the morning of August 28. Anticipation hovered quietly over the 24 buses that lined both sides of 125th Street. Cars and cabs stopped more and more frequently to pour forth bundle-laden, sleepy Marchers. Black, white, old, young zigzagged back and forth across the street trying to find their assigned buses. Bus captains marked by yellow ribbons and rumpled passenger lists stood guard at the bus doors. Small groups huddled around them.

Voices arose above the general din.

"You've got to switch me to Bus 10. It's a swingin' bus. There's nothin' but old ladies on this crate."

"Hey, is this bus air-conditioned?"

"Where can I get seat reservations?"

"Hey, chick, are you on this bus?"

"Yeah."

"Is your husband on this bus?"

"Yeah."

"That's all right. I'll make love to both of you. I'm compatible."

"Who the hell is on this bus?" cried George Johnson, the exasperated 30-year-old Negro captain of Bus 10 and organizer of New York CORE'S 24-bus caravan. "People shouldn't be swapping buses, especially CORE members. It only adds to the confusion. Now everybody get in a seat and stay there. You can't save seats. This isn't a cocktail party."

The reaction to George's gruffness was a tongue-in-cheek parody of the Mr. Charlie routine. "Yassir, anything you say, sir." "Don't you fret now, Mr. George." "Don't you go upsetting yourself, boss." "You knows I always listen to you captain sir."

There was a general shuffling of bundles on the bus. Index cards with emergency Washington phone numbers were filled out and kept by everyone. "Sit-In Song Books" were passed back.

Outside the window of Bus 10 an old Negro was standing with out-stretched arms reciting an impromptu ode to the Black Woman. "Black Woman, you are the queen of the universe. I would give my life for you." This was less comic than symptomatic. It was just one of many signs of the racial pride which is now surging through the Negro people.

A young Negro in the seat behind me, when asked why he was going on this March, replied, "Because it's like your sweater. It's Black. It's for the cause. If my people are in it, I am going to be in it fighting, even if I get killed."

Outside the window of Bus 10 was also a more extreme reminder of this racial pride. Young members of the Black Muslims, neatly dressed in suits and ties, were hawking copies of *Muhammad Speaks*. This paper is the official statement of the Black Muslim philosophy: Black is beautiful; Black is best; Black must be separate from white.

I swing off the bus to ask the young Muslim if he was going to Washington. With a faint trace of a smile on his lips, he answered, "No, ma'am, I have to sell papers. You people go to Washington." The implication was clear: he was too busy working for his own cause—separation—to be bothered working for integration.

An older man, converted to a Muslim later in life, was not so emotionally untouched by the March and what it stood for. When I asked him why the Muslims were not participating in the March, he gave all the proper answers. He said: "The Messenger has not spoken. If he says nothing, we sit still. If he says go, we go." But then, asked if as an individual rather than a Muslim he would have gone, he replied: "I would have gone."

Moving through the crowd, I encountered a Negro I knew to be a fence-sitter between the Muslim and integrationist philosophies. I asked him why he had decided to come on the March. He said, "It's like St. Patrick's Day to the Irish. I came out of respect for what my people are doing, not because I believe it will do any good. I thought it would do some good at the beginning, but when the March started to get all the official approval from Mastah Kennedy, Mastah Wagner, and Mastah Spellman, and they started setting limits on how we had to march peacefully, I knew that the March was going to be a mockery. That they were giving us something again. They were letting the niggers have their day to get all this nonsense out of their system, and then planning to go back to things as usual. Well, if the white man continues to sleep, continues to ignore the intensity of the black man's feelings and desires, all hell is going to break loose."

Moving back toward the bus I almost crashed into George Johnson. With a certain Hollywood director flourish, he was telling the driver to rev up the engine. George was being interviewed for radio, and they wanted the sound of departure. Followed by interviewers trailing microphone wires, George shouted, "I feel good because the Negroes are on the march and nothing is going to stop us." With that, he boarded the bus, signaled the driver, and we began to move. It was 3:40 a.m.

The 49 passengers on Bus 10 settled back. Among them were 10 CORE members, including Omar Ahmed and Wayne Kinsler, both typical of Harlem's Angry Young Men. Present also were 10 unemployed workers sent to Washington on money raised by CORE to protest the lack of jobs. Also among the passengers were Jim Peck, author of the book *The Freedom Riders*, who took a severe beating on one of the first freedom rides into the Deep South; six members of the Peace Corps who were scheduled to leave for Nigeria; three interviewers from French television, with cameras and sound equipment; and a slightly jaded reporter and a cameraman from the *Herald Tribune*, both of whom had seen too many Clark Gable reporter movies.

People began to talk and to question one another. Sue Brookway, a white member of the Peace Corps, was standing in the aisle speaking to George Johnson. She said, "I think the biggest influence of the March will be to create a greater national awareness of the issue and get more people to make a commitment to the cause. Although I agreed with CORE's goals, it never occurred to me to become active before this. But now I would join if I weren't going to Nigeria."

Omar Ahmed, who had overheard the word "Nigeria," turned around in his seat and said, "The Negro on this March has to be very glad of the existence of the Soviet Union. This government is so worried about wooing the African and Asian mind that it may even give the Negro what he wants."

"I don't think the Civil Rights Bill will get through," commented George Johnson from his seat across the aisle. "I have no faith in the white man. Even Kennedy & Kennedy Inc. isn't doing this for humanitarian reasons, but for political ones."

After a moment he continued: "CORE has been criticized for its new tactics of civil disobedience. Well, as far as I'm concerned, anything done to get our rights is O.K. It's remarkable that the Negro has taken it this long."

The whites in the group were startled at the vehemence in George's statement. Omar, noting their expressions, attempted to explain. "The white power structure has bred a New Negro," he said, "and he is angry and impatient. It's not just the Black Muslims. It's the man on the street. Come down to Harlem some night and listen to what's being said on the street corners. The cops go through and you can see fear on their faces. This isn't Birmingham. If anyone starts anything, we won't be passive."

The kids in the four adjacent seats were twisted around in their chairs listening. Heads pressed together, they formed a roundtable, minus the table. Into this group came Wayne Kinsler, a 19-year-old

Negro. He perched on one of the scat arms. Some crumbled cookies and overripe fruit were passed around.

The discussion turned to the Peace Corps. Frank Harman was asked why, since he was white, he wanted to go to Nigeria. He replied, "I want to go to help these people because they are human beings."

Suddenly Wayne shouted, "If this thing comes to violence, yours will be the first throat we slit. We don't need your kind. Get out of our organization."

Completely baffled by the outburst, Frank kept repeating the questions. "What's he talking about? What did I say?"

Wayne, straining forward tensely, screamed, "We don't need any white liberals to patronize us!"

Other Negroes joined in. "We don't trust you." "We don't believe you're sincere." "You'll have to prove yourself."

Frank shouted back, "I don't have to prove myself to anyone except myself."

"We've been stabbed in the back too many times."

"The reason white girls come down to civil rights meetings is because they've heard of the black man's reputation of sex."

"The reason white guys come down is because they want to rebel against their parents."

"I'll tell you this, proving that he is sincere when he is working in the civil rights groups is the last chance the white man has got to keep this thing from exploding."

The other passengers were urging us to stop the argument. Eventually we did. In the lull that followed, the reactions of the whites were mixed. The most widespread one was complete lack of understanding as to why this had all started. There was little comprehension of the effect words like "help you" or "work for you," with all their connotations of the Great-White-Father attitude, could have on the bristling black pride. Another attitude was one of revulsion at the ugliness which had been exhibited. Still others saw the argument as a sign that the walls between the races were beginning to come down, that people were really beginning to communicate instead of hiding behind masks of politeness. They felt that with a greater knowledge of one another's sensitivities, lack of understanding, and desires, it would be easier for the white liberal and the black man to work together.

People began to relax and joke again. Gradually they drifted off into an exhausted sleep. Bus 10 rolled on in silence.

With the coming of dawn, the French TV men started blinding everyone with their lights and interviewing those people who could speak French. Being Gallic, they made sure to get shots of the romantic duos pillowed against one another. Not to be left out, the *Herald Tribune*'s cameraman picked up his light meter and cord and started doing a mock interview of the interviewers.

Someone cheerfully yelled, "Everybody sing."

He was quickly put down by a voice from the lower depths: "You're nuts! At seven o'clock sane people don't even talk."

On we went. Sleeping, talking, anticipating. We passed other buses full of heads covered with caps printed with their organizations' names. On our right was a beat-up old cab with six people in it and March on Washington posters plastered on all its doors.

At 10:30—Washington. The city seemed strangely quiet and deserted except for a few groups of Negro children on corners. They stared curiously at the unending caravan of buses. Police and MPs were everywhere. Traffic moved swiftly. We parked at 117th and Independence, and the people of Bus 10 merged with the crowd moving up the street. The March was on.

The day was full of TV cameras, spontaneous singing, speeches, clapping, the green and white striped news tent, the P.A. system blasting "We Shall Not Be Moved," the ominous Red Cross symbol on a medical tent, March marshals with bright yellow arm bands and little white Nehru hats, the Freedom Walkers in faded blue overalls, Catholic priests in solemn black, posters proclaiming Freedom Now, feet soaking in the reflecting pool, portable drinking fountains, varicolored pennants and hats, warm Pepsi-Cola, the blanket of humanity sprawled in undignified dignity, a Nigerian student with his head bent in prayer, and the echo of Martin Luther King's phrase: "I have a dream . . ."

It was over. The bus moved out slowly. This time there were Negroes on every doorstep. As we passed, they raised their fingers in the victory sign. They clasped their hands over their heads in the prizefighter's traditional gesture. They clapped. They cheered. They smiled and the smile was reflected back from the buses.

On Bus 10 there was no one sitting at "the back of the bus." All the seats were in the front.

"We'll be back," said George Johnson. "If this doesn't work, we'll bring 500,000. And if that doesn't work, we'll bring all 20 million."

1994
Prime Time

By Henry Louis Gates, Jr.

Henry Louis Gates, Jr. is chairman of Harvard's Afro-American studies program, and a leading cultural critic. He was born in 1950, and grew up in West Virginia.

I GUESS SOME chafed more than others against the mundane

impediments of the color line. "It's no disgrace be colored," the black entertainer Bert Williams famously observed early in this century, "but it is awfully inconvenient." For most of my childhood, we couldn't eat in restaurants or sleep in hotels, we couldn't use certain bathrooms or try on clothes in stores. Mama insisted that we dress up when we went to shop. She was a fashion plate when she went to clothing stores, and wore white pads called shields under her arms so her dress or blouse would show no sweat. We'd like to try this on, she'd say carefully, articulating her words precisely and properly. We don't buy clothes we can't try on, she'd say when they declined, as we'd walk, in Mama's dignified manner, out of the store. She preferred to shop where we had an account and where everyone knew who she was.

As for me, I hated the fact that we couldn't sit down in the Cut-Rate. No one colored was allowed to, with one exception: my father. It was as if there were a permanent TAKE-AWAY ONLY sign for colored people. You were supposed to stand at the counter, get your food to go, and leave. I don't know for certain why Carl Dadisman, the proprietor, wouldn't stop Daddy from sitting down. But I believe it was in part because Daddy was so light-complected, and in part because, during his shift at the phone company, he picked up orders for food and coffee for the operators, and Dadisman relied on that business. At the time, I never wondered if it occurred to Daddy not to sit down at the Cut-Rate when neither his wife nor his two children were allowed to, although now that I am a parent myself, the strangeness of it crosses my mind on occasion.

Even when we were with Daddy, you see, we had to stand at the counter and order takeout, then eat on white paper plates using plastic spoons, sipping our vanilla rickeys from green-and-white paper cups through plastic flexible-end straws. Even after basketball games, when Young Doc Bess would set up the team with free Cokes after one of the team's many victories, the colored players had to stand around and drink out of paper cups while the white players and cheerleaders sat down in the red Naugahyde booths and drank out of glasses. Integrate? I'll shut it down first, Carl Dadisman had vowed. He was an odd-looking man, with a Humpty-Dumpty sort of head and bottom, and weighing four or five hundred pounds. He ran the taxi service, too, and was just as nice as he could be, even to colored people. But he did not want us sitting in his booths, eating off his plates and silverware, putting our thick greasy lips all over his glasses. He'd retire first, or die.

He had a heart attack one day while sitting in the tiny toilet at his place of business. Daddy and some other men tried to lift him up, while he was screaming and gasping and clutching his chest, but he was stuck in that cramped space. They called the rescue squad at the Fire Department. Lowell Taylor and Pat Amoroso came. Lowell was black and was the star of the soccer team at the high school across the river in Westernport. He looked like Pele, down to the shape of his head.

They sawed and sawed and sawed, while the ambulance and the rescue squad sat outside on Third Street, blocking the driveway to the town's parking lot. After a while, Carl Dadisman's cries and moans became quieter and quieter. Finally, they wedged in a couple of two-by-fours and dragged out his lifeless body. By then it made little difference to Carl that Lowell was black.

Maybe Carl never understood that the racial dispensation he took for granted was coming to an end. As a child, I must once have assumed that this dispensation could no more be contested than the laws of gravity, or traffic lights. And I'm not sure when I realized otherwise.

I know that I had rich acquaintance early on with the inconveniences to which Bert Williams alluded. But segregation had some advantages, like the picnic lunch Mama would make for the five-hour train ride on the National Limited to Parkersburg, where you had to catch the bus down to the state capital, Charleston, to visit her sister Loretta. So what if we didn't feel comfortable eating in the dining car? Our food was better. Fried chicken, baked beans, and potato salad . . . a book and two decks of cards . . . and I didn't care if the train ever got there. We'd sing or read in our own section, munching that food and feeling sorry for the people who couldn't get any, and play 500 or Tonk or Fish with Mama and Daddy, until we fell asleep.

The simple truth is that the civil rights era came late to Piedmont, even though it came early to our television set. We could watch what was going on Elsewhere on television, but the marches and sit-ins were as remote to us as, in other ways, was the all-colored world of *Amos 'n' Andy*—a world full of black lawyers, black judges, black nurses, black doctors.

Politics aside, though, we were starved for images of ourselves and searched TV to find them. Everybody, of course, watched sports, because Piedmont was a big sports town. Making the big leagues was like getting to Heaven, and everybody had hopes that they could, or a relative could. We'd watch the games day and night, and listen on radio to what we couldn't see. Everybody knew the latest scores, batting averages, rbi's, and stolen bases. Everybody knew the standings in the leagues, who could still win the pennant and how. Everybody liked the Dodgers because of Jackie Robinson, the same way everybody still voted Republican because of Abraham Lincoln. Sports on the mind, sports in the mind. The only thing to rival the Valley in fascination was the big-league baseball diamond.

I once heard Mr. James Helms say, "You got to give the white man his due when it comes to technology. One on one, though, and it's even-steven. Joe Louis showed 'em that." We were obsessed with sports in part because it was the only time we could compete with white people even-steven. And the white people, it often seemed, were just as obsessed with this primal confrontation between the races as we were. I think they integrated professional sports, after all those years of segregation, just to capitalize on this voyeuristic thrill of the forbidden contact. What interracial sex was to the seventies, interracial sports were to the fifties. Except for sports, we rarely saw a colored person on TV.

Actually, I first got to know white people as "people" through their flickering images on television shows. It was the television set that brought us together at night, and the television set that brought in the world outside the Valley. We were close enough to Washington to receive its twelve channels on cable. Piedmont was transformed from a radio culture to one with the fullest range of television, literally overnight. During my first-grade year, we'd watch *Superman, Lassie,* Jack Benny, Danny Thomas, *Robin Hood, I Love Lucy, December Bride,* Nat King Cole (of course), *Wyatt Earp, Broken Arrow,* Phil Silvers, Red Skelton, *The $64,000 Question, Ozzie and Harriet, The Millionaire, Father Knows Best, The Lone Ranger,* Bob Cummings, *Dragnet, The People's Choice, Rin Tin Tin, Jim Bowie, Gunsmoke, My Friend Flicka, The Life of Riley, Topper, Dick Powell's Zane Grey Theater, Circus Boy,* and Loretta Young—all in prime time. My favorites were *The Life of Riley,* in part because he worked in a factory like Daddy did, and *Ozzie and Harriet,* in part because Ozzie never seemed to work at all. A year later, however, *Leave It to Beaver* swept most of the others away.

With a show like *Topper,* I felt as if I was getting a glimpse, at last, of the life that Mrs. Hudson, and Mrs. Thomas, and Mrs. Campbell, must be leading in their big mansions on East Hampshire Street. Smoking jackets and cravats, spats and canes, elegant garden parties and martinis. People who wore suits to eat dinner! This was a world so elegantly distant from ours, it was like a voyage to another galaxy, light-years away.

Leave It to Beaver, on the other hand, was a world much closer, but just out of reach nonetheless. Beaver's street was where we wanted to live, Beaver's house where we wanted to eat and sleep, Beaver's father's firm where we'd have liked Daddy to work. These shows for us were about property, the property that white people could own and that we couldn't. About a level of comfort and ease at which we could only wonder. It was the world that the integrated school was going to prepare us to enter and that, for Mama, would be the prize.

If prime time consisted of images of middle-class white people who looked nothing at all like us, late night was about the radio, listening to *Randy's Record Shop* from Gallatin, Tennessee. My brother, Rocky, kept a transistor radio by his bed, and he'd listen to it all night, for all I knew, long after I'd fallen asleep. In 1956, black music hadn't yet broken down into its many subgenres, except for large divisions such as jazz, blues, gospel, rhythm and blues. On *Randy's,* you were as likely to hear The Platters doing "The Great Pretender" and Clyde McPhatter doing "Treasure of Love" as you were to hear Howlin' Wolf do "Smokestack Lightning" or Joe Turner do "Corrine, Corrine." My own favorite that year was the slow, deliberate sound of Jesse Belvin's "Goodnight, My Love." I used to fall asleep singing it in my mind to my Uncle Earkie's girlfriend, Ula, who was a sweet caffè latté brown, with the blackest, shiniest straight hair and the fullest, most rounded red lips. Not even in your dreams, he had said to me one day, as I watched her red dress slink down our front stairs. It was my first brush with the sublime.

We used to laugh at the way the disc jockey sang "Black Strap Lax-a-teeves" during the commercials. I sometimes would wonder if the kids we'd seen on TV in Little Rock or Birmingham earlier in the evening were singing themselves to sleep with *their* Ulas.

Lord knows, we weren't going to learn how to be colored by watching television. Seeing somebody colored on TV was an event.

"Colored, colored, on Channel Two," you'd hear someone shout. Somebody else would run to the phone, while yet another hit the front porch, telling all the neighbors where to see it. And *everybody* loved *Amos 'n' Andy*—I don't care what people say today. For the colored people, the day they took *Amos 'n' Andy* off the air was one of the saddest days in Piedmont, about as sad as the day of the last mill pic-a-nic.

What was special to us about *Amos 'n' Andy* was that their world was *all* colored, just like ours. Of course, *they* had their colored judges and lawyers and doctors and nurses, which we could only dream about having, or becoming—and we *did* dream about those things. Kingfish ate his soft-boiled eggs delicately, out of an egg cup. He even owned an acre of land in Westchester County, which he sold to Andy, using the facade of a movie set to fake a mansion. As far as we were concerned, the foibles of Kingfish or Calhoun the lawyer were the foibles of individuals who happened to be funny. Nobody was likely to confuse them with the colored people we knew, no more than we'd confuse ourselves with the entertainers and athletes we saw on TV or in *Ebony* or *Jet,* the magazines we devoured to keep up with what was happening with the race. And people took special relish in Kingfish's malapropisms. "I denies the allegation, Your Honor, and I resents the alligator."

In one of my favorite episodes of *Amos 'n' Andy,* "The Punjab of Java-Pour," Andy Brown is hired to advertise a brand of coffee and is required to dress up as a turbaned Oriental potentate. Kingfish gets the bright idea that if he dresses up as a potentate's servant, the two of them can enjoy a vacation at a luxury hotel for free. So attired, the two promenade around the lobby, running up an enormous tab and generously dispensing "rubies" and "diamonds" as tips. The plan goes awry when people try to redeem the gems and discover them to be colored glass. It was widely suspected that this episode was what prompted two Negroes in Baltimore to dress like African princes and demand service in a segregated four-star restaurant. Once it was clear to the management that these were not American Negroes, the two were treated royally. When the two left the restaurant, they took off their African headdresses and robes and enjoyed a hearty laugh at the restaurant's expense. "They weren't like our Negroes," the maitre d' told the press in explaining why he had agreed to seat the two "African princes."

Whenever the movies *Imitation of Life* and *The Green Pastures* would be shown on TV, we watched with similar hunger—especially *Imitation of Life*. It was never on early; only the late *late* show, like the performances of Cab Calloway and Duke Ellington at the Crystal Palace. And we'd stay up. Everybody colored. The men coming home on second shift from the paper mill would stay up. Those who had to go out on the day shift and who normally would have been in bed hours earlier (because they had to be at work at 6:30) would stay up. As would we, the kids, wired for the ritual at hand. And we'd all sit in silence, fighting back the tears, watching as Delilah invents the world's greatest pancakes and a down-and-out Ned Sparks takes one taste and says, flatly, "We'll box it." Cut to a big white house, plenty of money, and Delilah saying that she doesn't want her share of the money (which should have been *all* the money); she just wants to continue to cook, clean, wash, iron, and serve her good white lady and her daughter. (Nobody in our living room was going for *that*.) And then Delilah shows up at her light-complected daughter's school one day, unexpectedly, to pick her up, and there's the daughter, Peola, ducking down behind her books, and the white teacher saying, I'm sorry, ma'am, there must be some mistake. We have no little colored children here. And then Delilah, spying her baby, says, Oh, yes you do. Peola! Peola! Come here to your mammy, honey chile. And then Peola runs out of the room, breaking her poor, sweet mother's heart. And Peola continues to break her mother's heart, by passing, leaving the race, and marrying white. Yet her mama understands, always understands, and, dying, makes detailed plans for her own big, beautiful funeral, complete with six white horses and a carriage and a jazz band, New Orleans style. And she dies and is about to be buried, when, out of nowhere, comes grown-up Peola, saying, "Don't die. Mama, don't die, Mama, I'm sorry, Mama, I'm sorry," and throws her light-and-bright-and-damn-near-white self onto her mama's casket. By this time, we have stopped trying to fight back the tears and are boo-hooing all over the place. Then we turn to our *own* mama and tell her how much we love her and swear that we will *never, ever* pass for white. I promise. Mama. I promise.

Peola had sold her soul to the Devil. This was the first popular Faust in the black tradition, the bargain with the Devil over the cultural soul. Talk about a cautionary tale.

The Green Pastures was an altogether more uplifting view of things, our Afro Paradiso. Make way for the Lawd! Make way for the Lawd! And Rex Ingram, dressed in a long black frock coat and a long white beard, comes walking down the Streets Paved with Gold, past the Pearly Gates, while Negroes with the whitest wings of fluffy cotton fly around Heaven, playing harps, singing spirituals, having fish fries, and eating watermelon. Hard as I try, I can't stop seeing God as that black man who played Him in *The Green Pastures* and seeing Noah as Rochester from the Jack Benny show, trying to bargain with God to let him take along an extra keg of wine or two.

Civil rights took us all by surprise. Every night we'd wait until the news to see what "Dr. King and dem" were doing. It was like watching the Olympics or the World Series when somebody colored was on. The murder of Emmett Till was one of my first memories. He whistled at some white girl, they said; that's all he did. He was beat so bad they didn't even want to open the casket, but his mama made them. She wanted the world to see what they had done to her baby.

In 1957, when I was in second grade, black children integrated Central High School in Little Rock, Arkansas. We watched it on TV.

All of us watched it. I don't mean Mama and Daddy and Rocky. I mean *all* the colored people in America watched it, together, with one set of eyes. We'd watch it in the morning, on the *Today* show on NBC, before we'd go to school; we'd watch it in the evening, on the news, with Edward R. Murrow on CBS. We'd watch the Special Bulletins at night, interrupting our TV shows.

The children were all well scrubbed and greased down, as we'd say. Hair short and closely cropped, parted, and oiled (the boys); "done" in a "permanent" and straightened, with turned-up bangs and curls (the girls). Starched shirts, white, and creased pants, shoes shining like a buck private's spit shine. Those Negroes were clean. The fact was, those children trying to get the right to enter that school in Little Rock looked like black versions of models out of *Jack & Jill* magazine, to which my mama had subscribed for me so that I could see what children outside the Valley were up to. "They handpicked those children," Daddy would say. "No dummies, no nappy hair, heads not too kinky, lips not too thick, no disses and no dats." At seven, I was dismayed by his cynicism. It bothered me somehow that those children would have been chosen, rather than just having shown up or volunteered or been nearby in the neighborhood.

Daddy was jaundiced about the civil rights movement, and especially about the Reverend Dr. Martin Luther King, Jr. He'd say all of his names, to drag out his scorn. By the mid-sixties, we'd argue about King from sunup to sundown. Sometimes he'd just mention King to get a rise from me, to make a sagging evening more interesting, to see if I had *learned* anything real yet, to see how long I could think up counter arguments before getting so mad that my face would turn purple. I think he just liked the color purple on my face, liked producing it there. But he was not of two minds about those children in Little Rock.

The children would get off their school bus surrounded by soldiers from the National Guard and by a field of state police. They would stop at the steps of the bus and seem to take a very deep breath. Then the phalanx would start to move slowly along this gulley of sidewalk and rednecks that connected the steps of the school bus with the white wooden double doors of the school. All kinds of crackers would be lining that gulley, separated from the phalanx of children by rows of state police, who formed a barrier arm in arm. Cheerleaders from the all-white high school that was desperately trying to stay that way were dressed in those funny little pleated skirts, with a big red *C* for "Central" on their chests, and they'd wave their pompoms and start to cheer: "Two, four, six, eight—We don't want to integrate!" And all those crackers and all those rednecks would join in that chant as if their lives depended on it. Deafening, it was: even on our twelve-inch TV, a three-inch speaker buried along the back of its left side.

The TV was the ritual arena for the drama of race. In our family, it was located in the living room, where it functioned like a fireplace in the proverbial New England winter. I'd sit in the water in the galvanized tub in the middle of our kitchen, watching the TV in the next room while Mama did the laundry or some other chore as she waited for Daddy to come home from his second job. We watched people getting hosed and cracked over their heads, people being spat upon and arrested, rednecks siccing fierce dogs on women and children, our people responding by singing and marching and staying strong. Eyes on the prize. Eyes on the prize. George Wallace at the gate of the University of Alabama, blocking Autherine Lucy's way. Charlayne Hunter at the University of Georgia. President Kennedy interrupting our scheduled program with a special address, saying that James Meredith will *definitely* enter the University of Mississippi; and saying it like he believed it (unlike Ike), saying it like the big kids said "It's our turn to play" on the basketball court and walking all through us as if we weren't there.

Whatever tumult our small screen revealed, though, the dawn of the civil rights era could be no more than a spectator sport in Piedmont. It was almost like a war being fought overseas. And all things considered, white and colored Piedmont got along pretty well in those years, the fifties and early sixties. At least as long as colored people didn't try to sit down in the Cut-Rate or at the Rendezvous Bar, or eat pizza at Eddie's, or buy property, or move into the white neighborhoods, or dance with, date, or dilate upon white people. Not to mention try to get a job in the craft unions at the paper mill. Or have a drink at the white VFW, or join the white American Legion, or get loans at the bank, or just generally get out of line. Other than that, colored and white got on pretty well.

poverty

1930s
from *Hard Times*

BY STUDS TERKEL

Studs Terkel's 1970 oral history of the Great Depression
preserved memories of hunger and poverty.

PEGGY TERRY AND HER MOTHER, MARY OWSLEY

It is a crowded apartment in Uptown.[*] *Young people from the neighborhood wander in and out, casually. The flow of visitors is constant;
occasionally, a small, raggedy-clothed boy shuffles in, stares, vanishes.
Peggy Terry is known in these parts as a spokesman for the poor southern
whites. . . . "Hillbillies are up here for a few years and they get their guts
kicked out and they realize their white skin doesn't mean what they
always thought it meant."*

Mrs. Owsley is the first to tell her story.

*Kentucky-born, she married an Oklahoma boy "when he came back
from World War I. He was so restless and disturbed from the war, we just
drifted back and forth." It was a constant shifting from Oklahoma to
Kentucky and back again; three, four times the route. "He saw the
tragedies of war so vividly that he was discontented everywhere." From
1929 to 1936, they lived in Oklahoma.*

There was thousands of people out of work in Oklahoma City. They

---

[*] A Chicago area in which many of the southern white émigrés live; furnished flats in
most instances.

321

set up a soup line, and the food was clean and it was delicious. Many, many people, colored and white, I didn't see any difference, 'cause there was just as many white people out of work than were colored. Lost everything they had accumulated from their young days. And these are facts. I remember several families had to leave in covered wagons. To Californy, I guess.

See, the oil boom come in '29. People come from every direction in there. A coupla years later, they was livin' in everything from pup tents, houses built out of cardboard boxes and old pieces of metal that they'd pick up—anything that they could find to put somethin' together to put a wall around 'em to protect 'em from the public.

I knew one family there in Oklahoma City, a man and a woman and seven children lived in a hole in the ground. You'd be surprised how nice it was, how nice they kept it. They had chairs and tables and beds back in that hole. And they had the dirt all braced up there, just like a cave.

Oh, the dust storms, they were terrible. You could wash and hang clothes on a line, and if you happened to be away from the house and couldn't get those clothes in before that storm got there, you'd never wash that out. Oil was in that sand. It'd color them the most awful color you ever saw. It just ruined them. They was just never fit to use, actually. I had to use 'em, understand, but they wasn't very present-able. Before my husband was laid off, we lived in a good home. It wasn't a brick house, but it wouldn't have made any difference. These storms, when they would hit, you had to clean house from the attic to ground. Everything was covered in sand. Red sand, just full of oil.

The majority of people were hit and hit hard. They were mentally disturbed you're bound to know, 'cause they didn't know when the end of all this was comin'. There was a lot of suicides that I know of. From nothin' else but just they couldn't see any hope for a better tomorrow. I absolutely know some who did. Part of 'em were farmers and part of 'em were businessmen, even. They went flat broke and they committed suicide on the strength of it, nothing else.

A lot of times one family would have some food. They would divide. And everyone would share. Even the people that were quite well to do, they was ashamed. 'Cause they was eatin', and other people wasn't.

My husband was very bitter. That's just puttin' it mild. He was an intelligent man. He couldn't see why as wealthy a country as this is, that there was any sense in so many people starving to death, when so much of it, wheat and everything else, was being poured into the ocean. There's many excuses, but he looked for a reason. And he found one.

My husband went to Washington. To march with that group that went to Washington . . . the bonus boys.

He was a machine gunner in the war. He'd say them damn Germans gassed him in Germany. And he come home and his own Government stooges gassed him and run him off the country up there with the water hose, half drownded him. Oh, yes *sir,* yes sir, he was a hell-raiser (laughs—a sudden sigh). I think I've run my race.

Peggy Terry's Story:
I first noticed the difference when we'd come home from school in the evening. My mother'd send us to the soup line. And we were never allowed to cuss. If you happened to be one of the first ones in line, you didn't get anything but water that was on top. So we'd ask the guy that was ladling out the soup into the buckets—everybody had to bring their own bucket to get the soup—he'd dip the greasy, watery stuff off the top. So we'd ask him to please dip down to get some meat and potatoes from the bottom of the kettle. But he wouldn't do it. So we learned to cuss. We'd say: "Dip down, God damn it."

Then we'd go across the street. One place had bread, large loaves of bread. Down the road just a little piece was a big shed, and they gave milk. My sister and me would take two buckets each. And that's what we lived off for the longest time.

I can remember one time, the only thing in the house to eat was mustard. My sister and I put so much mustard on biscuits that we got sick. And we can't stand mustard till today.

There was only one family around that ate good. Mr. Barr worked at the ice plant. Whenever Mrs. Barr could, she'd feed the kids. But she couldn't feed 'em *all*. They had a big tree that had fruit on it. She'd let us pick those. Sometimes we'd pick and eat 'em until we were sick.

Her two daughters got to go to Norman for their college. When they'd talk about all the good things they had at the college, she'd kind of hush 'em up because there was always poor kids that didn't have anything to eat. I remember she always felt bad because people in the neighborhood were hungry. But there was a feeling of together. . . .

When they had food to give to people, you'd get a notice and you'd go down. So Daddy went down that day and he took my sister and me. They were giving away potatoes and things like that. But they had a truck of oranges parked in the alley. Somebody asked them who the oranges were for, and they wouldn't tell 'em. So they said, well, we're gonna take those oranges. And they did. My dad was one of the ones that got up on the truck. They called the police, and the police chased us all away. But we got the oranges.

It's different today. People are made to feel ashamed now if they don't have anything. Back then, I'm not sure how the rich felt. I think the rich were as contemptuous of the poor then as they are now. But among the people that I knew, we all had an understanding that it wasn't our fault. It was something that had happened to the machinery. Most people blamed Hoover, and they cussed him up one side and down the other—it was all his fault. I'm not saying he's blameless, but

I'm not saying either it was all his fault. Our system doesn't run by just one man, and it doesn't fall by just one man, either.

You don't recall at any time feeling a sense of shame?

I remember it was fun. It was fun going to the soup line. 'Cause we all went down the road, and we laughed and we played. The only thing we felt is that we were hungry and we were going to get food. Nobody made us feel ashamed. There just wasn't any of that.

Today you're made to feel that it's your own fault. If you're poor, it's only because you're lazy and you're ignorant, and you don't try to help yourself. You're made to feel that if you get a check from Welfare that the bank at Fort Knox is gonna go broke.

Even after the soup line, there wasn't anything. The WPA came, and I married. My husband worked on the WPA. This was back in Paducah, Kentucky. We were just kids. I was fifteen, and he was sixteen. My husband was digging ditches. They were putting in a water main. Parts of the city, even at that late date, 1937, didn't have city water.

My husband and me just started traveling around, for about three years. It was a very nice time, because when you're poor and you stay in one spot, trouble just seems to catch up with you. But when you're moving from town to town, you don't stay there long enough for trouble to catch up with you. It's really a good life, if you're poor and you can manage to move around.

I was pregnant when we first started hitchhiking, and people were really very nice to us. Sometimes they would feed us. I remember one time we slept in a haystack, and the lady of the house came out and found us and she said, "This is really very bad for you because you're going to have a baby. You need a lot of milk." So she took us up to the house.

She had a lot of rugs hanging on the clothesline because she was doing her house cleaning. We told her we'd beat the rugs for her giving us the food. She said, no, she didn't expect that. She just wanted to feed us. We said, no, we couldn't take it unless we worked for it. And she let us beat her rugs. I think she had a million rugs, and we cleaned them. Then we went in and she had a beautiful table, full of all kind of food and milk. When we left, she filled a gallon bucket full of milk and we took it with us.

You don't find that now. I think maybe if you did that now, you'd get arrested. Somebody'd call the police. The atmosphere since the end of the Second War—it seems like the minute the war ended, the propaganda started. In making people hate each other.

I remember one night, we walked for a long time, and we were so tired and hungry, and a wagon came along. There was a Negro family going into town. Of course, they're not allowed to stop and eat in restaurants, so they'd cook their own food and brought it with 'em. They had the back of the wagon filled with hay. We asked them if we could lay down and sleep in the wagon, and they said yes. We woke up, and it was morning, and she invited us to eat with 'em. She had this box, and she had chicken and biscuits and sweet potatoes and everything in there. It was just really wonderful.

I didn't like black people. In fact, I hated 'em. If they just shipped 'em all out, I don't think it woulda bothered me.

She recalls her feelings of white superiority, her discoveries. "If I really knew what changed me . . . I don't know. I've thought about it and thought about it. You don't go anywhere, because you always see yourself as something you're not. As long as you can say I'm better than they are, then there's somebody below you can kick. But once you get over that, you see that you're not any better off than they are. In fact, you're worse off 'cause you're believin' a lie. And it was right there, in front of us. In the cotton field, chopping cotton, and right over in the next field, there's these black people—Alabama, Texas, Kentucky. Never once did it occur to me that we had anything in common.

"After I was up here for a while and I saw how poor white people were treated, poor white southerners, they were treated just as badly as black people are. I think maybe that just crystallized the whole thing."

I didn't feel any identification with the Mexicans, either. My husband and me were migrant workers. We went down in the valley of Texas, which is very beautiful. We picked oranges and lemons and grape-fruits, limes in the Rio Grande Valley.

We got a nickel a bushel for citrus fruits. On the grapefruits you had to ring them. You hold a ring in your hand that's about like that (she draws a circle with her hands), and it has a little thing that slips down over your thumb. You climb the tree and you put that ring around the grapefruit. If the grapefruit slips through, you can't pick it. And any grapefruit that's in your box—you can work real hard, especially if you want to make enough to buy food that day—you'll pick some that aren't big enough. Then when you carry your box up and they check it, they throw out all the ones that go through the ring.

I remember this one little boy in particular. He was really a beau-tiful child. Every day when we'd start our lunch, we'd sit under the trees and eat. And these peppers grew wild. I saw him sitting there, and every once in a while he'd reach over and get a pepper and pop it in his mouth. With his food, whatever he was eating. I thought they looked pretty good. So I reached over and popped it in my mouth, and, oh, it was like liquid fire. He was rolling in the grass laughing. He thought it was so funny—that white people couldn't eat peppers like they could. And he was tearing open grapefruits for me to suck the juice, because my mouth was all cooked from the pepper. He used to run and ask if he could help me. Sometimes he'd help me fill my boxes of grapefruits, 'cause he felt sorry for me, 'cause I got burned on the peppers. (Laughs.)

But that was a little boy. I felt all right toward him. But the men and the women, they were just spies and they should be sent back to Mexico.

I remember I was very irritated because there were very few gringos in this little Texas town, where we lived. Hardly anybody spoke English. When you tried to talk to the Mexicans, they couldn't understand English. It never occurred to us that we should learn to speak Spanish. It's really hard to talk about a time like that, 'cause it seems like a different person. When I remember those times, it's like looking into a world where another person is doing those things.

This may sound impossible, but if there's one thing that started me thinking, it was President Roosevelt's cuff links. I read in the paper how many pairs of cuff links he had. It told that some of them were rubies and precious stones—these were his cuff links. And I'll never forget, I was setting on an old tire out in the front yard and we were poor and hungry. I was sitting out there in the hot sun, there weren't any trees. And I was wondering why it is that one man could have all those cuff links when we couldn't even have enough to eat. When we lived on gravy and biscuits. That's the first time I remember ever wondering why.

And when my father finally got his bonus, he bought a second-hand car for us to come back to Kentucky in. My dad said to us kids: "All of you get in the car. I want to take you and show you something." On the way over there, he'd talk about how life had been rough for us, and he said: "If you think it's been rough for us, I want you to see people that really had it rough." This was in Oklahoma City, and he took us to one of the Hoovervilles, and that was the most incredible thing.

Here were all these people living in old, rusted-out car bodies. I mean that was their home. There were people living in shacks made of orange crates. One family with a whole lot of kids were living in a piano box. This wasn't just a little section, this was maybe ten-miles wide and ten-miles long. People living in whatever they could junk together.

And when I read *Grapes of Wrath*—she bought that for me (indicates young girl seated across the room)—that was like reliving my life. Particularly the part where they lived in this Government camp. Because when we were picking fruit in Texas, we lived in a Government place like that. They came around, and they helped the women make mattresses. See, we didn't have anything. And they showed us how to sew and make dresses. And every Saturday night, we'd have a dance. And when I was reading *Grapes of Wrath* this was just like my life. I was never so proud of poor people before, as I was after I read that book.

I think that's the worst thing that our system does to people, is to take away their pride. It prevents them from being a human being. And wondering why the Harlem and why the Detroit. They're talking about troops and law and order. You get law and order in this country when people are allowed to be decent human beings. Every time I hear another building's on fire, I say: oh, boy, baby, hit 'em again. (Laughs.)

I don't think people were put on earth to suffer. I think that's a lot of nonsense. I think we are the highest development on the earth, and I think we were put here to live and be happy and to enjoy everything that's here. I don't think it's right for a handful of people to get ahold of all the things that make living a joy instead of a sorrow. You wake up in the morning, and it consciously hits you—it's just like a big hand that takes your heart and squeezes it—because you don't know what that day is going to bring: hunger or you don't know.

1936
from *The Harvest Gypsies*

By John Steinbeck

John Steinbeck toured squatters' camps in California for a series of articles on migrant workers three years before he wrote *The Grapes of Wrath*. The stories originally ran in *The San Francisco News*.

MIGRANT FAMILIES IN California find that unemployment relief, which is available to settled unemployed, has little to offer them. In the first place there has grown up a regular technique for getting relief; one who knows the ropes can find aid from the various state and Federal disbursement agencies, while a man ignorant of the methods will be turned away.

The migrant is always partially unemployed. The nature of his occupation makes his work seasonal. At the same time the nature of his work makes him ineligible for relief. The basis for receiving most of the relief is residence.

But it is impossible for the migrant to accomplish the residence. He must move about the country. He could not stop long enough to establish residence or he would starve to death. He finds, then, on application, that he cannot be put on the relief rolls. And being ignorant, he gives up at that point.

For the same reason he finds that he cannot receive any of the local benefits reserved for residents of a county. The county hospital was built not for the transient, but for residents of the county.

It will be interesting to trace the history of one family in relation to medicine, work relief and direct relief. The family consisted of five persons, a man of 50, his wife of 45, two boys, 15 and 12, and a girl of six. They came from Oklahoma, where the father operated a little ranch of 50 acres of prairie.

When the ranch dried up and blew away the family put its moveable possessions in an old Dodge truck and came to California. They arrived in time for the orange picking in Southern California and put in a good average season.

The older boy and the father together made $60. At that time the automobile broke out some teeth of the differential and the repairs, together with three second-hand tires, took $22. The family moved into Kern County to chop grapes and camped in the squatters' camp on the edge of Bakersfield.

At this time the father sprained his ankle and the little girl developed measles. Doctors' bills amounted to $10 of the remaining store, and food and transportation took most of the rest.

The 15-year-old boy was now the only earner for the family. The 12-year-old boy picked up a brass gear in a yard and took it to sell. He was arrested and taken before the juvenile court, but was released to his father's custody. The father walked in to Bakersfield from the squatters' camp on a sprained ankle because the gasoline was gone from the automobile and he didn't dare invest any of the remaining money in more gasoline.

This walk caused complications in the sprain which laid him up again. The little girl had recovered from measles by this time, but her eyes had not been protected and she had lost part of her eyesight.

The father now applied for relief and found that he was ineligible because he had not established the necessary residence. All resources were gone. A little food was given to the family by neighbors in the squatters' camp. A neighbor who had a goat brought in a cup of milk every day for the little girl.

At this time the 15-year-old boy came home from the fields with a pain in his side. He was feverish and in great pain. The mother put hot cloths on his stomach while a neighbor took the crippled father to the county hospital to apply for aid. The hospital was full, all its time taken by bona fide local residents. The trouble described as a pain in the stomach by the father was not taken seriously.

The father was given a big dose of salts to take home to the boy. That night the pain grew so great that the boy became unconscious. The father telephoned the hospital and found that there was no one on duty who could attend to his case. The boy died of a burst appendix the next day.

There was no money. The county buried him free. The father sold the Dodge for $30 and bought a $2 wreath for the funeral. With the remaining money he laid in a store of cheap, filling food—beans, oatmeal, lard. He tried to go back to work in the fields. Some of the neighbors gave him rides to work and charged him a small amount for transportation.

He was on the weak ankle too soon and could not make over 75¢ a day at piece-work, chopping. Again he applied for relief and was refused because he was not a resident and because he was employed. The little girl, because of insufficient food and weakness from measles, relapsed into influenza.

The father did not try the county hospital again. He went to a private doctor who refused to come to the squatters' camp unless he were paid in advance. The father took two days' pay and gave it to the doctor who came to the family shelter, took the girl's temperature, gave the mother seven pills, told the mother to keep the child warm and went away. The father lost his job because he was too slow.

He applied again for help and was given one week's supply of groceries.

This can go on indefinitely. The case histories like it can be found in their thousands. It may be argued that there were ways for this man to get aid, but how did he know where to get it? There was no way for him to find out.

California communities have used the old, old methods of dealing with such problems. The first method is to disbelieve it and vigorously to deny that there is a problem. The second is to deny local responsibility since the people are not permanent residents. And the third and silliest of all is to run the trouble over the county borders into another county. The floater method of swapping what the counties consider undesirables from hand to hand is like a game of medicine ball.

A fine example of this insular stupidity concerns the hookworm situation in Stanislaus County. The mud along water courses where there are squatters living is infected. Several business men of Modesto and Ceres offered as a solution that the squatters be cleared out. There was no thought of isolating the victims and stopping the hookworm.

The affected people were, according to these men, to be run out of the county to spread the disease in other fields. It is this refusal of the counties to consider anything but the immediate economy and profit of the locality that is the cause of a great deal of the unsolvable quality of the migrants' problem. The counties seem terrified that they may be required to give some aid to the labor they require for their harvests.

According to several Government and state surveys and studies of large numbers of migrants, the maximum a worker can make is $400 a year, while the average is around $300, and the large minimum is $150 a year. This amount must feed, clothe and transport whole families.

Sometimes whole families are able to work in the fields, thus making an additional wage. In other observed cases a whole family, weakened by sickness and malnutrition, has worked in the fields, making less than the wage of one healthy man. It does not take long at the migrants' work to reduce the health of any family. Food is scarce always, and luxuries of any kind are unknown.

Observed diets run something like this when the family is making money:

Family of eight—Boiled cabbage, baked sweet potatoes, creamed carrots, beans, fried dough, jelly, tea.

Family of seven—Beans, baking-powder biscuits, jam, coffee.

Family of six—Canned salmon, cornbread, raw onions.

Family of five—Biscuits, fried potatoes, dandelion greens, pears.

These are dinners. It is to be noticed that even in these flush times there is no milk, no butter. The major part of the diet is starch. In slack times the diet becomes all starch, this being the cheapest way to fill up. Dinners during lay-offs are as follows:

Family of seven—Beans, fried dough.

Family of six—Fried cornmeal.

Family of five—Oatmeal mush.

Family of eight (there were six children)—Dandelion greens and boiled potatoes.

It will be seen that even in flush times the possibility of remaining healthy is very slight. The complete absence of milk for the children is responsible for many of the diseases of malnutrition. Even pellagra is far from unknown.

The preparation of food is the most primitive. Cooking equipment usually consists of a hole dug in the ground or a kerosene can with a smoke vent and open front. If the adults have been working 10 hours in the fields or in the packing sheds they do not want to cook. They will buy canned goods as long as they have money, and when they are low in funds they will subsist on half-cooked starches.

The problem of childbirth among the migrants is among the most terrible. There is no prenatal care of the mothers whatever, and no possibility of such care. They must work in the fields until they are physically unable or, if they do not work, the care of the other children and of the camp will not allow the prospective mothers any rest.

In actual birth the presence of a doctor is a rare exception. Sometimes in the squatters' camps a neighbor woman will help at the birth. There will be no sanitary precautions nor hygienic arrangements. The child will be born on newspapers in the dirty bed. In case of a bad presentation requiring surgery or forceps, the mother is practically condemned to death. Once born, the eyes of the baby are not treated, the endless medical attention lavished on middle-class babies is completely absent.

The mother, usually suffering from malnutrition, is not able to produce breast milk. Sometimes the baby is nourished on canned milk until it can eat fried dough and cornmeal. This being the case, the infant mortality is very great.

The following is an example: Wife of family with three children. She is 38; her face is lined and thin and there is a hard glaze on her eyes. The three children who survive were born prior to 1929, when the family rented a farm in Utah. In 1930 this woman bore a child which lived four months and died of "colic."

In 1931 her child was born dead because "a han' truck fulla boxes run inta me two days before the baby come." In 1932 there was a miscarriage. "I couldn't carry the baby 'cause I was sick." She is ashamed of this. In 1933 her baby lived a week. "Jus' died. I don't know what of." In 1934 she had no pregnancy. She is also a little ashamed of this. In 1935 her baby lived a long time, nine months.

"Seemed for a long time like he was gonna live. Big strong fella it seemed like." She is pregnant again now. "If we could get milk for um I guess it'd be better." This is an extreme case, but by no means an unusual one.

1936

from *Let Us Now Praise Famous Men*

By James Agee

James Agee spent four weeks living with a sharecropper
family in the Deep South while researching an assignment
for *Fortune*. The story was too lengthy for the magazine, so
Agee published it in book form.

> *You are farmers; I am a farmer myself.*
> —Franklin Delano Roosevelt

Woods and Ricketts work for Michael and T. Hudson Margraves,
two brothers, in partnership, who live in Cookstown. Gudger
worked for the Margraves for three years; he now (1936) works for
Chester Boles, who lives two miles south of Cookstown.

On their business arrangements, and working histories, and on
their money, I wrote a chapter too long for inclusion in this volume
without sacrifice of too much else. I will put in its place here as
extreme a précis as I can manage.

Gudger has no home, no land, no mule; none of the more important farming implements. He must get all these of his landlord. Boles,
for his share of the corn and cotton, also advances him rations money
during four months of the year, March through June, and his fertilizer.

Gudger pays him back with his labor and with the labor of
his family.

At the end of the season he pays him back further: with half his
corn; with half his cotton; with half his cottonseed. Out of his own
half of these crops he also pays him back the rations money, plus

interest, and his share of the fertilizer, plus interest, and such other debts, plus interest, as he may have incurred.

What is left, once doctors' bills and other debts have been deducted, is his year's earnings.

Gudger is a straight half-cropper, or sharecropper.

Woods and Ricketts own no home and no land, but Woods owns one mule and Ricketts owns two, and they own their farming implements. Since they do not have to rent these tools and animals, they work under a slightly different arrangement. They give over to the landlord only a third of their cotton and a fourth of their corn. Out of their own parts of the crop, however, they owe him the price of two thirds of their cotton fertilizer and three fourths of their corn fertilizer, plus interest; and, plus interest, the same debts on rations money.

Woods and Ricketts are tenants: they work on third and fourth.

A very few tenants pay cash rent: but these two types of arrangement, with local variants (company stores; food instead of rations money; slightly different divisions of the crops) are basic to cotton tenantry all over the South.

From March through June, while the cotton is being cultivated, they live on the rations money.

From July through to late August, while the cotton is making, they live however they can.

From late August through October or into November, during the picking and ginning season, they live on the money from their share of the cottonseed.

From then on until March, they live on whatever they have earned in the year; or however they can.

During six to seven months of each year, then—that is, during exactly such time as their labor with the cotton is of absolute necessity to the landlord—they can be sure of whatever living is possible in rations advances and in cottonseed money.

During five to six months of the year, of which three are the hardest months of any year, with the worst of weather, the least adequacy of shelter, the worst and least of food, the worst of health, quite normal and inevitable, they can count on nothing except that they may hope least of all for any help from their landlords.

Gudger—a family of six—lives on ten dollars a month rations money during four months of the year. He has lived on eight, and on six. Woods—a family of six—until this year was unable to get better than eight a month during the same period; this year he managed to get it up to ten. Ricketts—a family of nine—lives on ten dollars a month during this spring and early summer period.

This debt is paid back in the fall at eight per cent interest. Eight per cent is charged also on the fertilizer and on all other debts which tenants incur in this vicinity.

At the normal price, a half-sharing tenant gets about six dollars a bale from his share of the cottonseed. A one-mule, half-sharing tenant makes on the average three bales. This half-cropper, then, Gudger, can count on eighteen dollars, more or less, to live on during the picking and ginning: though he gets nothing until his first bale is ginned.

Working on third and fourth, a tenant gets the money from two thirds of the cottonseed of each bale: nine dollars to the bale. Woods, with one mule, makes three bales, and gets twenty-seven dollars. Ricketts, with two mules, makes and gets twice that, to live on during the late summer and fall.

• • •

What is earned at the end of a given year is never to be depended on and, even late in a season, is never predictable. It can be enough to tide through the dead months of the winter, sometimes even better: it can be enough, spread very thin, to take through two months, and a sickness, or six weeks, or a month: it can be little enough to be completely meaningless: it can be nothing: it can be enough less than nothing to insure a tenant only of an equally hopeless lack of money at the end of his next year's work: and whatever one year may bring in the way of good luck, there is never any reason to hope that that luck will be repeated in the next year or the year after that.

The best that Woods has ever cleared was $1300 during a war year. During the teens and twenties he fairly often cleared as much as $300; he fairly often cleared $50 and less; two or three times he ended the year in debt. During the depression years he has more often cleared $50 and less; last year he cleared $150, but serious illness during the winter ate it up rapidly.

The best that Gudger has ever cleared is $125. That was in the plow-under year. He felt exceedingly hopeful and bought a mule: but when his landlord warned him of how he was coming out the next year, he sold it. Most years he has not made more than $25 to $30; and about one year in three he has ended in debt. Year before last he wound up $80 in debt; last year, $12; of Boles, his new landlord, the first thing he had to do was borrow $15 to get through the winter until rations advances should begin.

Years ago the Ricketts were, relatively speaking, almost prosperous. Besides their cotton farming they had ten cows and sold the milk, and they lived near a good stream and had all the fish they wanted. Ricketts went $400 into debt on a fine young pair of mules. One of the mules died before it had made its first crop; the other died the year after; against his fear, amounting to full horror, of sinking to the half-crop level where nothing is owned, Ricketts went into debt for other, inferior mules; his cows went one by one into debts and desperate exchanges and by sickness; he got congestive chills; his wife got pellagra; a number of his children died; he got appendicitis and lay for days on end under the ice cap; his wife's pellagra got into her brain; for ten consecutive years now, though they have lived on so little rations money, and have turned nearly all their cottonseed money toward their debts, they have not cleared or had any hope of clearing a cent at the end of the year.

It is not often, then, at the end of the season, that a tenant clears enough money to tide him through the winter, or even an appreciable part of it. More generally he can count on it that, during most of the four months between settlement time in the fall and the beginning of work and resumption of rations advances in the early spring, he will have no money and can expect none, nor any help, from his landlord: and of having no money during the six midsummer weeks of laying by, he can be still more sure. Four to six months of each year, in other words, he is much more likely than not to have nothing whatever, and during these months he must take care for himself: he is no responsibility of the landlord's. All he can hope to do is find work. This is hard, because there are a good many chronically unemployed in the towns, and they are more convenient to most openings for work and can at all times be counted on if they are needed; also there is no increase, during these two dead farming seasons, of other kinds of work to do. And so, with no more jobs open than at any other time of year, and with plenty of men already convenient to take them, the whole tenant population, hundreds and thousands in any locality, are desperately in need of work.

A landlord saves up certain odd jobs for these times of year: they go, at less than he would have to pay others, to those of his tenants who happen to live nearest or to those he thinks best of; and even at best they don't amount to much.

When there is wooded land on the farm, a landlord ordinarily permits a tenant to cut and sell firewood for what he can get. About the best a tenant gets of this is a dollar a load, but more often (for the market is glutted, so many are trying to sell wood) he can get no better than half that and less, and often enough, at the end of a hard day's peddling, miles from home, he will let it go for a quarter or fifteen cents rather than haul it all the way home again: so it doesn't amount to much. Then, too, by no means everyone has wood to cut and sell: in the whole southern half of the county we were working mainly in, there was so little wood that the negroes, during the hard winter of 1935–36, were burning parts of their fences, outbuildings, furniture and houses, and were dying off in great and not seriously counted numbers, of pneumonia and other afflictions of the lungs.

WPA work is available to very few tenants: they are, technically, employed, and thus have no right to it: and if by chance they manage to get it, landlords are more likely than not to intervene. They feel it spoils a tenant to be paid wages, even for a little while. A tenant who so much as tries to get such work is under disapproval.

There is not enough direct relief even for the widows and the old of the county.

Gudger and Ricketts, during this year, were exceedingly lucky. After they, and Woods, had been turned away from government work, they found work in a sawmill. They were given the work on condition that they stay with it until the mill was moved, and subject strictly to their landlords' permission: and their employer wouldn't so much as hint how long the work might last. Their landlords quite grudgingly gave them permission, on condition that they pay for whatever help was needed in their absence during the picking season. Gudger hired a hand, at eight dollars a month and board. Ricketts did not need to: his family is large enough. They got a dollar and a quarter a day five days a week and seventy-five cents on Saturday, seven dollars a week, ten hours' work a day. Woods did not even try for this work: he was too old and too sick.

1998

from *Nickel and Dimed*

By Barbara Ehrenreich

After two years of research that included several months working low-wage jobs, Barbara Ehrenreich learned first-hand why so many of the working poor live in a perpetual state of emergency.

THE ECONOMIC POLICY Institute recently reviewed dozens of studies of what constitutes a "living wage" and came up with an average figure of $30,000 a year for a family of one adult and two children, which amounts to a wage of $14 an hour. This is not the very minimum such a family could live on; the budget includes health insurance, a telephone, and child care at a licensed center, for example, which are well beyond the reach of millions. But it does not include restaurant meals, video rentals, Internet access, wine and liquor, cigarettes and lottery tickets, or even very much meat. The shocking thing is that the majority of American workers, about 60 percent, earn less than $14 an hour. Many of them get by by teaming up with another wage earner, a spouse or grown child. Some draw on government help in the form of food stamps, housing vouchers, the earned income tax credit, or—for those coming off welfare in relatively generous states—subsidized child care. But others—single mothers for example—have nothing but their own wages to live on, no matter how many mouths there are to feed.

Employers will look at that $30,000 figure, which is over twice what they currently pay entry-level workers, and see nothing but bankruptcy ahead. Indeed, it is probably impossible for the private sector to provide everyone with an adequate standard of living through wages, or even wages plus benefits, alone: too much of what we need, such as reliable child care, is just too expensive, even for middle-class families. Most civilized nations compensate for the inadequacy of wages by providing relatively generous public services such as health insurance, free or subsidized child care, subsidized housing, and effective public transportation. But the United States, for all its wealth, leaves its citizens to fend for themselves—facing market-based rents, for example, on their wages alone. For millions of Americans, that $10—or even $8 or $6—hourly wage is all there is.

It is common, among the nonpoor, to think of poverty as a sustainable condition—austere, perhaps, but they get by somehow, don't they? They are "always with us." What is harder for the nonpoor to see is poverty as acute distress: The lunch that consists of Doritos or hot dog rolls, leading to faintness before the end of the shift. The "home" that is also a car or a van. The illness or injury that must be "worked through," with gritted teeth, because there's no sick pay or health insurance and the loss of one day's pay will mean no groceries for the next. These experiences are not part of a sustainable lifestyle, even a lifestyle of chronic deprivation and relentless low-level punishment. They are, by almost any standard of subsistence, emergency situations. And that is how we should see the poverty of so many millions of low-wage Americans—as a state of emergency.

In the summer of 2000 I returned—permanently, I have every reason to hope—to my customary place in the socioeconomic spectrum. I go to restaurants, often far finer ones than the places where I worked, and sit down at a table. I sleep in hotel rooms that someone else has cleaned and shop in stores that others will tidy when I leave. To go from the bottom 20 percent to the top 20 percent is to enter a magical world where needs are met, problems are solved, almost without any intermediate effort. If you want to get somewhere fast, you hail a cab. If your aged parents have grown tiresome or incontinent, you put them away where others will deal with their dirty diapers and dementia. If you are part of the upper-middle-class majority that employs a maid or maid service, you return from work to find the house miraculously restored to order—the toilet bowls shit-free and gleaming, the socks that you left on the floor levitated back to their normal dwelling place. Here, sweat is a metaphor for hard work, but seldom its consequence. Hundreds of little things get done, reliably and routinely every day, without anyone's seeming to do them.

The top 20 percent routinely exercises other, far more consequential forms of power in the world. This stratum, which contains what I have termed in an earlier book the "professional-managerial class," is the home of our decision makers, opinion shapers, culture creators—our professors, lawyers, executives, entertainers, politicians, judges, writers, producers, and editors.[1] When they speak, they are listened to. When they complain, someone usually scurries to correct the problem and apologize for it. If they complain often enough, someone far below them in wealth and influence may be chastised or even fired. Political power, too, is concentrated within the top 20 percent, since its members are far more likely than the poor—or even the middle class—to discern the all-too-tiny distinctions between candidates that can make it seem worthwhile to contribute, participate, and vote. In all these ways, the affluent exert inordinate

---

[1] *Fear of Falling: The Inner Life of the Middle Class* (Pantheon, 1989).

power over the lives of the less affluent, and especially over the lives of the poor, determining what public services will be available, if any, what minimum wage, what laws governing the treatment of labor.

So it is alarming, upon returning to the upper middle class from a sojourn, however artificial and temporary, among the poor, to find the rabbit hole close so suddenly and completely behind me. You were *where,* doing *what?* Some odd optical property of our highly polarized and unequal society makes the poor almost invisible to their economic superiors. The poor can see the affluent easily enough—on television, for example, or on the covers of magazines. But the affluent rarely see the poor or, if they do catch sight of them in some public space, rarely know what they're seeing, since—thanks to consignment stores and, yes, Wal-Mart—the poor are usually able to disguise themselves as members of the more comfortable classes. Forty years ago the hot journalistic topic was the "discovery of the poor" in their inner-city and Appalachian "pockets of poverty." Today you are more likely to find commentary on their "disappearance," either as a supposed demographic reality or as a shortcoming of the middle-class imagination.

In a 2000 article on the "disappearing poor," journalist James Fallows reports that, from the vantage point of the Internet's *nouveaux riches,* it is "hard to understand people for whom a million dollars would be a fortune . . . not to mention those for whom $246 is a full week's earnings."[2] Among the reasons he and others have cited for the blindness of the affluent is the fact that they are less and less likely to share spaces and services with the poor. As public schools and other public services deteriorate, those who can afford to do so send their children to private schools and spend their off-hours in private spaces—health clubs, for example, instead of the local park. They don't ride on public buses and subways. They withdraw from mixed

---

[2] "The Invisible Poor," *New York Times Magazine,* March 19, 2000.

neighborhoods into distant suburbs, gated communities, or guarded apartment towers; they shop in stores that, in line with the prevailing "market segmentation," are designed to appeal to the affluent alone. Even the affluent young are increasingly unlikely to spend their summers learning how the "other half" lives, as lifeguards, waitresses, or housekeepers at resort hotels. The *New York Times* reports that they now prefer career-relevant activities like summer school or interning in an appropriate professional setting to the "sweaty, low-paid and mind-numbing slots that have long been their lot." [3]

Then, too, the particular political moment favors what almost looks like a "conspiracy of silence" on the subject of poverty and the poor. The Democrats are not eager to find flaws in the period of "unprecedented prosperity" they take credit for; the Republicans have lost interest in the poor now that "welfare-as-we-know-it" has ended. Welfare reform itself is a factor weighing against any close investigation of the conditions of the poor. Both parties heartily endorsed it, and to acknowledge that low-wage work doesn't lift people out of poverty would be to admit that it may have been, in human terms, a catastrophic mistake. In fact, very little is known about the fate of former welfare recipients because the 1996 welfare reform legislation blithely failed to include any provision for monitoring their postwelfare economic condition. Media accounts persistently bright-side the situation, highlighting the occasional success stories and downplaying the acknowledged increase in hunger.[4] And sometimes there seems to be almost deliberate deception. In June 2000, the press rushed to hail a study supposedly showing that

---

[3] "Summer Work Is Out of Favor with the Young," *New York Times,* June 18, 2000.
[4] The *National Journal* reports that the "good news" is that almost six million people have left the welfare rolls since 1996, while the "rest of the story" includes the problem that "these people sometimes don't have enough to eat" ("Welfare Reform, Act 2," June 24, 2000, pp. 1,978–93).

Minnesota's welfare-to-work program had sharply reduced poverty and was, as *Time* magazine put it, a "winner." [5] Overlooked in these reports was the fact that the program in question was a pilot project that offered far more generous child care and other subsidies than Minnesota's actual welfare reform program. Perhaps the error can be forgiven—the pilot project, which ended in 1997, had the same name, Minnesota Family Investment Program, as Minnesota's much larger, ongoing welfare reform program.[6]

You would have to read a great many newspapers very carefully, cover to cover, to see the signs of distress. You would find, for example, that in 1999 Massachusetts food pantries reported a 72 percent increase in the demand for their services over the previous year, that Texas food banks were "scrounging" for food, despite donations at or above 1998 levels, as were those in Atlanta.[7] You might learn that in San Diego the Catholic Church could no longer, as of January 2000, accept homeless families at its shelter, which happens to be the city's largest, because it was already operating at twice its normal capacity.[8] You would come across news of a study showing that the percentage of Wisconsin food-stamp families in "extreme poverty"—defined as less than 50 percent of the federal poverty line—has tripled in the last decade to more than 30 percent.[9] You might discover that, nationwide, America's food banks are experiencing "a torrent of need which [they] cannot meet" and that, according to a survey conducted by the U.S.

---

[5] "Minnesota's Welfare Reform Proves a Winner," *Time,* June 12, 2000.

[6] Center for Law and Social Policy, "Update," Washington, D.C., June 2000.

[7] "Study: More Go Hungry since Welfare Reform," *Boston Herald,* January 21, 2000; "Charity Can't Feed All while Welfare Reforms Implemented," *Houston Chronicle,* January 10, 2000; "Hunger Grows as Food Banks Try to Keep Pace," *Atlanta Journal and Constitution,* November 26, 1999.

[8] "Rise in Homeless Families Strains San Diego Aid," *Los Angeles Times,* January 24, 2000.

[9] "Hunger Problems Said to Be Getting Worse," *Milwaukee Journal Sentinel,* December 15, 1999.

Conference of Mayors, 67 percent of the adults requesting emergency food aid are people with jobs.[10]

One reason nobody bothers to pull all these stories together and announce a widespread state of emergency may be that Americans of the newspaper-reading professional middle class are used to thinking of poverty as a consequence of unemployment. During the heyday of downsizing in the Reagan years, it very often was, and it still is for many inner-city residents who have no way of getting to the proliferating entry-level jobs on urban peripheries. When unemployment causes poverty, we know how to state the problem—typically, "the economy isn't growing fast enough"—and we know what the traditional liberal solution is—"full employment." But when we have full or nearly full employment, when jobs are available to any job seeker who can get to them, then the problem goes deeper and begins to cut into that web of expectations that make up the "social contract." According to a recent poll conducted by Jobs for the Future, a Boston-based employment research firm, 94 percent of Americans agree that "people who work full-time should be able to earn enough to keep their families out of poverty."[11] I grew up hearing over and over, to the point of tedium, that "hard work" was the secret of success: "Work hard and you'll get ahead" or "It's hard work that got us where we are." No one ever said that you could work hard—harder even than you ever thought possible—and still find yourself sinking ever deeper into poverty and debt.

When poor single mothers had the option of remaining out of the labor force on welfare, the middle and upper middle class

---

[10] Deborah Leff, the president and CEO of the hunger-relief organization America's Second Harvest, quoted in the *National Journal,* op. cit.; "Hunger Persists in U.S. despite the Good Times," *Detroit News,* June 15, 2000.

[11] "A National Survey of American Attitudes toward Low-Wage Workers and Welfare Reform," Jobs for the Future, Boston, May 24, 2000.

tended to view them with a certain impatience, if not disgust. The welfare poor were excoriated for their laziness, their persistence in reproducing in unfavorable circumstances, their presumed addictions, and above all for their "dependency." Here they were, content to live off "government handouts" instead of seeking "self-sufficiency," like everyone else, through a job. They needed to get their act together, learn how to wind an alarm clock, get out there and get to work. But now that government has largely withdrawn its "handouts," now that the overwhelming majority of the poor are out there toiling in Wal-Mart or Wendy's—well, what are we to think of them? Disapproval and condescension no longer apply, so what outlook makes sense?

Guilt, you may be thinking warily. Isn't that what we're supposed to feel? But guilt doesn't go anywhere near far enough; the appropriate emotion is shame—shame at our *own* dependency, in this case, on the underpaid labor of others. When someone works for less pay than she can live on—when, for example, she goes hungry so that you can eat more cheaply and conveniently—then she has made a great sacrifice for you, she has made you a gift of some part of her abilities, her health, and her life. The "working poor," as they are approvingly termed, are in fact the major philanthropists of our society. They neglect their own children so that the children of others will be cared for; they live in substandard housing so that other homes will be shiny and perfect; they endure privation so that inflation will be low and stock prices high. To be a member of the working poor is to be an anonymous donor, a nameless benefactor, to everyone else. As Gail, one of my restaurant coworkers put it, "you give and you give."

Someday, of course—and I will make no predictions as to exactly when—they are bound to tire of getting so little in return and to demand to be paid what they're worth. There'll be a lot of anger when that day comes, and strikes and disruption. But the sky will not fall, and we will all be better off for it in the end.

2003
How the Other Half Still Lives

By Jack Newfield

Journalist Jack Newfield looks at the current state of
poverty in America in this story which originally appeared
in *The Nation*.

IN 1890 THE great photojournalist Jacob Riis published his now
classic book about immigrant tenement poverty in lower Manhattan, called *How the Other Half Lives.* During the past few
months I have tried to retrace some of Riis's steps through modern
New York's pain and deprivation. As New York's (and America's)
economy turned bleaker and bleaker, I hung out in unemployment
offices, food-stamp application centers and the occasional job fair,
where lines of job-seekers were never short. I traveled around in a
van with volunteers from the Coalition for the Homeless as they
distributed free hot meals at night to the city's most defeated and
destitute inhabitants.

I visited union halls, food pantries, immigrant community centers
and the dreadful Emergency Assistance Unit (EAU) in the Bronx. I
interviewed community organizers, economists, politicians, leaders of
nonprofit advocacy groups—as well as the jobless, homeless and
hopeless. I wanted to understand better how the other half lives now,
and who was responsible for this misery in the midst of this new,
twenty-first-century Gilded Age of excess produced by the money culture, corporate scandal and the concentration of wealth and power.

What I learned was that in some ways little has changed since Riis
published his reportorial findings in 1890. The poor are still largely
invisible to the complacent majority. Most Americans don't see the

everydayness of poverty. It is segregated in "bad neighborhoods" and in impersonal government waiting rooms. We don't see all the people being told there are no applications for food stamps available at that location; all the people postponing medical treatment for their children because they don't have health insurance; all the people trying to find a job with their phone service shut off because they couldn't pay the bill; or all the deliverymen for drugstores and supermarkets paid only $3 an hour, which is illegal.

In one way we are even worse off than we were 113 years ago: We have no Jacob Riis now humanizing poverty, making the satisfied see it and smell it. We have no American Dickens or Orwell, no James Agee and Walker Evans, no Michael Harrington, no John Steinbeck, no Edward R. Murrow.

Something else in addition to poverty's invisibility that harks back to the first Gilded Age is the widening economic disparity between the rich and poor. During the Reagan presidency, the poor lost tremendous ground. And during the Clinton presidency, the rich did fabulously well. In 1998 the top 1 percent of households collected almost 17 percent of the nation's income. And now Bush is proposing a tax cut that gives the richest 5 percent of taxpayers most of the economic gain. This is a class-warfare policy of shooting the wounded and looting the amputees.

What is amazing is that this expansion of inequality took place without ever becoming a noticeable issue in American politics. This growing concentration of wealth has given the superrich domination over politics through extravagant campaign contributions and media ownership, which has made large elements of the media sound like Republican echo chambers. The increasing gap between rich and poor and the erosion of democracy by vast wealth are not hot-button talk-show issues because so few politicians with a national following agitate about them with continuing conviction. Only Ted Kennedy, John McCain and the late Paul Wellstone come to mind. None of the leading Democrats seeking the 2004 presidential nomination are talking about the maldistribution of wealth or mobilizing a new war on poverty or a massive jobs program. Cerebral, suburban Gary Hart was quoted in a February 2 *New York Times Magazine* profile as saying: "How do you make the principles of equality and justice and fairness work in a time when everyone's well off?" I would gladly take Hart on a tour of New York's communities of sorrow.

I conceived this piece as a way to dramatize the growth of poverty in liberal, pro-labor New York City. But there is also a bigger, national picture that frames the local reporting. This big picture has many layers. It is not only the Republican ascendancy in Washington, Albany and the courts. It is not just the capitulating silences of Democrats. It is not just the fading power of the AFL-CIO. It is not just the historical forces well beyond New York's capacity to influence—like global terrorism, the recessions of the business cycle, the bursting of the Internet technology bubble, the crushing state and city deficits made worse by Bush's radicalism for the rich. It's all of the above and more. For all of New York's real estate, banking, media, marketing and cultural power—and for all its mystique—it is still just a cork bobbing on the ocean of capitalism.

Only during FDR's New Deal was economic disparity significantly reduced. More recently, in addition to the dramatic redistribution of income upward, wealth (property, investments, stocks, bonds and other assets) has become even more concentrated in a few hands than income is. The wealthy fared as well under Clinton as they did under Grover Cleveland—also a Democrat—during the original Gilded Age. The top 5 percent of Americans now own almost 60 percent of the country's wealth—the same 5 percent who would receive most of the benefit from Bush's proposed tax cut.

Downward mobility is the hot new trend in the city of buzz and billionaires. By every measure, unemployment, homelessness and hunger are on the rise in New York. In December, unemployment jumped up to 8.4 percent, the highest it has been in five years, the highest of any of the country's big cities. New York has lost 176,000 jobs in the past two years, more than any other city. Today more than 1.6 million New Yorkers (20.2 percent of the population) are living below the federal poverty line; another 13 percent are barely above it.

And, as always, poverty is more severe among people of color. Blacks and Latinos comprise 47.5 percent of the city's labor force but account for 61.2 percent of the jobless. The city's poverty rate is 25 percent for blacks, 28 percent for Hispanics and 12 percent for whites. It's been double for people of color for generations. There are now 38,000 homeless people in city shelters each winter night—and 17,000 of them are children. Homelessness has increased by 82 percent since 1998. In 2002 the city's network of 1,000 soup kitchens and food pantries affiliated with the New York Food Bank—many faith-based—fed 45 percent more hungry people than they did two years earlier. And about 90 percent of these hungry people are not homeless, and do have a history of work.

"Hunger among the working poor is a growing trend," Joel Berg, the director of the Coalition Against Hunger, told me. "It's caused by skyrocketing rents, a minimum wage that has been stagnant at $5.15 an hour since 1997, rising costs for health insurance and the city restricting access to food stamps while Giuliani was mayor." Every day the city's soup kitchens and food pantries provide about 1 million people with meals. The Coalition Against Hunger reports that because of increased demand, in 2001, the soup kitchens and food pantries have had to turn away 350,000 New Yorkers—including 85,000 children.

Every Thursday morning, at the Yorkville Common Pantry, on 109th Street in East Harlem, there is a long line of silent, dejected women with shopping carts, waiting for fresh meats and canned goods to be distributed by volunteers when the doors open at 11:30 am. On my occasional visits to this line, I saw that most of these Hispanic women were mothers with children who had sporadic histories of at least part-time work. I also met a recent Russian immigrant who had no coat and a woman attending some night classes who had lost her job, exhausted her health insurance and suffered serious depression but could not afford the medication to treat it. Her grandest dream, she said, is "to move to a safer block."

New York's economy has declined for seven consecutive quarters. Consumer confidence is vaporizing. Inflation is rising faster than wages. Personal bankruptcies are up as a consequence of credit-card debt and predatory lending by the jackals of recession. And to make future prospects even darker, the state has a $10 billion budget deficit while the city's is $3 billion, at a time when the President is refusing to assist the states. New York City now faces state-imposed transit-fare increases, college tuition increases and a $1.2 billion cut in state education funding.

The Low-Wage World

Most poor people work. The roughly $10,700 a year that $5.15-an-hour minimum-wage jobs pay is without question not sufficient to hold a family together in New York. But a big part of the city's poverty crisis is the World of Low-Wage Work, just above the legal minimum—"McJobs," as organizers call them. There are hundreds of thousands of New Yorkers who are trapped in such jobs, from which they can be fired or lose shifts on the whim of a supervisor, at big chain franchises like McDonald's, Tower Records, Duane Reade drugstores and Gristedes supermarkets.

In testimony before the City Council on behalf of a living-wage bill, David Jones, president of the Community Service Society, a non-profit social service agency, said that "one-in-five New York workers earns less than $8.10 an hour. Three-quarters of those earning less than $8.10 an hour are living in poverty." According to a comprehensive CSS study, 52.6 percent of low-wage workers are women; six out of ten have a high school diploma; and more than one in ten is a college graduate. Eight in ten are people of color. They are not teenagers working part-time jobs or subsidized members of middle-income households. More than 90 percent of those trapped in low-wage jobs are adults. More than 75 percent are now working full-time. They are not substance abusers, alcoholics or the mentally ill.

More than 600,000 New Yorkers earn between $5.15 an hour and $10 an hour. Some 56 percent of these low-wage workers have no health insurance for their families, 52 percent have no pension or 401(k) plan and 37 percent receive no paid leave. The CSS survey found that 27 percent of these workers fell behind in rent payments during the past year, 18 percent had their utilities shut off and 14 percent had to postpone necessary medical treatment. This low-wage world includes busboys, waitresses, janitors, food-service workers, store clerks, security guards, porters, maids, home health aides, day laborers and deliverymen. In late January, a federal judge in Manhattan ruled that more than 200 deliverymen were being paid less than $3 an hour by the Duane Reade drugstore chain. Most of these workers are immigrants from West Africa; as a group, they had been cheated out of $1 million in back pay.

A political tragedy is that only three unions are aggressively trying to organize the most underpaid workers: Local 1199 of the Service Employees International Union, Local 32BJ, also of the SEIU, and the Hotel Trades Council, which is unionizing maids, housekeepers and employees of private clubs. Without the protection of unionization, collective bargaining and job security, low-wage workers are powerless in this savage season of high unemployment and intense competition for bad jobs. The simultaneous trend of Republican electoral ascendancy shoves these low-wage workers into a deeper hole, since Republican policies like tax cuts for the rich and budget cuts for the poor increase poverty and diminish the standard of living.

But late last year, the overwhelmingly Democratic City Council did pass two important laws to protect low-wage workers. They were enacted mostly because of the intense lobbying and targeted campaign donations of Local 1199 and Local 32BJ. First, the Council passed a compromise version of the living-wage law that gave 50,000 home healthcare workers—Local 1199 members—a minimum wage of $8.10 an hour if they have health insurance, $9.60 if not. This will become $10 an hour by 2006. The law covers employees of companies that receive homecare contracts from the city government—the basis for the legislative jurisdiction over wages. The scope of the bill was narrowed during negotiations between Council Speaker Gifford Miller and Mayor Mike Bloomberg, with about 2,000 building and other service workers deleted from coverage. But Local 32BJ got something else in return that they desired almost as much. This was the Displaced Building Service Worker Protection Act, which requires landlords, managers and contractors of newly acquired commercial properties of fifty units or more to retain on the payroll all union and nonunion workers for a ninety-day grace period.

32BJ was a notoriously corrupt union a few years ago. But now, under president Mike Fishman, and with an engaged membership of 70,000, it made its presence felt at the City Council. Every time there was a hearing on this bill, there were seventy-five or a hundred union members in purple union T-shirts, filling the chamber. A recent court-authorized wiretap recorded unsolicited praise for this union under Fishman's leadership. A Genovese crime family capo known as "Sammy Meatballs" was overheard talking about the union. "It's a very good union for the men," the gangster was complaining. "Y'know what I mean? Usually whoever belongs to it don't want to give that up. The men get treated good and they get good salaries." In the bad old days, this union was in collusion with the mob, selling labor peace and signing sweetheart contracts that screwed the membership. Now Local 32BJ is starting to demonstrate that even in this harsh economic and political climate, a democratic union can make a positive difference.

The difficulty is that too many private-sector unions are too timid or too much a part of the Establishment to hire the best organizers, think big, take risks and embrace an activist mission. Fishman, Dennis Rivera of Local 1199 and Peter Ward, the leader of the Hotel and Motel Trades Union Council, are the exceptions. Unfortunately, they don't have the jurisdiction to organize the exploited workers at the large nonunion chains.

It is hard for people in low-wage jobs to break out of the cycle of poverty. They obey the law, pay their bills, try to improve their education, stay away from drugs—and they still remain where they are, in bad jobs and in bad neighborhoods. Unionization is almost the equivalent of the lottery for them. When I asked Fishman about his philosophy of unionism, he replied: "Our power comes from our ability to take to the street. It is the only power we have. We can create chaos. I believe unions have to risk everything every day. I know our members are always one contract away from destitution."

CHINATOWN

Every evening at about 7:30, a van from the Coalition for the Homeless stops on the fringe of Chinatown in lower Manhattan. And every evening about fifty or sixty women step out of the shadows to receive a free meal of hot soup, fruit and bread in polite silence. They almost all had seamstress jobs in garment sweatshops or worked in restaurants before 9/11. Now they barely survive on family help, extensions of unemployment insurance and charity. Most of them live doubled up, or tripled up, in Chinatown, which has by far the highest population density of any New York neighborhood: 189 people per acre compared with eighty-two people per acre in the rest of Manhattan.

Chinatown—located a mile from Ground Zero—was also the community hardest hit by the terrorist attack. Because of security checkpoints, traffic congestion during the season in which garments had to be trucked and a sudden drop in tourism, Chinatown's economy collapsed in the weeks after 9/11. Sixty-five garment factories in the neighborhood closed in the year after the attack. Three-quarters of Chinatown's work force temporarily lost their jobs in the weeks after the attack, according to the Asian American Federation, a community advocacy group. Although Chinatown employees were only about 1 percent of New York City's work force, they suffered 10 percent of the unemployment caused by the calamity. Even three months after 9/11, the Asian American Federation estimates, about 8,000 Chinatown workers were still unemployed. Making all this worse is Chinatown's immigrant character. This includes a cash-based economy, a dearth of documentation and credit histories that are needed for government or charitable assistance, and many middle-aged workers with a limited command of English. Chinatown also suffers from internal political feuds and divisions. Moreover, most of Chinatown's housing stock dates back to the nineteenth century.

Because of all this disproportionate deprivation, the city's Department of Business Services commissioner, Rob Walsh, nominated Chinatown to be one of the state's new Empire Zones, which would provide lower taxes and cheaper utilities to attract new businesses, creating jobs. But in December 2002 the city's application for Chinatown was rejected by Governor Pataki. He chose six upstate and rural areas to be designated as Empire Zones, but not the city's neighborhood most in need of help. The last economic development zone selected by Pataki was upstate Rensselaer County, which happens to be represented by Joe Bruno, the GOP majority leader of the State Senate. Chinatown happens to be part of the district represented by Democrat Sheldon Silver, Speaker of the Assembly. As Tip O'Neill said, "All politics is local." Walsh was outraged. He told me, "This is wrong. When you analyze the numbers of poverty, of job losses, of the concentration of small businesses that are hurting, there is no comparison between the needs of Chinatown and the needs of well-to-do Rensselaer County. Chinatown is the hardest-hit community in the whole state." New York City contains 40 percent of the state's population but has only ten of the state's seventy-two Empire Zones.

The two Georges—Pataki and Bush—seem to harbor some deep resentment against New York City, and keep denying the city the revenue and assistance it deserves. Pataki's hostility seems to be primarily political—the city is predominantly Democratic in state elections and Pataki has never carried it. The President's antagonism seems deeper and more personal. Bush is the evangelical cowboy for whom New York seems to be emblematic of the diversity, cultural experimentation, religious pluralism, individual freedom, social programs and now antiwar feeling that he loathes. Friends of mine who knew Bush well when he was the owner of the Texas Rangers baseball franchise say that even then, early in his intolerant, born-again fanaticism, he made disparaging remarks about New York in the context of welfare, drugs, immigration and disorder. So even as Bush exploited the patriotic passions unleashed by the mass murder of 9/11, he did not do anything to rescue a community like Chinatown, or help with Medicaid, or revenue sharing, or block grants to the state, or education funds to make the city whole.

CHEATING THE POOR OUT OF FOOD STAMPS

About 800,000 city residents are eligible for food stamps, but do not receive them. During Mayor Rudolph Giuliani's second term, barriers to access were intentionally created, causing a 42 percent drop in recipients. A federal judge, the federal Agriculture Department and Governor Pataki's social service commissioner all found that poor people were being denied access improperly. City officials were claiming to visitors that they had no applications. The applications that were distributed were sixteen pages long and unnecessarily complex. Other bureaucratic games were played to discourage participation in the program. Giuliani's administration fostered a subtle culture of rejection.

Giuliani came to see—and speak of—food stamps as a costly "welfare program" that increased what he called "a culture of dependency." But in fact, food stamps were started as a nutrition program to combat hunger. The program's original federal sponsors included Republican senators from farm states, like Bob Dole, who saw the program as assisting their home state economies through subsidized urban food purchases.

In November 2002, with food pantries swamped by rising demand, New York City somehow removed 11,000 qualified people from the food stamp program. City officials quickly admitted this was a mistake—paperwork errors causing delays in recertifications. The City Council then dispatched undercover investigators to the offices where food stamp applications are supposed to be easily available to the public. But one-third of these undercover testers were sent away without applications, even when they were insistent with clerks and bureaucrats. These rejections were a clear violation of the law. At a December 16, 2002, City Council public hearing, the city's Human Resources commissioner, Verna Eggleston, and her deputy, Giuliani holdover Seth Diamond, told the stunned Councilmembers they were concerned about the cost of enrolling more recipients. They seemed indifferent to the fact that food stamps are often the last barrier between crying children and the cramps of hunger. The chairman of the Council's committee, Bill de Blasio of Brooklyn, reminded the commissioner that not only is the program 100 percent federally funded but that the federal government also pays half of the city's administrative costs.

Only malice, or the most wretched incompetence, could explain the city's failure to provide food stamps to half the city's poor population. Food stamps add at most $4,000 of food to the table of a family living on less than $15,000 a year. They also recycle the money immediately back into the poor community's economy of supermarkets and bodegas. And if every poor New Yorker who is eligible received food stamps, it would inject almost $1 billion in federal benefits into the city's economy. Food stamps are the mother of all win/win propositions. At the Council's hearing, de Blasio asked commissioner Eggleston, "Why is it you can find someone when there is a problem, but you can't find someone when you have a benefit to offer them?"

Homeless Children and "Generous Anger"

When the economy is strong, the homeless population contracts. When the economy is weak, the homeless population expands. The Emergency Assistance Unit—the gateway homeless intake office in the Bronx—is a more reliable economic barometer than the computerized Dow Jones. When mothers and children applying for shelter are sleeping on the floor, or on desks in the office, you know the economy is lousy.

With the recession now in its third year, New York's homeless population is larger than it has ever been. In the late 1980s the shelter population peaked at 28,700. Now it is 38,200. More than 85 percent of the city's homeless population are families, including 17,000 children. Forty percent of these nomadic children suffer from asthma and have no regular doctor. Two years ago, so many mothers with young children started showing up at the office of the Coalition for the Homeless that a playspace and toys were added to the waiting room.

A year ago, with the help of advocates and union members, I was able to sneak into the EAU office. It was something straight out of Dickens or Jacob Riis. Desperate mothers and crying children with running noses were searched for contraband. With the shelter system clogged, the homeless often had to sleep in these offices for two or three days under bright lights before being offered a place to stay. A court order precluding applicants from sleeping overnight in the EAU was routinely violated. Seeing this place gave me a feeling of "generous anger"—the phrase Orwell invoked to describe Dickens's writing about the poorhouse.

To be sure, not all of the homeless want help. These days the street homeless seem to be "more hard-core than before," in the words of Patrick Markee, the senior policy analyst for the coalition, who also helps deliver meals to them on many nights. Based on my own interviews, most of the single adult men on the streets don't want social services, medication or Medicare. They prefer to be left alone. Many appear to suffer from serious mental problems, but the state does not provide nearly enough supportive housing units for the mentally ill. This group does not like shelters; they prefer sleeping in subways or in the waiting room of the Staten Island Ferry terminal in winter. Some of these street people tell me they have been homeless for years. They profess no interest in job training, medication or counseling. They present an intractable problem that seems immune to charity, common sense or romantic liberalism.

Every governmental attempt to ameliorate poverty seems to attract its own breed of parasite and leech. New York has had scandals involving poverty programs, community school boards, nursing home operators and Medicaid fraud, kickbacks to politicians for helping get state contracts for drug and alcohol rehab facilities, and politicians monopolizing twenty-year no-bid care leases. Now there are rapacious landlords getting paid by the city to house homeless families. This racket started as a temporary experiment under Mayor Giuliani in August 2000 but grew to 2,000 apartments, dozens of landlords and millions of dollars paid to them out of the city's treasury. The city has been paying these landlords an average of $2,900 a month—a total of $33 million since last July. But the volume of the homeless flood is so large that the city has no time to verify the backgrounds of these bottom-feeder landlords and the conditions of their squalid apartments. One complex of buildings, where the Human Resources Administration placed 260 families, had so many hazardous and unsanitary violations of the building code that a judge took ownership away from the landlord and placed the complex in receivership. Tenants of another Brooklyn complex have sued, charging that they were evicted so their landlord could rent to 125 homeless families.

There are two silver linings on the horizon. In December, Mayor Bloomberg announced an ambitious five-year plan to build or rehabilitate 60,000 units of low- and middle-income housing, some of which would be set aside for the homeless. Bloomberg also doubled the number of rent vouchers and public housing apartments immediately available to homeless families. And on January 17 the Bloomberg administration and advocates for the homeless, led by the Legal Aid Society, reached an agreement that settled twenty years of rancorous litigation. This agreement codified the existing court order requiring the city to provide shelter to the homeless as a permanent legal right. It also granted to the city the authority to eject from the shelter system—whenever the temperature was above freezing—people who refused an appropriate apartment or engaged in misconduct like assault or theft.

THE FRONTIER OF THE POSSIBLE

Michael Harrington, the author of *The Other America* and my mentor, used to recommend "locating the frontier of the possible" when it came to devising a strategy to shrink poverty. A recent frontier-defining survey by the Community Service Society disclosed a broad common agenda shared by the poor and middle-income and even high-income voters. This included raising the minimum wage, national health insurance, a larger investment in public education and more afford-able housing. (Affordable housing was the highest priority among low-income voters.)

The November 2002 local elections did offer some hopeful signs that can be duplicated. The intransigently progressive State Senator Liz Krueger was re-elected on Manhattan's Upper East Side, in a dis-trict that had been held by a Republican for thirty years. Krueger was outspent by her Republican opponent, Andrew Eristoff, by six to one but was elected by a margin of almost 60-40. In terms of advocating for the poor and creating coalitions, Krueger is the frontier of the possible in electoral politics. The new union-based Working Families Party received 90,000 votes statewide, winning a permanent position on the ballot and serious leverage in swing districts. David Paterson was elected New York's first black party leader in the state legislature, as rank-and-file Democrats in the State Senate revolted and threw out Martin Connor as their leader. Paterson then named maverick Eric Schneiderman as his deputy. Schneiderman had survived a Republican and Democratic deal to end his career by redistricting him into a Hispanic district, where it was hoped he would lose a pri-mary. But Schneiderman prevailed, with the support of the heavily black and Latino healthcare workers' union Local 1199/SEIU.

There is also little doubt that the near-suburbs are trending Democratic. The black and Latino populations of Nassau and Westchester counties are growing. If the Democrats can gain six seats in the State Senate over the next six years, they can become the majority. Paterson, Krueger, the WFP and organizer Jonathan Rosen of the New York Unemployment Project are now planning exactly such a long-term strategy of grassroots membership organizing and registering of low-income voters in the suburbs.

I hear a lot of talk about how "all we need" is one good liberal talk-show host on network radio or cable television, or all we need is a liberal policy think tank to compete with the conservative Manhattan Institute with its easy access to op-ed pages. But I think the frontier of the possible is also community-based organizing, the grunt drudgery of real voter registration and a renewed union militancy on behalf of the nickel-and-dimed low-wage workers. We need phone banks and Spanish-speaking union organizers as much as we need a left-wing Limbaugh.

Change comes from the bottom up. Change comes from ordinary people in political motion. This has been true from the 1936-37 sit-down auto factory strike in Flint, Michigan, to the strike-filled rise of New York's garment, transit and healthcare unions, to the marchers from Selma to Montgomery, who wrote the 1965 Voting Rights Act with their mud-caked boots, to today's growing antiwar movement.

The message of history is that only a participatory democracy can challenge a predatory plutocracy.

civil liberties

Testimony Before House Un-American Activities Committee

Screenwriter John Howard Lawson was the first of nineteen unfriendly witnesses to testify before Joseph McCarthy's House Un-American Activities Committee. Larson eventually went to jail for contempt of Congress.

OCTOBER 27, 1947

Staff members present: Mr. Robert E. Stripling, Chief Investigator; Messrs. Louis J. Russell, H.A. Smith, and Robert B. Gaston, Investigators; and Mr. Benjamin Mandel, Director of Research.

THE CHAIRMAN: The record will show that a Subcommittee is present, consisting of Mr. Vail, Mr. McDowell, and Mr. Thomas.

MR. LAWSON: Mr. Chairman, I have a statement here which I wish to make—

THE CHAIRMAN: Well, all right, let me see your statement. *(Statement handed to the Chairman.)*

THE CHAIRMAN: I don't care to read any more of the statement. The statement will not be read. I read the first line.

MR. LAWSON: You have spent one week vilifying me before the American public—

THE CHAIRMAN: Just a minute—

MR. LAWSON: —and you refuse to allow me to make a statement on my rights as an American citizen.

THE CHAIRMAN: I refuse to let you make the statement because of the first sentence. That statement is not pertinent to the inquiry. Now, this is a Congressional Committee set up by law. We must have orderly procedure, and we are going to have orderly procedure. Mr. Stripling, identify the witness.

MR. LAWSON: The rights of American citizens are important in this room here, and I intend to stand up for those rights, Congressman Thomas.

MR. STRIPLING: Mr. Lawson, will you state your full name, please?

MR. LAWSON: I wish to protest against the unwillingness of this Committee to read a statement, when you permitted Mr. Warner, Mr. Mayer, and others to read statements in this room. My name is John Howard Lawson.

MR. STRIPLING: When and where were you born?

MR. LAWSON: New York City.

MR. STRIPLING: What year?

MR. LAWSON: 1894.

MR. STRIPLING: Give us the exact date.

MR. LAWSON: September 25.

MR. STRIPLING: Mr. Lawson, you are here in response to a subpoena which was served upon you on September 19, 1947; is that true?

MR. LAWSON: That is correct.

MR. STRIPLING: What is your occupation, Mr. Lawson?

MR. LAWSON: I am a writer.

MR. STRIPLING: How long have you been a writer?

MR. LAWSON: All my life—at least thirty-five years—my adult life.

MR. STRIPLING: Are you a member of the Screen Writers Guild?

MR. LAWSON: The raising of any question here in regard to membership, political beliefs, or affiliation—

MR. STRIPLING: Mr. Chairman—

MR. LAWSON: —is absolutely beyond the powers of this Committee.

MR. STRIPLING: Mr. Chairman—

MR. LAWSON: But—

(The chairman pounding gavel.)

MR. LAWSON: It is a matter of public record that I am a member of the Screen Writers Guild. . . .

Mr. Stripling: I repeat the question, Mr. Lawson: Have you ever held any position in the Screen Writers Guild?

Mr. Lawson: I stated that it is outside the purview of the rights of this Committee to inquire into any form of association—

The Chairman: The Chair will determine what is in the purview of this Committee.

Mr. Lawson: My rights as an American citizen are no less than the responsibilities of this Committee of Congress.

The Chairman: Now, you are just making a big scene for yourself and getting all "het up." *(Laughter.)* Be responsive to the questioning, just the same as all the witnesses have. You are no different from the rest. Go ahead, Mr. Stripling.

Mr. Lawson: I am being treated differently from the rest.

The Chairman: You are not being treated differently.

Mr. Lawson: Other witnesses have made statements, which included quotations from books, references to material which had no connection whatsoever with the interest of this Committee.

The Chairman: We will determine whether it has connection. Now, you go ahead—

Mr. Lawson: It is absolutely beyond the power of this Committee to inquire into my association in any organization.

The Chairman: Mr. Lawson, you will have to stop or you will leave the witness stand. And you will leave the witness stand because you are in contempt. That is why you will leave the witness stand. And if you are just trying to force me to put you in contempt, you won't have to try much harder. You know what has happened to a lot of people that have been in contempt of this Committee this year, don't you?

MR. LAWSON: I am glad you have made it perfectly clear that you are going to threaten and intimidate the witnesses, Mr. Chairman.

(The Chairman pounding gavel.)

MR. LAWSON: I am an American and I am not at all easy to intimidate, and don't think I am.

(The Chairman pounding gavel.)

MR. STRIPLING: Mr. Lawson, I repeat the question. Have you ever held any position in the Screen Writers Guild?

MR. LAWSON: I have stated that the question is illegal. But it is a matter of public record that I have held many offices in the Screen Writers Guild. I was its first president in 1933, and I have held office on the board of directors of the Screen Writers Guild at other times.

MR. STRIPLING: You have been employed in the motion-picture industry, have you not?

MR. LAWSON: I have.

MR. STRIPLING: Would you state some of the studios where you have been employed?

MR. LAWSON: Practically all of the studios, all the major studios.

MR. STRIPLING: As a screen writer?

MR. LAWSON: That is correct.

MR. STRIPLING: Would you list some of the pictures which you have written the script for?

MR. LAWSON: I must state again that you are now inquiring into the freedom of press and communications, over which you have no control whatsoever. You don't have to bring me here three thousand miles to find out what pictures I have written. The pictures that I have written are very well known. They are such pictures as *Action in the North Atlantic, Sahara*—. . . .

MR. STRIPLING: Mr. Lawson, are you now or have you ever been a member of the Communist Party of the United States?

MR. LAWSON: In framing my answer to that question I must emphasize the points that I have raised before. The question of Communism is in no way related to this inquiry, which is an attempt to get control of the screen and to invade the basic rights of American citizens in all fields.

MR. McDOWELL: Now, I must object—

MR. STRIPLING: Mr. Chairman—

(The Chairman pounding gavel.)

MR. LAWSON: The question here relates not only to the question of my membership in any political organization, but this Committee is attempting to establish the right—

(The Chairman pounding gavel.)

MR. LAWSON: —which has been historically denied to any committee of this sort, to invade the rights and privileges and immunity of American citizens, whether they be Protestant, Methodist, Jewish, or Catholic, whether they be Republicans or Democrats or anything else.

THE CHAIRMAN *(pounding gavel)*: Mr. Lawson, just quiet down again. Mr. Lawson, the most pertinent question that we can ask is whether or not you have ever been a member of the Communist Party. Now, do you care to answer that question?

MR. LAWSON: You are using the old technique, which was used in Hitler Germany in order to create a scare here—

THE CHAIRMAN *(pounding gavel)*: Oh—

MR. LAWSON: —in order to create an entirely false atmosphere in which this hearing is conducted—

(The Chairman pounding gavel.)

MR. LAWSON: —in order that you can then smear the motion-picture industry, and you can proceed to the press, to any form of communication in this country.

THE CHAIRMAN: You have learned—

Mr. Lawson: The Bill of Rights was established precisely to prevent the operation of any committee which could invade the basic rights of Americans. Now, if you want to know—

Mr. Stripling: Mr. Chairman, the witness is not answering the question.

Mr. Lawson: If you want to know—

(The Chairman pounding gavel.)

Mr. Lawson: —about the perjury that has been committed here and the perjury that is planned—

The Chairman: Mr. Lawson—

Mr. Lawson: —permit me and my attorneys to bring in here the witnesses that testified last week and permit us to cross-examine these witnesses, and we will show up the whole tissue of lies—

The Chairman *(pounding gavel)*: We are going to get the answer to that question if we have to stay here for a week. Are you a member of the Communist Party, or have you ever been a member of the Communist Party?

Mr. Lawson: It is unfortunate and tragic that I have to teach this Committee the basic principles of American—

The Chairman *(pounding gavel)*: That is not the question. That is not the question. The question is: Have you ever been a member of the Communist Party?

Mr. Lawson: I am framing my answer in the only way in which any American citizen can frame his answer to a question which absolutely invades his rights.

The Chairman: Then you refuse to answer that question; is that correct?

Mr. Lawson: I have told you that I will offer my beliefs, affiliations, and everything else to the American public, and they will know where I stand.

The Chairman (*pounding gavel*): Excuse the witness—

Mr. Lawson: As they do from what I have written.

The Chairman (*pounding gavel*): Stand away from the stand—

Mr. Lawson: I have written Americanism for many years, and I shall continue to fight for the Bill of Rights, which you are trying to destroy.

The Chairman: Officers, take this man away from the stand—.

1950
Declaration of Conscience

By Margaret Chase Smith

Margaret Chase Smith persuaded six fellow Republican senators to sign her statement, a response to the growing power
of anti-Communist Senator Joseph McCarthy. The
McCarthy era lasted another four years, as McCarthy and his
cohorts destroyed countless careers and lives in their campaign against the supposed influence of Communist conspir-
ators in Washington, Hollywood and around the nation.

Mr. President:

I would like to speak briefly and simply about a serious national
condition. It is a national feeling of fear and frustration that could
result in national suicide and the end of everything that we Americans hold dear. It is a condition that comes from the lack of effective
leadership in either the Legislative Branch or the Executive Branch of
our Government.

That leadership is so lacking that serious and responsible proposals
are being made that national advisory commissions be appointed to
provide such critically needed leadership.

I speak as briefly as possible because too much harm has already
been done with irresponsible words of bitterness and selfish political
opportunism. I speak as simply as possible because the issue is too
great to be obscured by eloquence. I speak simply and briefly in the
hope that my words will be taken to heart.

I speak as a Republican, I speak as a woman. I speak as a United
States Senator. I speak as an American.

The United States Senate has long enjoyed worldwide respect as the greatest deliberative body in the world. But recently that deliberative character has too often been debased to the level of a forum of hate and character assassination sheltered by the shield of congressional immunity.

It is ironical that we Senators can in debate in the Senate directly or indirectly, by any form of words impute to any American, who is not a Senator, any conduct or motive unworthy or unbecoming an American—and without that non-Senator American having any legal redress against us—yet if we say the same thing in the Senate about our colleagues we can be stopped on the grounds of being out of order.

It is strange that we can verbally attack anyone else without restraint and with full protection and yet we hold ourselves above the same type of criticism here on the Senate Floor. Surely the United States Senate is big enough to take self-criticism and self-appraisal. Surely we should be able to take the same kind of character attacks that we dish out to outsiders.

I think that it is high time for the United States Senate and its members to do some soul searching—for us to weigh our consciences—on the manner in which we are performing our duty to the people of America—on the manner in which we are using or abusing our individual powers and privileges.

I think that it is high time that we remembered that we have sworn to uphold and defend the Constitution. I think that it is high time that we remembered; that the Constitution, as amended, speaks not only of the freedom of speech but also of trial by jury instead of trial by accusation.

Whether it be a criminal prosecution in court or a character prosecution in the Senate, there is little practical distinction when the life of a person has been ruined.

Those of us who shout the loudest about Americanism in making character assassinations are all too frequently those who, by our own words and acts, ignore some of the basic principles of Americanism—

The right to criticize;
The right to hold unpopular beliefs;
The right to protest;
The right of independent thought.

The exercise of these rights should not cost one single American citizen his reputation or his right to a livelihood nor should he be in danger of losing his reputation or livelihood merely because he happens to know some one who holds unpopular beliefs. Who of us doesn't? Otherwise none of us could call our souls our own. Otherwise thought control would have set in.

The American people are sick and tired of being afraid to speak their minds lest they be politically smeared as "Communists" or "Fascists" by their opponents. Freedom of speech is not what it used to be in America. It has been so abused by some that it is not exercised by others. The American people are sick and tired of seeing innocent people smeared and guilty people whitewashed. But there have been enough proved cases to cause nationwide distrust and strong suspicion that there may be something to the unproved, sensational accusations.

As a Republican, I say to my colleagues on this side of the aisle that the Republican Party faces a challenge today that is not unlike the challenge that it faced back in Lincoln's day. The Republican Party so successfully met that challenge that it emerged from the Civil War as the champion of a united nation—in addition to being a Party that unrelentingly fought loose spending and loose programs.

Today our country is being psychologically divided by the confusion and the suspicions that are bred in the United States Senate to spread like cancerous tentacles of "know nothing, suspect everything" attitudes. Today we have a Democratic Administration that has developed a mania for loose spending and loose programs. History is repeating itself—and the Republican Party again has the opportunity to emerge as the champion of unity and prudence.

The record of the present Democratic Administration has provided us with sufficient campaign issues without the necessity of resorting to political smears. America is rapidly losing its position as leader of the world simply because the Democratic Administration has pitifully failed to provide effective leadership.

The Democratic Administration has completely confused the American people by its daily contradictory grave warnings and optimistic assurances—that show the people that our Democratic Administration has no idea of where it is going.

The Democratic Administration has greatly lost the confidence of the American people by its complacency to the threat of communism here at home and the leak of vital secrets to Russia through key officials of the Democratic Administration. There are enough proved cases to make this point without diluting our criticism with unproved charges.

Surely these are sufficient reasons to make it clear to the American people that it is time for a change and that a Republican victory is necessary to the security of this country. Surely it is clear that this nation will continue to suffer as long as it is governed by the present ineffective Democratic Administration.

Yet to displace it with a Republican regime embracing a philosophy that lacks political integrity or intellectual honesty would prove equally disastrous to this nation. The nation sorely needs a Republican victory. But I don't want to see the Republican Party ride to political victory on the Four Horsemen of Calumny—Fear, Ignorance, Bigotry and Smear.

I doubt if the Republican Party could—simply because I don't believe the American people will uphold any political party that puts political exploitation above national interest. Surely we Republicans aren't that desperate for victory.

I don't want to see the Republican Party win that way. While it might be a fleeting victory for the Republican Party, it would be a more lasting defeat for the American people. Surely it would ultimately be suicide for the Republican Party and the two-party system that has protected our American liberties from the dictatorship of a one party system.

As members of the Minority Party, we do not have the primary authority to formulate the policy of our Government. But we do have the responsibility of rendering constructive criticism, of clarifying issues, of allaying fears by acting as responsible citizens.

As a woman, I wonder how the mothers, wives, sisters and daughters feel about the way in which members of their families have been politically mangled in Senate debate—and I use the word "debate" advisedly.

As a United States Senator, I am not proud of the way in which the Senate has been made a publicity platform for irresponsible sensationalism. I am not proud of the reckless abandon in which unproved charges have been hurled from this side of the aisle. I am not proud of the obviously staged, undignified countercharges that have been attempted in retaliation from the other side of the aisle.

I don't like the way the Senate has been made a rendezvous for vilification, for selfish political gain at the sacrifice of individual reputations and national unity. I am not proud of the way we smear outsiders from the Floor of the Senate and hide behind the cloak of congressional immunity and still place ourselves beyond criticism on the Floor of the Senate.

As an American, I am shocked at the way Republicans and Democrats alike are playing directly into the Communist design of "confuse, divide and conquer." As an American, I don't want a Democratic Administration "white wash" or "cover up" any more than I want a Republican smear or witch hunt.

As an American, I condemn a Republican "Fascist" just as much as I condemn a Democrat "Communist." I condemn a Democrat "fascist" just as much as I condemn a Republican "Communist."

They are equally dangerous to you and me and to our country. As an American, I want to see our nation recapture the strength and unity it once had when we fought the enemy instead of ourselves.

It is with these thoughts I have drafted what I call a "Declaration of Conscience." I am gratified that Senator Tobey, Senator Aiken, Senator Morse, Senator Ives, Senator Thye and Senator Hendrickson, have concurred in that declaration and have authorized me to announce their concurrence.

2002
Sunday A16
By Starhawk

The loosely defined global justice movement that has emerged during the past decade has staged creative and attention-getting street actions in cities such as Seattle, Washington, D.C., Quebec City, Genoa, and New York City. Here veteran activist and writer Starhawk describes the movement's tactics in Washington, D.C. and the police response.

We have been blockading all day in a giant spiderweb, an intersection entirely surrounded by webs of yarn that effectively prevent free movement into the street. We have been drawn here by Wilow's nose, following the energy. The intersection is held by a cluster from Asheville that includes many labor union people. In Seattle, we were cheered in jail to hear that the ILWU had shut down every port on the West Coast in solidarity with our action. Here on the streets of Washington, D.C., we are blockading arm in arm with the Ecofeminist Teamsters. In front of the police blockade, an affinity group is locked down, sitting in a line with their arms locked together. Their supporters surround them, bring them water, administer sunscreen, and hold the keys.

I am really, really happy to be part of a movement that includes a group of ecofeminist teamsters. They ask us for some help in shifting the energy, which is loud, raucous, and confrontational. I join the group of drummers in the center. I don't have my own drum today, just a bucket and sticks, which works fairly well except when it falls off the rope tied around my waist. I start to drum with the group in the center, trying to entrain as I know the only way to shift a rhythm is first to join with it. With the help of some of the singers in our group, we manage to shift into a song: "We have come too far, we won't turn around, we'll flood the streets with justice, we are freedom bound."

I'm thinking about all the energies we'd invoked at the ritual the night before, Brigid, Oya, the Norns, the Red Dragon. At that moment, a red dragon made of cloth and ribbons dances into the intersection atop of line of smiling young protesters. It circles the intersection, and the energy shifts.

This magic is played out against a background of stark though unacknowledged fear. In all our affinity group's discussions about who to invoke and how to arrange early-morning transport, I don't think we've ever simply said, "I'm afraid." I haven't said it because I've pushed the fear down so far it doesn't easily surface, and because what I'm most afraid of is that someone else, someone I persuaded to come to this action, will get hurt. And also, I suppose, because I think the group looks to me to project calm and confidence, when really what might help us all most would be to simply be able to say, "I'm scared. Are you scared, too?"

We're scared because we are out on the street risking arrest in a city that has been turned into a police state. Sixty square blocks have been barricaded off. The day before, 600 people were arrested in a preemptive strike at a peaceful march. They weren't warned or allowed to leave. Our Convergence Center was shut down the same morning, with thousands of people arriving that day to be trained. Our puppets and medical supplies were confiscated. Although the puppets were eventually released, the medical supplies remain under lock and key.

I spent Saturday morning wandering in the rain with a group of about eighty people for whom I was trying to do a nonviolence training. The church we headed to was flanked by police and so overcrowded we could not possibly squeeze in. We set off for a park, but a runner informed us that the police were throwing people out of it. Eventually, I just stopped on the corner and said to the group, "Look, you can come back in the afternoon and try to get into a training, or we can just do it in the road." "Let's do it!" they cried, and so we ducked into an alley, arranged a fallback point in case we had to scatter, and did the training right there, with police cruising half a block away. "I must be a Witch," I said to Wilow after she finally found us toward the end of the morning. "I just disappeared eighty people!"

We are afraid of the police: they have guns, clubs, tear gas, pepper spray, and all the power of the state at their disposal. They can beat, gas, or jail us with relative impunity. What's hard to grasp is how much they are afraid of us. Some of our group are wearing black and covering their faces and look like the folks in Seattle that broke windows and made the police look bad. Mostly, I think, the police are afraid of the unknown. Someone in the crowd could have a bomb. Those bubbling vats in the convergence kitchen could be homemade pepper spray instead of lunch. Those bottles of turpentine could have some nefarious purpose other than removal of the paint used in banner making.

Now the two groups, each perceiving themselves as righteous and the other side as potentially violent, are squaring off on the streets of our nation's capital.

Later: Wilow, Evergreen, and I are returning from a trek to the bathrooms blocks away. We see a barricade half-built across the street. A dumpster has been dragged into the middle of the street, and a few broken pieces of furniture lie atop it. Other pieces of debris strew the roadside. A couple of cars have been lifted up and set down at forty-five-degree angles. Our much-debated nonviolence guidlelines state that we will not damage property. The cars are unharmed, but moving them has certainly put them in harm's way. It is an action right on the edge of what the guidelines allow—but then we know many people are unhappy at having guidelines at all, and agree to them with the greatest reluctance.

Behind the dumpster, a circle of people stands engrossed in a heated meeting. They are discussing the barricade. David, my partner, is in the midst of them. As I listen, I soon realize what has happened. The young man in black, the tall Rasta from the Caribbean, and some of the others have built the barricade. David has been taking it down even as they built it up. Now they are having a spokescouncil meeting. A young woman from the Ecofeminist Teamsters is facilitating.

The people who built the barricade see it as protective. We hear rumors that the cops have been running over people with motorcycles. The barricade builders view it as our defense. David sees it as endangering us, as upping the ante of confrontation and potentially provoking violence. Most of the barricade builders are young; he is middle-aged, he looks and sounds like somebody's dad, which in fact he is. He's somebody's granddad, for that matter. He's also a man who burned his draft card in the Vietnam War and spent two years of his youth in Federal Prison. His lifelong pacifism is staunch and unshakable, and I've never known him to back down on a matter of principle. Next to him is a young, black-clad, masked protester who looks like the classic image of the anarchist/terrorist. He is listening thoughtfully to the discussion.

I look at that circle and see all the tensions, fears, and hopes that have surrounded this action. I've been here for close to a week, doing trainings, going to meetings, sitting in on every spokescouncil. I know that we have deep divisions among us on the question of how this action should be conducted. In the spokescouncils, the strongest voice generally seems to belong to those who want a more confrontational action, who chafe against the nonviolence guidelines and are ready to do battle in the streets. But in the nonviolence trainings I've done, and on the street itself, I hear the voices of those for whom the guidelines are vitally important and who want a stronger commitment to nonviolence, to communication as well as confrontation.

This is the kind of issue that has torn movements apart. Those of us who are old enough to remember the sixties have seen it happen again and again. We know how easy it is for this energy to turn sour and dissipate. We've seen strong organizations splinter apart around questions of tactics. Much stronger than any fear I might have of the police is my fear that this blessed wild unlooked-for movement, this rising tide of rage and passion for justice, will founder in the same way I've seen movements founder before, that we'll end up denouncing each other instead of the IMF, or that small splinter groups will take us too quickly into forms of action so extreme they leave our base of support far behind.

This energy is rare and precious. It's the one thing that can't be organized or created. When it's present, it's unstoppable, but when it goes, it's gone. And in thirty years of political activism, I've learned how quickly it can go.

"What's amazing," I say to the group, "is that we're having this dialogue. Under all this tension and in the middle of the action, we're willing to discuss this and listen to each other. That may be as important as anything else we do on the street today."

The black-masked anarchist, the Rasta, the Ecofeminist Teamster facilitator, the other affinity group representatives, and even David are all nodding in agreement. Eventually, a compromise is reached: David will not take down any more of the barricade, and no one else will add to it or build it up. I don't know which amazes me more: that the barricade builders agree or that David does. By the end of the day, the dumpster has become a giant drum, a symbol both of our differences and of the process we use to resolve them, a living testimony to the true democracy we have brought to confront the systems of political and economic control.

We are in the Ellipse. The blockade is over. The march and rally are done. We are lying in the shade, napping after an exhausting day, when someone comes running.

"The cops are trying to sweep the park! There's Riot Cops massing over there in the corner!"

We can't really believe the police would do something so unprovoked and stupid, but a few of us go to see what is happening. A line of Park Police on horseback are threading their way through clumps of people seated on the grass and alarming a small contingent of the Daughters of the American Revolution in pink suits and pearls, who scatter toward their building across the way. We follow the horses, and they move out into Constitution Avenue, form a line, and begin, or so it seems, to try to push the crowd off the street. Half the crowd is panicking and the other half are shouting at the cops and challenging the horses and in a moment, many people are going to get badly hurt. It's a situation so dangerous and unprovoked that I'm ready to get arrested just in protest of its stupidity, or so I tell Dan Fireheart, who is right behind me. But suddenly I know that I have to get to the front of the crowd. I catch hold of some lightning bolt of energy and streak through, checking myself as I go, "Is this really for me to do?" I know it is because suddenly I'm there, doing it, yelling, "Sit down! Sit down!" And doing it myself with enough conviction that others follow suit. In a moment, the crowd is sitting down or lying in front of the horses, who stop.

I am sitting with my legs out toward a horse whose feet stand between my ankles. One of my arms is outstretched as if to say, "Stop!" I can't seem to move it or put it down. Dan Fireheart reaches forward from behind me and takes my other hand. The horse is very big. The policeman on his back will not look me in the eye. Down the line, a cop tells a young woman protester, "I don't want to trample you but if my boss orders me to move forward, I'll have to." I've been teaching people for twenty years in nonviolence trainings that horses do not like to walk into uneven ground and won't trample people if you sit down or lie down in a group in front of them, but I've never tested it before. The horse shifts its weight. I remember that we called on the spirits of the land itself to support us. I can feel all the rings of magical energy and protection being sent to this action. They surround me like ripples in a pond, converging toward me instead of dispersing out. I still cannot seem to put my hand down.

Half the people around me look like they're part of the black bloc. In this moment, we have total solidarity. There are no more questions of tactics or style or guidelines; we are simply there together, facing the same threat, making the same stand, facing the same fear.

There's a line of riot cops behind the horses, so they can't move back. We all sit, frozen in time. I reach up, let the horse sniff my hand. The horse and I, we're in complete agreement. He doesn't want to step on me, and I don't want him to. Behind us, someone from the Committee for Full Enjoyment begins a chant: "It's not about the cops, it's about the IMF!" The crowd takes it up, and the energy unifies.

Then I realize there is a second line of horses behind our horses, facing the other way. It seems as if they've just come in from some-where. They form a kind of open V with the riot cops in the middle. The crowd facing those horses begins to shout and panic. They're yelling at the horses and trying to push them back and throwing horse manure at the cops. The riot cops get out of the way. The horses are dancing and stumbling and being pushed into our horses who will have nowhere to move and stumble except on top of us. We begin chanting at the other crowd to sit down. They don't listen. "Sit down! Sit down! Sit down!" we chant. Finally they get it. They sit down. The horses stop. We breathe again. At some point in the melee, one young man does get stepped on and is left with a broken leg.

Now the horses are trapped. They have nowhere to go. I look up at the policeman who still won't meet my eye. "Officer, you have cre-ated an incredibly dangerous situation here, for us, for yourselves, for the horses! What were you thinking of? And how can we get you out of this?" I am fully prepared to try to negotiate with the crowd to let the horses out, but he still won't look at me. Off to the side, the riot cops move in. They begin literally throwing people around, until they clear a passage where the horses can file out. We scoot forward and then stand up and follow them, taking over the street, chanting, "Whose streets? Our streets!" At the other end of Constitution Avenue, a line of riot cops stands, batons ready. We are willing to be arrested, but they don't move, simply hold their own blockade as the drums thunder and the victory dance begins.

2003
The Silencing of Gideon's Trumpet

BY ANTHONY LEWIS

A prisoner's right to counsel is an important element of our democracy. That right isn't always enforced—and George W. Bush's administration thinks it doesn't always exist. This story originally appeared in *The New York Times Magazine.*

FORTY-ONE YEARS ago, a poor, isolated prisoner in Florida, the least influential of Americans, wrote a letter to the Supreme Court—a letter in pencil, on lined prison paper—claiming that he had been wrongly denied the right to a lawyer when he was convicted. The Supreme Court agreed to hear his case and found that the Constitution required counsel to be provided in all serious criminal cases for defendants too poor to hire their own. Clarence Earl Gideon would have a new trial, this time with a lawyer.

The new jury found him not guilty: a happy ending not only for him but also for the principle that a lawyer's help is crucial for criminal defendants.

After the Supreme Court decision, I recognized that it would be, as I wrote then, "an enormous social task to bring to life the dream of Gideon v. Wainwright—the dream of a vast, diverse country in which every man charged with crime will be capably defended . . . sure of the support needed to make an adequate defense." On this 40th anniversary, how have we done? I take my answer from a recent paper by Bruce Jacob, the lawyer who represented the State of Florida in the Supreme Court, arguing against Gideon's claim of a right to counsel. "I hoped that legislatures would meet the challenge," Jacob wrote.

"That was at a time in my life when I still believed that legislators want to do the right thing. . . . The record of the courts in fulfilling the hopes represented by Gideon is a dismal one."

I was covering the Supreme Court when it decided Gideon v. Wainright, and the case has always had special meaning for me. It is painful to hear Bruce Jacob express disappointment at today's courtroom inadequacies. Even more alarming is the assertion by the Bush administration that in a whole new class of cases it can deny the right to counsel altogether. Those are the cases of American citizens designated by Bush as "enemy combatants." One of them is Jose Padilla, born in Brooklyn in 1970 and arrested by federal agents last May at O'Hare International Airport in Chicago. The administration claims that it can hold Padilla in solitary confinement indefinitely, without trial and without access to a lawyer.

Bruce Jacob's judgment rests on endless failures to bring the promise of Gideon to life. Many states and localities offer not even the minimal level of financial support needed for an adequate defense. And far too often the lawyers provided for indigent defendants have not met the barest standards of competence. Take the case of the sleeping lawyer. Calvin Burdine was on trial for his life in Texas when his appointed counsel, Joe Frank Cannon, fell asleep several times during the trial. The Texas Court of Criminal Appeals held that that was no reason to set aside Burdine's conviction. The United States Court of Appeals, considering the issue on habeas corpus, disagreed, but only by a vote of 9 to 5. That is, five of those distinguished federal judges thought a lawyer who fell asleep during a capital trial did not do enough harm to matter.

The truth of the proposition that a lawyer is essential was vividly demonstrated to me by something that happened in Gideon's second trial. Gideon had been charged with breaking and entering the Bay Harbor Poolroom in Panama City, Florida, in the early morning hours and taking some coins and wine. At his first trial, a taxi driver, Preston

Bray, testified that Gideon had telephoned him and that he had gone to the poolroom and picked him up. When he got into the cab, Bray said, Gideon told him not to tell anyone about it. That was damaging testimony. And Gideon, without a lawyer, let it stand without any cross-examination.

In the second trial, Gideon had a lawyer: Fred Turner. After Preston Bray testified again that Gideon had told him not to say anything about picking him up that morning, Turner asked whether Gideon had ever said that to him before. The taxi driver answered, yes, Gideon said that every time he called a cab. "Why?" "I understand it was his wife—he had trouble with his wife."

Nothing could demonstrate more clearly the value of having a lawyer. But we know now that it has to be a competent lawyer. Fred Turner was competent, and then some. He not only destroyed the taxi driver's evidence against Gideon. He destroyed the chief prosecution witness, one Henry Cook, who said he had seen Gideon near the time of the break-in. Turner suggested to the jury that it was really Cook himself who had committed the crime. He was in a good position to speak about Cook because he had represented Cook in two other cases.

Lawyers themselves bear some of the responsibility for the failures since the Gideon decision. Of the 13 people on death row in Illinois released between 1987 and 2000 after they were found innocent, four had been represented by lawyers who were later disbarred or suspended from practice. But so do the authorities who pick indifferent, sleepy, incompetent lawyers to defend men and women on matters as serious as life and death. Calvin Burdine's lawyer, Joe Frank Cannon, was appointed by judges in Houston to other cases after he slept through Burdine's trial. In Texas and other places, some appointments of counsel are regarded as sinecures to be given to friends and supporters.

Then there is the question of resources. Even a competent lawyer may not be able to mount an adequate defense against the state, with all its resources, if he has next to nothing for investigation and effectively works for starvation wages. Bobby Houston spent 19 months in jail in Indianapolis without ever being tried, four of them after the charge against him, child molesting, had been dismissed. The public defender handling his case never told him, or told the prison authorities, about the dismissal.

We can surely say that Houston's lawyer lacked due diligence. But politics and money were also involved. At the time of the case, public defenders in Marion County, Ind.—working part time or more than part time—were paid $20,800 a year, plus $60 a month for all office expenses. They were so grossly underpaid and overworked that many could not even accept collect calls.

Why does the dream of the Gideon decision—the dream of a country in which every person charged with crime will be capably defended—remain just that, a dream? Why do judges countenance mockeries of legal representation? Why do we, the citizens, tolerate such unfairness? These are profound questions, and I can do no more than speculate on possible explanations.

One answer is plain. Criminal defendants and prisoners have little or no political power. Legislators see no votes in assigning competent lawyers for poor defendants or giving lawyers the resources to do their job properly. The Clarence Earl Gideons of this world are constituents who can safely be ignored. Many are barred from voting, and the rest seldom bother.

There is more to it than defendants' and prisoners' lack of political power. This country differs from all other Western countries in its attitude toward crime and criminals. We are tough on crime, as the advocates of harsh measures put it. Critics might use a stronger term, like "brutal." American prisons tend to be more unpleasant than they are elsewhere; sentences, much longer. And of course we impose the death penalty, which has been abandoned everywhere else in the trans-Atlantic world as a savage relic. Why the United States takes so different a view of how to treat criminals is a question too deep for exploration here. But there is no doubt that the harsh view exists, exacerbated by politicians, starting with Richard Nixon and his "war on crime."

Manifestations of this harshness are widespread. The United States Court of Appeals for the Eighth Circuit recently approved the involuntary administration of antipsychotic drugs to a death-row inmate so he could be made sane enough to be executed. Then there was the prosecutor who argued that an execution should proceed even if the prisoner were to offer last-minute DNA evidence of his innocence.

DNA is at the center of an extraordinary recent development that sheds some light on attitudes toward criminal justice. The discovery of incompetence—or worse—at the Houston Police crime laboratory in recent months may affect hundreds of prosecutions in Harris County, where Houston is located, including many capital cases. More defendants from Harris County have been executed than from any other county in the United States. Now it turns out that the work of the laboratory is suspect. What about the defense lawyers? Many simply did not have the resources to check the authenticity of the evidence that sent their clients to jail—or to death.

Among them were the lawyers for Josiah Sutton, convicted of rape four years ago and prosecuted in part on the basis of a DNA report from the Houston lab. After a Houston television station raised questions about the laboratory last fall, the sample used to help convict Sutton was retested by an independent laboratory in Houston, which found that it did not match Sutton's DNA.

The case of Josiah Sutton and the Houston crime lab is one more proof of what Justice Black told us in Gideon: when the state brings its weight down on an individual, he or she cannot get justice without the help—the effective help—of a lawyer. That is a fundamental truth, an obvious truth, as Black said. But on the anniversary of the decision in Gideon v. Wainwright, that truth is being challenged in a way that I did not believe was possible in our country.

In two cases now before the courts, Attorney General John Ashcroft is asserting that President Bush has the power to detain any American citizen indefinitely, in solitary confinement, without access to a lawyer, if he, the president, designates the detainee an "enemy combatant." The detainee cannot effectively challenge that designation. A court may hold a habeas corpus proceeding, but the government need produce only its own assertions of evidence, not subject to cross-examination. "Some evidence" will suffice—that is, any evidence, however unchecked and second-hand. That is the claim being made by the law officers of the United States.

I would not have believed that an attorney general would argue that an American could be held indefinitely without being able to speak to a lawyer. I seriously doubt that any attorney general in the years since Gideon, except the present occupant of the office, would have made that claim.

One of the pending cases concerns Jose Padilla, who became a gang member, was arrested half a dozen times and served several jail sentences. He became a Muslim. After traveling, in Pakistan among other places, Padilla flew into O'Hare Airport last May 8 and was arrested by federal agents. He was first detained as a material witness before a New York federal grand jury investigating the September 11 terrorist attack on the World Trade Center. A judge appointed a lawyer for him and set a hearing for June 11. But on June 10 Ashcroft, who happened to be in Moscow, made a televised statement about Padilla. "We have captured a known terrorist," Ashcroft said. His arrest "disrupted an unfolding terrorist plot to attack the United States by exploding a radioactive 'dirty bomb.' " There has been no way for Padilla, or his lawyer, to challenge that statement, or for the news media to test its truth. It was a conviction by government announcement.

Padilla is confined in a Navy brig in South Carolina. The lawyer originally appointed to represent him in the material witness proceeding, Donna R. Newman, has been trying to see him—without success. A federal judge, Michael Mukasey, decided that she should have a chance to talk with him for the limited purpose of examining the evidence produced by the government in support of his designation as an "enemy combatant." But that decision was challenged anew by government lawyers.

They offered an affidavit by the director of the Defense Intelligence Agency, Vice Adm. Lowell E. Jacoby. He said successful interrogation of a prisoner depends largely on "creating an atmosphere of dependency and trust between the subject and interrogator. Developing the kind of relationship . . . necessary for effective interrogations . . . can take a significant amount of time. There are numerous examples of situations where interrogators have been unable to obtain valuable intelligence from a subject until months, or even years, after the interrogation process began." Admiral Jacoby said any access to counsel, however brief, "can undo months of work and may permanently shut down the interrogation process."

There is a certain paradox in Admiral Jacoby's affidavit. The very fact that extended interrogation in the absence of counsel may break a subject's will is one reason that the right to counsel is guaranteed in the criminal law. It is the basis of the Miranda rule.

The government argues, and in the other "enemy combatant" case the United States Court of Appeals for the Fourth Circuit agreed, that the Sixth Amendment's guarantee of the right to counsel "in all criminal prosecutions" does not apply because Padilla is not being prosecuted. In other words, the government can hold an American in prison for life without letting him see a lawyer if it takes care not to charge him with a crime and try him. James Madison and the others who added the Sixth Amendment and the rest of the Bill of Rights to the Constitution in 1791 would surely have regarded that argument as sophistry.

Bruce Jacob has served on both the defense and the prosecution side of criminal justice. Forty years after Gideon v. Wainwright was decided, he takes a broad view of the constitutional right to counsel. It should include civil as well as criminal proceedings, he says in his paper: "The due process and equal protection clauses do not differentiate between criminal and civil cases." Paraphrasing Black's opinion, Jacob concludes: "Certainly any person haled into court or brought before any tribunal, whether criminal, civil or administrative. . . should, if indigent, be afforded counsel at public expense." With an eye on the enemy combatant cases, I would amend that statement to include any person deprived of his liberty by the state.

Clarence Earl Gideon was not a clear thinker, a man of the world or, least of all, an easy person to deal with. He was a petty criminal, a habitual one, worn out beyond his years by a difficult life. But he knew what he wanted. He turned down the first two lawyers offered him, when it came time for his second trial. He wanted Fred Turner, and that was a wise choice.

Fred Turner told Bruce Jacob that Gideon came to him with "a valise full of motions." Among other things, he wanted to move for a change of venue, to Tallahassee. Turner pointed out that he knew people in Panama City—in fact, he knew most of the jurors—but none in Tallahassee. Gideon agreed to drop the idea of a change of venue. Then Turner told him, "I'll only represent you if you will stop trying to be the lawyer and let me handle the case." Gideon agreed.

Clarence Gideon, who died in 1972, would be disappointed today at the imperfect realization of his dream. He would regret especially, I think, the failure of the Supreme Court to hold that the Constitution requires a meaningfully competent lawyer for the poor defendant— the court's countenancing, even in capital cases, of lawyers who scarcely go through the motions while their clients are convicted.

On the other hand, the Supreme Court has held fast to the principle that the right to consult a lawyer is, as Justice Black said, "fundamental." It is a far more conservative court than the one that decided the Gideon case, with William Rehnquist as chief justice instead of Earl Warren. It has overruled or narrowed many precedents. But it has repeatedly reaffirmed its holding in Gideon v. Wainwright.

That is what makes the Bush administration's claim in the "enemy combatant" cases so extraordinary. Of course, Jose Padilla and the other man being held, Yasser Esam Hamdi, are not in precisely Gideon's position. They are not being prosecuted; they are being held indefinitely, without charges, in solitary confinement. They are not looking for counsel; they both already have lawyers, highly competent ones appointed by federal judges. But they are not allowed to talk to them. Those differences from Gideon's situation seem to make their need to consult the lawyers they have, if anything, more compelling.

The constitutional argument made by Ashcroft and his aides also seems imperfect. Perhaps the Sixth Amendment guarantee of counsel "in all criminal prosecutions" can be reasoned away as inapplicable to indefinite detention without charge, though I think the framers would have been astonished at the invention of a severe penalty for a suspect with fewer rights than he would have as a criminal defendant.

But the Constitution also includes the Fifth Amendment. It provides that "no person shall . . . be deprived of life, liberty or property, without due process of law." Jose Padilla has been deprived of his liberty—forever, for all he knows. Has he had due process of law?

The Bush administration's answer to that question is essentially this: in a war against terrorism, any process that the president says is essential to the war is due process. Government lawyers argue that in wartime, courts must defer to the president's judgment.

The denial of counsel to Jose Padilla, then, is an aspect of something larger. About the time the Gideon case was decided, we began to hear about the imperial presidency. The terrorist attacks of September 11, 2001, and now the war on Iraq have renewed that concept in even more extreme form. Bush has little trouble with a supine Congress. He wants the Constitution, too, as our judges enforce it, to yield to the supremacy of the president.

2003
State of the Union

By Charles P. Pierce

Americans sometimes like to say that the Constitution is "a living document". Lately, it seems all too mortal. This story originally appeared in *Esquire*.

THE UNITED STATES Constitution went missing from the Rotunda of the National Archives in July 2001. Its disappearance is an easy metaphor for the restrictions on our civil liberties that war has made possible—some say necessary. While the Constitution, along with the Bill of Rights, has been away, our country has changed.

Every few days, the Constitution of the United States and the Bill of Rights are brought out into a quiet room to the Maryland woods. In that room, which is part of the National Archives' research complex, the five individual parchments are gently moved—always with four hands on each of them, and never with gloves—and placed flat on boards or laid flat in a tray. The documents have not been on public display since July 4, 2001. Since that day, the Constitution of the United States, and the Bill of Rights appended thereto, have been stored in an undisclosed location.

And every few days they are delivered in their undisclosed location to the tender care and scientific ministrations of two women who look like the jovial hosts of an NPR quilting program. For the past two years, Mary Lynn Ritzenthaler and Catherine Nicholson have been working with the so-called Charters of Freedom—the Constitution, the Bill of Rights, and the Declaration of Independence—as part of a $4.8 million effort by the National Archives to restore the documents and to build new encasements in which they will be placed when they go back on public display later this year.

The encasements themselves are high-tech marvels; each page will be housed in a titanium frame behind a half inch of laminated glass and will have its own argon atmosphere monitored by sensors built beneath the frame. (The glass in the old encasements developed tiny cracks, thereby threatening the fragile parchments.) The new encasements are the province of the engineers in another part of the complex; atmospheric scientists from NASA were brought in on the job.

Ritzenthaler and Nicholson work most closely with the documents within the encasements, and with the words within the documents. "I think there's a sense of awareness and some degree of awe," says Ritzenthaler. "But I think we also become a little bit more familiar with them, and a nice relationship develops."

"They almost become like friends," says Nicholson. "We've worked with them for so long and gotten to know their problems and their concerns. It's like they're real, physical entities."

Through the years, it was the Declaration that people wanted to see. From 1841 until 1876, it hung in a simple frame opposite a window in the U. S. Patent Office. From 1877 to 1894, it hung in the State Department library, where its parchment took a fearful beating from woodsmoke and generations of cigars. Meanwhile, the Constitution never was in much demand. Mostly, it was packed up and stored like a throw rug in the attic. From 1866 to 1875, as historian Michael Kammen points out, it was stashed away at the Washington Orphan Asylum. In 1921, it joined the Declaration in the Library of Congress, where some of the parchments were later displayed. The Bill of Rights, however, was stored in the State Department cellar next to the ceremonial sword of an obscure loon who'd once declared himself emperor of Haiti. People venerated the Constitution in their minds, but hardly anyone ever saw the actual parchments. It was as though the document was a strange, iconic cabala containing the secret American spells and chants.

"I don't think there ever was a broadside of the Constitution published at the time," says Ritzenthaler. "It didn't have, I don't know, the excitement. It was just kind of an organizational document." The Declaration and the Constitution traveled together occasionally, though—in 1921, in the bed of a mail truck; in 1941, during World War II, when they were locked away at Fort Knox; and again in 1952, when twelve MPs and two tanks escorted them to the Rotunda of the National Archives. The Declaration, of course, got the prime spot in the Archives—up on the front wall, where the crucifix would be in a cathedral. The Constitution—well, some of it, anyway—got spread out beneath it like an altar rail, a visible gap between theory and practice, between big ideas and hard choices. They stayed there until July 2001, when they were moved to an undisclosed location and, from there, handed over to Mary Lynn Ritzenthaler and Catherine Nicholson.

It's the ink that's giving them the most trouble. The ink used on the parchments is slightly acidic, with iron in its base and a little tooth to it. It attaches itself to the animal-hide parchment, which was treated specially to accept the ink's shallow bite. The ink, then, does not become part of the substance of the parchment, soaking deeply into it the way it would soak into paper. Instead, the ink fastens the words to the surface of the parchments, as though the words were ornaments hung upon them.

So, gradually, over two hundred years or more, the ink scatters and the letters migrate. The words begin to fade as the ink grows toothless with age and wear. Flakes of it dislodge. They disperse amid the Articles and the Sections. They spread among the Amendments. The tail of a J that began in the phrase "establish Justice" tumbles down to Article I, Section 3, finding itself amid "two Senators from each State." The foot of the A from "All bills for raising revenue" finds its way into the white space between "the Writ of Habeas Corpus shall not be suspended" and "unless when in Cases of Rebellion." The peak of the W from "no Warrants shall issue, but upon probable cause" meanders into the far margin, where nothing is written at all. These are the tiniest fragments of the words, the merest motes of the ideas of which the words are fragments themselves, and you need a microscope to find them. Nobody noticed when they went missing. Nobody would ever notice if they were gone.

In 1814, only a few steps ahead of the Royal Marines, the parchments of the Constitution were rolled up, stuffed in linen sacks, and shipped off to an empty mill in Virginia by President James Madison, whose masterwork it had been twenty-seven years earlier in Philadelphia. The United States was at war with England, and British troops were on their way to torch the White House and most of official Washington. It was the first engagement conducted under the new Constitution that had been given a formal declaration of war from Congress, living up to what Madison had once written, that it was wise to separate the power to declare war from the power to conduct it so as "to exclude the danger of its being declared for the sake of its being conducted." With the war coming to his doorstep, Madison sent the Constitution to an undisclosed location in the hills. However, as historian Garry Wills points out, President Madison "was truer to [the Constitution's] strictures than any subsequent war president. . . . War is a constant temptation to demagogy and he never succumbed to it." By hiding it away, he preserved, protected, and defended the Constitution, the way he swore to do, in its parchments and in its spirit.

So maybe it is just a metaphor, then: the Constitution being packed up and shipped off to an undisclosed location—out of sight, out of mind—just in time for the country to change itself over the past year and a half, just in time for the conversation about liberty and safety to move from the language of balance into the language of sacrifice, just in time for the syntax of democracy to slip imperceptibly into the passive voice. The country has not changed, it has been changed. We are protected more than we protect ourselves. We are governed more than we govern, and we are hidden more than we hide.

Trust us, our leaders say. Give us arrests without cause, trials without counsel, imprisonment without charge, and searches without warrant. Give us these because you've already given us wars without battlefields, without formal declarations, without clear objectives or signs of ending. We will do it to them, they say. We will curtail our enemies' liberties and not yours. Give us these things, and we will give you a place to go where you can feel safe. We will put you in an undisclosed location.

Trust us, they say.

And we do.

In late 2001, the USA Patriot Act (Uniting and Strengthening America by Providing Appropriate Tools Required to Intercept and Obstruct Terrorism) was passed without amendment and without even the pretense of debate. A ragbag of proposals that had been kicking around the law-enforcement community for decades, this act crystallized the changes wrought by the country upon itself in the wake of September 11. It gives to the executive branch unprecedented authority to abridge established civil liberties in order to combat the threat of terrorism. It allows extensive monitoring of computer usage and of library transactions. It allows the government to jail American citizens indefinitely without counsel and without a charge being brought against them, based on secret evidence gathered without warrant, and to act on that evidence whether or not it has anything to do with possible terrorist acts, and its decisions are not subject to review by any higher court. The Justice Department repeatedly has denied Congress any authority over how the executive branch is using these sweeping new powers. The act passed the Senate with only a single dissenting vote—Russell Feingold of Wisconsin—and. without either amendment or debate.

Elsewhere, the CIA can now engage again in domestic intelligence gathering, and the FBI can "coordinate" with local law enforcement. There was even a proposal for something called Operation TIPS (Terrorism Information and Prevention System), whereby every mail carrier, meter reader, and cable guy could be employed as a government snitch. A college student in North Carolina was visited by the Secret Service because she had a poster critical of the president in her apartment. The president's spokesman warned us to watch what we say. And on PBS last September, a national-security expert named Frank Gaffney Jr. reassured the country that "the contention that this [country] is a police state is laughable."

I don't speak the language of the undisclosed location. I don't have the vocabulary. I get tangled in the new syntax. I fall all over myself trying to make myself understood. Maybe I'm just lost, a naive foreigner in a changed country, stumbling down the wrong alley, opening the wrong doors, asking the wrong people for directions to the wrong place. Maybe the Constitution being hidden is only a metaphor, and maybe the ideas are not really coming apart in tiny pieces the way the ink loses its grip on the parchment. I just don't recall ever needing to be reassured that I don't live in a police state.

It would be easier if this were the story of America being in an undisclosed location, like the Constitution is. Then this would be a story about the search for America, and everybody loves those stories because America is cast as both the map and the treasure. There are whispers in them of secret wonders and hints of sacred fountains. That's an easy story to tell. I would tell it if I could.

There are few places as quiet as an empty courthouse at the end of a business day. This afternoon, as a gale blows itself out into the Atlantic, the United States Courthouse in Norfolk, Virginia, is silent in the dull light of the late afternoon. Rain pounds vainly on the granite walls, and the thick glass of the high windows deadens the sound of the wind.

Robert Doumar works here, a seventy-three-year-old federal judge with a slow drawl, manners out of a gentler age, and a canny fisherman's squint that makes him look like the kind of old gentleman whom you don't try to bluff with a low pair. His family has lived in Norfolk for almost a hundred years after coming to America from Syria and opening Doumar's, a restaurant on Monticello Avenue.

The Doumars threw themselves so deeply into their new country that, in 1904, Robert's uncle Abe went all the way to St. Louis for the big World's Fair, and, while there, he began selling ice cream in round cookie holders, making the Doumars one of several American families with a claim to having invented the ice-cream cone. In 1981, Ronald Reagan made Robert a United States district judge.

Twenty years later, Robert Doumar had one of the worst days of his life.

On September 11, 2001, Doumar was in Boston, where he'd

been assigned as a visiting judge to the First Circuit's Court of Appeals. That morning, two planes left from Logan Airport there and were flown by hijackers into the World Trade Center's twin towers in New York. Watching the disaster unfold on TV, Robert Doumar remembered that his son Charles routinely walked through the World Trade Center to get to his office at Merrill Lynch. Doumar called his daughter-in-law, and she told him that there had been a problem with their baby that morning but that Charles had left for work.

Doumar was frantic. The phone system in New York had collapsed, and Boston was locking itself down. Finally, late in the afternoon, he heard from Charles, who'd never actually made it to the office because he'd been so late leaving home. Robert Doumar began to breathe again. The next day, he went back to work in federal court in Boston.

"That Wednesday morning," Doumar says, "the day after the incident, there were people out there with automatic weapons and soldiers everywhere, and it sort of scared you. You're walking into a courthouse, and to see all this weaponry exhibited, it's hard to place it in a decent context. I never saw anything like it before, and I hope we don't ever live in a situation where that becomes necessary."

Doumar returned to Norfolk, and over the next several months, he watched a number of measures passed in reaction to September 11, most notably the USA Patriot Act. "Unfortunately, legislators, I think, are not supposed to read the bills they vote on anymore," Doumar says. Not long before the act passed, the United States went to war in Afghanistan. During the fighting there, a twenty-one-year-old Saudi Arabian named Yaser Esam Hamdi was taken prisoner by Northern Alliance forces while allegedly fighting for the Taliban government.

Hamdi was designated an "enemy combatant" by the Pentagon, which maintained that, as such, he could be held indefinitely without charge and without the benefits of due process. He was first held at

Guantánamo Bay and later tossed into a Navy brig in Norfolk. A problem arose when it was discovered that Hamdi was an American citizen, born in Baton Rouge, Louisiana, while his father worked for an oil company there.

Hamdi's father petitioned Doumar to allow his son access to an attorney. Doumar granted the petition. The government responded with a two-page, nine-paragraph document, written by a Defense Department official named Michael Mobbs, that argued that, as an enemy combatant, Hamdi could be held indefinitely, without counsel, based on evidence that the government declined to produce, on the authority of some bureaucrat who wasn't even in his courtroom that day, and that, essentially, Doumar and the rest of the federal judiciary could go climb a tree.

Doumar was furious. First, he grilled the government's lawyer on who Mobbs was and from whence he derived his authority. The government lawyers replied that Mobbs was an undersecretary of defense, a "special adviser" who'd been involved in issues regarding detainees. Doumar was unimpressed. He moved on to the case at hand.

"How long does it take to question a man?" Doumar asked the government lawyers. "A year? Two years? Ten years? A lifetime?"

The present detention is lawful, the government replied. (Trust us.)

"Well," Doumar asked, "what if we just sit him in boiling oil, then? Would that be lawful?"

The present detention is lawful, the government replied. (Trust us.)

It became comic. At one point, Doumar called the government's argument "idiotic." He kept hammering at three questions: Who in the hell was Michael Mobbs? Where did he get this power? And who gave it to him? Finally, in ruling against the government and determining that Hamdi should have a lawyer, Doumar had one last thing to say to the government lawyers:

"So," he asked, "the Constitution doesn't apply to Mr. Hamdi?"

In January, the government won its appeal of Doumar's ruling.

Applauding the reversal, John Ashcroft called it an important step in the president's effort to "protect the American people"—intimating, of course, that Doumar's excessive zeal as regards the Sixth Amendment had somehow put those same Americans in peril. It is the language of the new world, and, to Doumar, it might as well be Urdu.

"The right to counsel is part of our system," Doumar says. "It's our government, what we have fought for and tried to preserve. You can't change that—can't teach an old dog new tricks. I can't accept that which I was taught was an undeniable right is . . . just a privilege, and you can't take away people's undeniable rights, as far as I was concerned.

"Now, truly, you can limit those rights. You can make them reasonably limited, but to take away someone's undeniable rights is different. In times of war, you have to curtail rights, but you can't just eliminate or abdicate your responsibility of preserving rights. Because if we do that, it's no longer worth protecting."

The easier story would end there—the story of a lonesome pilgrim, a conservative judge, no less—finding America deep in its undisclosed location, tracking it through secret passages that lead to sacred fountains. It's a story that's been told by everyone from de Tocqueville to Paul Simon, but it's a story of an old country, and its essential elements—the limitless frontier, the idea that freedom lives in the open places and that democracy dies in secret—have lost their power to make us question our doubts that people can govern themselves, and, at last, you find that America is not in the undisclosed location, hidden away like something precious. America is the undisclosed location, secret and windowless, deaf to whatever dissonant optimism is left outside, soundproof as a tomb.

The rain falls harder as the storm blows out to sea. It falls on Doumar's restaurant, where a man came from Syria and made a life for himself, and it falls on the courthouse, where his son now works. It is the fulfillment of a golden immigrant dream, right there along

Monticello Avenue, and it looks, in the gathering darkness, like the measure of another country.

Look at that guy down the block, the guy selling the hot dogs out of his wagon, the guy at whom you toss a smile on a spring afternoon, and maybe you tell him to keep the change because you're feeling so light and easy and free. Tomorrow, that guy could be gone. Forever, or long enough to feel like forever to his wife and to his family and to his friends. Nobody else would notice, though, if he were gone. Him, not you.

We have moved ourselves to the place where we feel safe, a place designed in an architecture of possibility. Possibility is both the reason for the undisclosed location and the steel and concrete from which it was constructed. Something probably won't happen, but it could, and that is all that matters. I probably won't die in a terrorist attack, but the possibility is there now, more clearly than it was before. I probably won't get rounded up, or have my mail read, or have my home entered without a warrant. But I could.

Maybe I'm wrong to see all the possibilities, to see the shiny, brilliant acronym of the USA PATRIOT Act and to be reminded of the great Bogart line from *The Maltese Falcon*: "The cheaper the crook, the gaudier the patter." Maybe, since I don't have the vocabulary of the undisclosed location, I can't follow its logic, either. The unthinkable was done, so why should anything be unthinkable in response? Just because I can't follow the rules of logic is not to deny that they exist.

Maybe I'm seeing the ghosts of things, jumping at the possibilities that now exist the way people who are lost jump, startled by what John Ashcroft derided before Congress as the "phantoms of lost liberty." Trust us, he says. We will use these powers against them. We will not use them against you. Lost is the oldest syllogism of all: If it can happen to them, then it's already happened to me.

After all, so very little of this is new. Upton Sinclair got arrested in 1923 simply for reading the Bill of Rights during a rally for striking dockworkers in Los Angeles. There were Red scares and Palmer raids, the McCarthy period, the 1960s and all their attendant insanity. Keep us safe, people said, and there were always people willing to do it. More recently, the war on drugs brought new strategies by which the Constitution became a series of fascinating hurdles to be overcome in the quest for the public good. No-knock warrants and secret informants. Forfeiture laws. My son now goes to high school, and as soon as he crosses the threshold, he loses any protection from the Fourth and Fifth Amendments. The principal can search his locker without probable cause. He can be forced to take a drug test without even suspicion. And last year the Supreme Court said that was fine. It was a popular decision.

Long before September 11, 2001, the Constitution had been transformed into a puzzle to be solved—an eighteenth-century riddle, a cunning postcolonial entertainment to while away the hours in the undisclosed location. We've been moving in this direction for most of my lifetime. So maybe I'm something of a creationist, in denial of inexorable evolution, wasting everybody's time here in the new world by polishing the bones of the old. What if I stand up, right there in the middle of the undisclosed location, and somebody sees me? What if I give the whole thing away?

"It deserves to be well-considered also that actual war is not the only state which may supply the means of usurpation. The real or pretended apprehensions of it are sometimes of equal avail to the projects of ambition . . . . Hence the propagation and management of alarms has grown into a kind of system."

—James Madison
Aurora General Advertiser, February 23, 1799

He wrote this, the little fellow did, looking out these very windows, looking off over the broad sweep of the lawns and off toward the distant mountains. James Madison did his best work here at Montpelier, the family estate about two hours southwest into Virginia from Washington, or he did it scurrying between the back rooms and closed committees and all the other undisclosed locations in Philadelphia, where they first hung the ink onto the parchment, where it has scattered and migrated through the years until the words began to fade.

He was never a superstar, not even among his contemporaries. And he was a terrible president—the mark of Cain in American political history, which demands that All Great Men Be Great Presidents and Do Great Things. His home never became a shrine—not the way Washington's Mount Vernon has, with its million annual visitors. Barely fifty-five thousand people come here every year to stand on James Madison's lawns, wander through his house, and sit in the room where he looked out at the mountains and thought about how a free people might govern themselves. "The Father of the Constitution," it says in the main foyer of the house. But that's not nearly enough to bring in tourists by the busload. Down at the tiny gift shop, there are nearly as many Jefferson trinkets as there are Madison tchotchkes.

James and Dolley Madison died without heirs, so Montpelier was sold like any other home. In 1901, it was purchased by the du Pont family, which built on, added to, and refurbished the place until the original Montpelier disappeared like Troy vanishing into a Turkish hillside. Finally, in 1983, Marion du Pont Scott died, and the estate was transferred to the National Trust for Historic Preservation. Since then, the Trust has begun the slow work of freeing the original Montpelier from the encrustations of gilded-age plutocracy. It is a place of holes and exposed beams now, a discreet archaeological dig being reassembled from its tiniest parts, the way words are reassembled by the smallest slivers of the migrating ink.

"Right there," says Randy Huwa, the director of communications for Montpelier, pointing to a deep gouge in the plaster, "that's probably a fireplace from the original home.

"We're a stop on a few people's personal life list. Mostly, it's people who come here to walk where Madison walked, and to feel some of the spirit of the place, as a kind of a shrine to the Constitution."

Somewhere, north beyond the mountains, Mary Lynn Ritzenthaler and Catherine Nicholson are trying to restore the tiniest fragments of Madison's words, the way people are trying to restore his house. Their work is ending for the day, and the Constitution is being returned, again, to its undisclosed location, and maybe that really is just a metaphor. I am not likely to die that way. But now, it seems, I could, which is all the difference. Just as, in response, nobody is likely to round me up, or read my mail, or search my house when I am not home. But they could. Which is all the difference.

Am I afraid? Of course I am. A monstrous crime was committed. The unthinkable happened, and the unthinkable has been proposed—and, in some cases, engaged—in response, and the undisclosed location has swallowed us all, a place to be hidden and not to hide. A place where we are sent while feeling that we chose to go there.

There are still holes in the architecture at Montpelier through which you can see the old place as they dig out Madison's house from the extravagance of the du Ponts. I think of those tiny bits of ink that are being rounded up, one at a time, and being put back to strengthen the words that seem to so many people now as quaint as gas lamps and rail fences.

And maybe I'm wrong, un-American even, but I'll stay awhile in the little fellow's home and watch the mountains go purple in the twilight. I will hide, if I hide, and not be hidden. I will govern and not be governed. This is where I'll stand, for awhile longer anyway. To hell with it. My location is disclosed.

Acknowledgments

Many people made this anthology.

At Thunder's Mouth Press and Avalon Publishing Group:
Thanks to Will Balliett, Kristen Couse, Maria Fernandez, Linda Kosarin, Dan O'Connor, Neil Ortenberg, Susan Reich, David Riedy, Michelle Rosenfield, Simon Sullivan and Mike Walters for their support, dedication, and hard work.

At The Writing Company:
Nate Hardcastle and Taylor Smith took up slack on other projects.

At the Portland Public Library in Portland, Maine:
The librarians helped collect books from around the country.

Finally, we are grateful to the writers whose work appears in this book—with particular thanks due to James W. Loewen.

Permsissions

We gratefully acknowledge everyone who gave permission for written material to appear in this book. We have made every effort to trace and contact copyright holders. If an error or omission is brought to our notice we will be pleased to correct the situation in future editions of this book. For further information, please contact the publisher.

Bibliography

The selections used in this anthology were taken from the editions and sources listed below. In some cases, other editions may be easier to find. Hard-to-find or out-of-print titles often are available through interlibrary loan services or through Internet booksellers.

Adams, Judith Porter. *Peacework: Oral Histories of Women Peace Activists.* Boston: Twayne Publishers, 1991.

Agee, James and Walker Evans. *Let Us Now Praise Famous Men.* Boston: Houghton Mifflin Co., 1941.

Ball, Eve with Nora Henn and Lynda Sanchez. *Indeh: An Apache Odyssey.* Provo, UT: Brigham Young University Press, 1980.

Brecher, Jeremy, Jerry Lombardi and Jan Stackhouse. *Brass Valley: The Story of Working People's Lives and Struggles in an American Industrial Region.* Philadelphia: Temple University Press, 1982. (For "The 1920s Strike.")

Byrd, Robert. Senate Speech delivered February 12, 2003. http://www.senate.gov/~byrd/byrd_newsroom/byrd_news_feb/news_2003_february/news_2003_february_9.html.

Corrie, Rachel. "Rachel's War." Originally appeared in *The Guardian,* March 18, 2003. (For "Dispatch from Rafah, Occupied Palestine.")

DuBois, Ellen Carol, ed. *Elizabeth Cady Stanton, Susan B. Anthony: Correspondence, Writings, Speeches.* New York: Schocken Books, 1981. (For "Speech on Women's Rights.")

Ducas, George with Charles Van Doren, eds. *Great Documents In Black American History.* New York: Praeger Publishers, 1970. (For "The Negro Artist and the Racial Mountain.")

Ehrenreich, Barbara. *Nickel and Dimed: On (Not) Getting By in America.* New York: Metropolitan Books, 2001.

Foner, Philip S. *The Life And Writings Of Frederick Douglass.* New York: International Publishers, 1955. (For "A July 4, 1852 Speech.")

Fried, Albert. *McCarthyism: The Great American Red Scare: A Documentary History.* New York: Oxford University Press, 1997. (For "Testimony Before House Un-American Activities Committee.")

Friedan, Betty. "Demanding Full Equality." Originally appeared in *Time,* March 31, 2003.

Gates, Henry Louis, Jr. *Colored People.* New York: Knopf, 1994. (For "Prime Time.")

Grimké, Sarah Moore. *Letters on the Equality of the Sexes, and the Condition of Women.* Boston: Isaac Knapp, 1838. (For "Legal Disabilities of Women.")

Harper's Magazine, May 1999. (for "Transcript from a Class Action Suit Against the U.S. Government").

Hofstadter, Richard, ed. *American Violence: A Documentary History.* New York: Vintage Books, 1971. (For "Sand Creek Massacre" and "Dearborn Massacre.")

Hurtado, Albert L. and Peter Iverson, eds. *Major Problems in American Indian History: Documents and Essays.* Boston: Houghton Mifflin, 2001. (For "Address to President Monroe," "A California Law for the Government and Protection of the Indians," "Back on the War Ponies," and "Whose History Do We Celebrate?")

Ladd, William. *Address Delivered At The Tenth Anniversary Of The Massachusetts Peace Society.* Boston: Published at the office of the Christian Register, 1826.

Lawson, Don, ed. *Ten Fighters for Peace: An Anthology.* New York: Lothrop, Lee & Shepard, 1971. (For "My Country Right or Wrong.")

Lewis, Anthony. "The Silencing of Gideon's Trumpet." Originally appeared in *The New York Times Magazine,* April 20, 2003.

Loewen, James W. *Lies My Teacher Told Me: Everything Your American History Textbook Got Wrong.* New York: Touchstone, 1995.

Mieskowski, Katharine. "Can My Mommy Have Her Paycheck?" Originally appeared on www.salon.com, May 1, 2001.

Moody, Anne. *Coming of Age in Mississippi.* New York: Laurel Books, 1968.

Morgan, Robin, ed. *Sisterhood is Powerful.* New York: Random House, 1970. (For "Do You Know the Facts About Marriage?" and "Principles.")

Newfield, Jack. "How the Other Half Still Lives." Originally appeared in *The Nation*, March 17, 2003.

Pierce, Charles. "State of the Union." Originally appeared in *Esquire,* April, 2003.

Pringle, Cyrus. "The Record of A Quaker Conscience." Originally appeared in *The Atlantic Monthly,* February 1913.

Reporting Civil Rights Part One: American Journalism 1941-1963. New York: Library of America, 2003. (For "Non-Violence vs. Jim Crow" and "Adventures in Dining.")

Reporting Civil Rights Part Two: American Journalism 1963-1973. New York: Library of America, 2003. (For "The View from the Front of the Bus.")

Slave Narratives. New York: Library of America, 2000. (For "The Life of Olaudah Equiano" and "The Narrative of William W. Brown, A Fugitive Slave.")

Smith, Margaret Chase. "Declaration of Conscience". http://www.mcs library.org/program/library/declaration.htm

Standing Bear, Luther. *Land of the Spotted Eagle.* Lincoln, NE: University of Nebraska Press, 1978.

Starhawk. *Webs of Power: Notes from the Global Uprising.* Gabriola Island, BC: New Society Publishers, 2002. (For "Sunday A16.")

Steinbeck, John. *The Harvest Gypsies.* Berkely, CA: Heyday Books, 1988.

Terkel, Studs. *Hard Times: An Oral History of the Great Depression.* New York: Pantheon, 1970.

Terkel, Studs. *The Great Divide: Second Thoughts on the American Dream.* New York: Pantheon, 1988.

Tisdale, Sallie. "We Do Abortions Here." Originally appeared in *Harper's Magazine,* October 1987.

Washington, Booker T. *Up From Slavery: An Autobiography.* New York: Dodd, Mead & Co., 1965.

Williams, Juan. *Eyes on the Prize.* New York: Penguin, 1988.

Young, Joseph. "An Indian's Views of Indian Affairs". Originally appeared in *The North American Review,* April 1879.

Index

Nathaniel May's anthologies include *Oval Office: Stories of Presidents in Crisis from Washington to Bush*. He lives in Portland, Maine.

Clint Willis has edited more than 30 anthologies on subjects ranging from mountaineering *(Epic: Stories of Survival from the World's Highest Peaks)* to the Dalai Lama *(A Lifetime of Wisdom)*. Clint lives with his family in Maine.

James W. Loewen's books include *Lies My Teacher Told Me, Lies Across America: What Our Historic Sites Get Wrong,* and *The Mississippi Chinese: Between Black and White.* He lives in Washington, D.C.